CW00690012

MICHAEL CARDEW
A PIONEER
POTTER

MICHAEL CARDEW

A PIONEER POTTER

AN AUTOBIOGRAPHY

COLLINS

First published in 1988
by William Collins Sons & Co., Ltd
London · Glasgow · Sydney
Auckland · Toronto · Johannesburg

British Library Cataloguing in Publication Data

Cardew, Michael
A pioneer potter: an autobiography.
1. Cardew, Michael   2. Potters—Great
Britain—Biography
I. Title
738.3′092′4   NK4210.C29

ISBN 0-00-412288-7

Edited by Josephine Christian

Printed and bound in Great Britain
by Robert Hartnoll (1985) Ltd, Bodmin

CONTENTS

ILLUSTRATIONS

PREFACE

This book is shortened from the lengthy manuscript left by Michael Cardew. The original thirty-three chapters in my father's hand, together with some of his other papers, are now in the keeping of the Craft Study Centre at the Holborne of Menstrie Museum, Bath, where they are available to students.

Other papers, film of Michael Cardew and many of his pots can be seen here at Wenford Bridge Pottery. The following museums and institutions also have interesting collections of pots by Michael Cardew. In Britain: the Ashmolean Museum, Oxford; the British Council, London; the City of Bristol Museum and Art Gallery; the Holborne of Menstrie Museum, Bath; the University College of Wales Ceramics Collection at Aberystwyth Arts Centre; the Victoria and Albert Museum, London. In the United States: Everson Museum of Art, Syracuse, New York; the Garth Clark Gallery, New York; Los Angeles County Museum of Art; Pomona College Art Gallery, Claremont, California; the Smithsonian Institute, Washington, D.C. In Australia: the Australian National Gallery, Canberra. In New Zealand: Canterbury Museum, Christchurch; the Institute and Museum, Auckland.

I wish to thank Jenny-Louise, who typed the full-length manuscript; my wife, Jutta, who helped edit and who sought out references for the quotations used; Tanya Harrod, who supplied the informative Appendix on Achimota College and the West African Institute; and particularly William Ismay, who writes briefly but so perceptively of my father, his friend, in his Introduction to this book.

Seth Cardew, Wenford Bridge Pottery, Bodmin, *August 1987*

INTRODUCTION

No one who ever met Michael Cardew and savoured the qualities of his personality and his later life-style (and of the slipware pots he made at Winchcombe and the equally warm and vibrant and more durable stonewares from Africa and Wenford Bridge) is ever likely to forget him. For my own part I would say that of all the remarkable men and women whom I've met and who are no longer with us in the flesh, he is the one I miss the most. Hence I found enthralling this incomplete account of what he himself called his 'potter's progress'.

That it is incomplete is due I think to an optimism on Michael's part about his prospects of longevity, which was not unreasonable in view of his vigour at eighty. It was the sudden stroke which in a few days ended his life at eighty-one which has robbed us of what we would much have liked to have, his own retrospective view of Abuja and Wenford Bridge and the later travels. Yet in a curious way it is not inappropriate that what we do have is a kind of skeleton key to his enigma, written with an at times bleak and ferocious honesty about his motivations and his mistakes, glancing almost obliquely at what went right, and ending in mid-story with an interlude after what seems a disaster at Vumë. Yet this was an essential part of the 'progress' – nor should it be forgotten that there were triumphs too in these earlier days, and that a selection of his best work needs pots from Winchcombe and Vumë to be truly representative.

What people and particularly his fellow-potters, his family and his neighbours thought of him in later days was evident whenever any assembly of them came together to look at his pots or to hear him talk and see him demonstrate, as I saw for myself in several countries, and it is clear that the same happened further afield. So others have written and will write about those later days. We already have *Pioneer Pottery*, and film and video of him moving and talking, and many briefer writings as yet uncollected – yet nothing else perhaps so intimate and revealing as what we have here.

W. A. Ismay, Wakefield, *August 1987*

I

THE BEGINNINGS

'There is always one moment in childhood when the door opens and lets the future in.'

(Graham Greene, *The Power and the Glory*)

There must have been a door marked 'Pottery' in my childhood, but I can't remember the exact moment when it opened. Our house always seemed to be full of pots. My father was not rich enough to be a collector, but, nevertheless, he was continually acquiring the things. The four-storey semi-detached house on Wimbledon Common, already filled to capacity with father, mother, six children, Nanny Mason and three maids, was also crammed with antique furniture and pieces of 'china'. Visitors used to say, 'The house is like a museum.'

I rather hated the china. Some of it was in an antique glass case at the foot of the stairs, and once when I was bouncing a ball there, it bounced through the glass and broke a valuable cup and saucer inside. I was in disgrace. No doubt that accounts for my dislike of glass cases.

Besides the early English china and the late Chinese porcelain, there were other kinds of pots in the Wimbledon house. There was some eighteenth-century Whieldon ware, condemned in my eyes because under the mottled glaze you could see that they were not really made of clay but of some nasty, dead, cold, white composition. But round the fireplaces in the day nursery and the music room there were polychrome Dutch tiles with irresistible pictures of tulips, fritillaries, houses, boats and men skating. There were also some delft drug jars with mysterious inscriptions painted in blue capitals, TORMENTIL, SAMBUCUS . . . and there were a few pots by Mr Fishley.

Only the drug jars seemed to me to be classifiable as *pots*, in the sense that Mr Fishley's pots were pots. There were not many of those at Wimbledon; but the house at Saunton, in north Devon, was full of them.

Saunton was different. It was heaven. Wimbledon was where you went to school; Saunton restored your animal integrity. You gulped the Atlantic wind and it went right down to the bottom of your body and made you gasp for more. When you reached the house after the long railway journey and the bike ride from Braunton, you burst into the hall and there, still in their old places, smelling just the same and waiting to greet you, were the harvest jugs from Mr Fishley's pottery at Fremington, three big yellow pitchers. The biggest had a hunting scene drawn on it, and a long rhyme:

> The fearfull hare doth run apace
> Because the hounds are on their chace
> The country he is forced to fly
> While they are out with hue and cry
> Nature hath taught him in this strife
> To seek for to presarve his life
> Which he by running doth obtain
> And then the hounds return again
> The huntsman seeing this doth cry
> Let him go his meat is dry
> Ile to thy landlady with speed
> For i of her have greater need.

There were Fremington pots all over the house, not only for ornament but for use. Scalded cream (when we got it) was baked in the oval combed dishes, and pies made from whortleberries, plums or blackberries and apples were eaten from green-glazed bowls. Upstairs in the bedroom the wash-stands had Fremington pitchers, basins, beakers and soap dishes.

Sometimes we explored the attic – one of the mansions of heaven. It contained, besides the water tank with its unpredictable garglings, various other numinous objects, especially a pair of large revolving globes on wooden tripods. One of them had the familiar continents and oceans all over it. The other had strange mythical creatures and personages with names like Gemini, Ursa Major, Scorpio, Serpens or Capricorn. They squeaked slightly when you turned them and emitted strange rattlings from bits of plaster which had come loose inside.

There were also two huge terracotta pots with lids. 'Do you realize', said my brother Richard in that didactic elder-brother tone which I always rather resented, 'that Mr Fishley made those pots with his thumb?' The pots were enormous: much too heavy for us to lift. 'Thumb indeed! What rot!' I thought privately to myself. Up till then I had imagined that like certain specially sacred Byzantine icons, they were *acheiropoiëta* – things-not-made-with-hands.

The earliest memory of seeing pots actually being made is unfortunately a 'non-memory': that is, my own mind is a total blank. But the fact that I was already addicted and obsessed is confirmed by a reliable witness, Alison Bagenal (*née* Hogg), who wrote, *à propos des neiges d'antan*,

> ... the best time of my life was a holiday in Devon when I was a girl. We were a big family and there was another family – a lot of boys and a big girl Penelope who was my friend. The boys were all very vigorous and different. There was a little one called Michael who used to spend all his time watching an old Mr Fishley making pots. He watched him all day, and used to kick Pen and me on the shins when we came to bring him back for dinner ...

I remember being in love with Alison. I'm sorry I kicked her shins, though. No wonder my memory is a blank.

Those visits to Mr Fishley's pottery only happened once a year. They involved a complicated expedition. The whole party had to walk or bicycle four miles along the sands to the lighthouse, and from there we hailed one of the boatmen in Appledore across the water, and hired him and his boat for the day. Then we rowed or sailed up the tidal estuary of the River Taw till we reached Fremington Creek, and from there it was only a short walk up a lane to the pottery.

The pottery was one of the few survivors of an ancient tradition which had flourished in this part of north Devon since before the time of the first Queen Elizabeth. Those early potters made a complete range of household wares. They made the pots from the local Fremington clay, dipped them in a white slip made from cutty clay and then drew their remarkably free and inventive designs by cutting through the white slip coating to the underlying red clay. They glazed them with a single-fire galena glaze and fired them in open saggars set in large updraught round kilns. The finished pots were bright yellow over the white slip and a warm brown where the clay body was exposed. This ware had much more in common with the early sgraffito pottery of Southern Europe and the Mediterranean countries than with the slip-trailed styles cultivated in other parts of England.

About the middle of the seventeenth century the demand for this country pottery began to decline; it was being superseded by white tin-glazed delft ware which was now being made in England and becoming fashionable. However, the north Devon potters found a new outlet overseas, selling vast quantities of their wares to the American plantations or colonies, chiefly Virginia and Maryland. Small ocean-going schooners and ketches were continually sailing from Bideford Bay bound for America and laden with 'parcels of earthenware'. Malcolm Watkins, to whose labours we owe all this information, quotes lists from the Port Books of Barnstaple and Bideford for the years 1665 to 1690, which give an idea of the size of the industry at that time. Almost nothing from this large production has survived in Britain, but Malcolm Watkins illustrates many beautiful examples, excavated mostly at Jamestown and carefully repaired and reconstructed at the National Museum in Washington.[1]

In the second quarter of the eighteenth century even this market was coming to an end – the colonists were now making their own pots. At the beginning of the present century the north Devon potters' work was limited to a few standard types made for the villages: water pitchers, baking dishes, milk pans, washing pans, salting pans and 'cloam ovens' – beautiful one-piece bread ovens the shape of giant tortoises, which in every north Devon and Cornish home were built into the wall near the kitchen fireplace. But they still made a few special pieces for special occasions or people – things like harvest jugs and puzzle mugs. Edwin Beer Fishley was the proud inheritor of this ancient tradition, and being a potter with original ideas and a sense of form, he was already finding that there were a few people – like my father and mother – who were interested, and bought his pots whenever they got the chance.

Life in the pottery at Fremington is described in the autobiography of Fishley's grandson, William Fishley Holland.[2] The buildings enclosed an irregular rectangle: a square dwelling house on one side, the big beehive-shaped kiln in one of the corners. This had a damper at the top of the chimney which could be raised by pulling a chain attached to the trunk of an apple tree. On the other sides of the quadrangle there were low dark sheds full of the good smell of damp clay; a wheel-house; and in the courtyard there was a circle where a horse walked round and round to work the pugmill.

When it was time to go home all the family (except me) went happily: father and mother with more pots for the house, children with big lumps of lovely brown clay wrapped in damp calico and decaying newspaper. (Plastic bags were still forty or fifty years in the future.)

These excursions came to an end about 1912 when old Mr Fishley died. None of his sons had chosen to be a potter; and though his grandson Willie Holland had joined the pottery as a boy and had now become an efficient potter, his uncles were not interested and insisted on selling the place.

---

[1] C. Malcolm Watkins, *North Devon Pottery and its Export to America in the 17th Century*, The Smithsonian Institution, Washington D.C., 1960.
   C. Malcolm Watkins and Ivor Noel Hume, *The 'Poor Potter' of Yorktown*, Smithsonian Institution Press, Washington D.C., 1967.
[2] William Fishley Holland, *Fifty Years a Potter, Pottery Quarterly*, Tring, Hertfordshire, 1958.

Barnstaple Market used to be the normal place for buying Fremington pots. Every Friday the farmers' wives or daughters, from a radius of several miles, drove their two-wheeled traps to market, loaded with cream, butter, honey, poultry, eggs, fruit and vegetables of every kind. Then there were the stalls of the basket-makers, and Mr Fishley also used to drive his wagon to town and lay out his wares on the pottery stalls, side by side with those of the rival pottery firms in Barnstaple. We also bought some of our pots here; and to get them home we handed them over to Minnie Tucker from the farm at Saunton whose trap would be returning comparatively empty at the end of the day.

But now the Fremington Pottery stall was deserted. The flow of Fishley pots came to an end and was replaced by the pale and lifeless products of the rival firms. I don't know whether the rest of the world noticed anything at all; but all through the years after 1912 we were aware of a change for the worse. (I speak for myself; but I think my parents felt the same.)

However, although I missed Mr Fishley and his pots, I was too busy growing up to think much about it. Then the First World War came, and as it dragged on through four horrible years the minor deprivation was forgotten among the major tragedies. When at last the seemingly everlasting war came to a sudden end, I was seventeen and a half. My elder brother Richard had been killed in France, at the age of nineteen, in April of the same year; and I by the accident of my birthday had survived to see the future. Survivors of my age were convinced that nothing would ever be the same again. We were right there. Some of us also assumed as a matter of course that henceforward everything was going to be 'nicer'. Unfortunately, we had no evidence of any kind to support that assumption.

Among the things around me which I now examined, with a newly critical eye, were the ordinary cups, saucers, plates, bowls, jugs and teapots of daily use; and I found I did not like them. I began to wonder why we could not throw them away and use pots like Mr Fishley's instead, for all our eating, drinking and cooking, at Wimbledon as well as at Saunton. Since they were soft-fired lead-glazed earthenware they could not have stood up well to continuous family use. But at that age I would have been scornful of such frivolous 'technical' objections. Still less was I conscious of any dangers from lead release. That was something which even the technical men were only just beginning to worry about.

It was now that I became aware that the drying-up of the supply of Fremington pots was a permanent and serious deprivation. I looked around to see if it was possible to get more pots of this kind. They told me that Mr Fishley's grandson, Willie Holland, was now in charge of a new pottery at Braunton, which was financed and owned by a Barnstaple solicitor. So I went to Braunton and found the pottery. Mr Holland was a very good thrower and I stood fascinated, watching him for hours on end, just as I had watched his grandfather in my forgotten childhood.

I was hoping to find the same kind of pots which we used to get from Fremington; but the things which came from the kiln at Braunton were not the same. They were made from the same Fremington clay and the kiln was a similar kiln. But now it was fired entirely with coal; there was no faggot firing, and the pots were all set in sealed saggars. They were given a biscuit-fire as high as the glaze-fire, and then dipped with red-lead-based glazes – hard, efficient greens and blues, and none of the old soft yellows and browns. The shapes themselves had undergone a change. They had become tight and stiff; their rims and lips were sharp and thin, instead of warm and kind and generous. Once I even naïvely asked Mr Holland why he did not make pots like those of his grandfather, but I could not convince him that there had ever been much merit in them. He said, 'I never could understand why grandfather used to make his pots so thick. It was not that he could not throw them thin if he wanted to.'

He was very kind and helpful to me. He told me about galena, the glaze which gave the old yellows and browns. He took me to his home and introduced me to his mother, Mr Fishley's daughter. I asked her too about the Fremington pots, and she said much the same thing, adding, 'One thing about Father, he never bothered about what anybody else said or thought. *So long as he pleased himself,* that was all he cared about.' I thought to myself, 'Ah yes, that's the difference between grandfather and grandson. The old man was an artist, and this proves it.'

I don't know how long it took me to come round to thinking that if I wanted pots like Mr Fishley's, I would somehow have to try to make them myself. I began to wonder whether I could persuade Willie Holland to teach me how to throw. But I was a timid youth and was afraid he would refuse because it was one of his trade secrets. At last I screwed up my courage to ask him, and to my surprise and relief he immediately said, 'Of course I can give you lessons. It will cost you £1 a week.'

So I arranged to come to the pottery every day. He taught me how to centre the clay and to pull it up with a steady hand while kicking the wheel, and how to 'bow a pot' – that is, to make handles. He tried to show me how to shape the pots with the help of a rib (called a 'spoon' at Braunton), but I never took the trouble to learn this, obstinately – perhaps wrongheadedly – preferring to do it all with my fingers.

The lessons only lasted three weeks. Braunton Pottery was undergoing a crisis. The Barnstaple solicitor was bankrupt, and Willie Holland was full of hope that the pottery would be sold at a knock-down price and that he would become the sole owner. But that solicitor in Barnstaple was too clever for him. Willie Holland found that the pottery had already been registered in the name of the solicitor's wife. Disappointed of his hopes, he accepted an offer to go up to Somerset as thrower for the Clevedon Court Pottery, which was then being revived by Sir Ambrose Elton, nephew of the original producer of the once famous Elton ware.

Braunton Pottery continued. They put in a manager to run the business side and engaged a thrower from Barnstaple to look after the making, with the help of two apprentices. The new manager allowed me to come in every day after five o'clock to practise on the wheel after the others had left; and so all through that long summer vacation, every evening I continued, teaching myself to throw.

It was the hot summer of 1921. I was just twenty and was an undergraduate at Exeter College, Oxford. I was half-way through the four-year Greats (classics) course. This was the Long Vacation, which ran from mid-June to early October – an eternity of summer in which there were no limits to what I could do if I wanted to do it. Of course I knew that the Long Vacation was not officially a holiday at all, but a time when students were supposed to prepare themselves by an intensive course of reading and study for the coming academic term. But at the age of twenty, one is intellectually cocksure. I was perfectly confident that all this reading and study could be got through without interfering with pottery; in fact, that I could easily do both these things without cutting out any of the other delights of Saunton life – fishing, lobstering, swimming, rock-climbing and family music.

2

ARE YOU GOING
TO MAKE NEW SHAPES?

When I got back to Oxford in October the first thing we had to do was 'Collections'. This was a sort of full-scale dress rehearsal examination, lasting two or three days, in all the things we had been supposed to be studying during the Long Vacation. My performance was deplorable. I was summoned by the Rector of the College, Dr Lewis Farnell, who was also the husband of my Aunt Sylvia, the youngest and best-loved of my father's surviving sisters. He pointed out that if I continued to neglect my studies in this way, I would fail in my final examinations. This would be a disgraceful result for a Scholar of the College, and would be felt as a personal disgrace by my father, and by Dr Farnell himself. 'I am told,' he said,

> ... that you have spent a great part of the Vacation learning to make pottery. ... If you seriously intend to take up pottery, it is your duty to resign your scholarship and leave the University without taking a degree. This would be a perfectly honourable course of action. But if you decide that you sincerely want to continue your studies and to take your degree, you must give us an undertaking that you will drop all this pottery and concentrate yourself properly on your work here – that is to say, an undertaking that you can be relied upon to pass your finals with distinction and not let us all down.

I seemed to hesitate. Dr Farnell was really trying to be kind, he himself being an expert on Greek vases – things which were anathema to me at that time. He asked, 'What makes you so interested in pottery? Is there any future in it? Will you be able to earn your living at it? *Are you going to make new shapes?*'

My jaw dropped. I thought, 'What on earth does he mean?' At this time I had not yet got any consistent philosophy about shapes; but I dimly thought to myself, 'No! Not *new* shapes: rather, old shapes revived and rescued from decay.' But I think Dr Farnell meant something like this: 'Shapes are finite things, definable and defined; mathematically determined entities whose perfect paradigms, like the Platonic Ideas, are static, fixed and stored up for all eternity in a kind of celestial Museum of Archetypes. The Greek vase-makers (as is well known) aimed at perfection. They made all the best shapes, once and for all. Can anything remain for a modern upstart to do in this field?'

I had no articulate answer then; now I would say, 'Certainly, shapes are universal, but they are never new, never old. They are continually in need of being re-created. What you make of them depends on you – you can kill them or bring them to life. That's part of what Blake meant when he said in the "Proverbs of Hell", "Eternity is in love with the productions of time."'

It was a bad moment, and a difficult decision. I felt inarticulate and dumb. Two years later, when I arrived at the Leach Pottery and began to find out how amateurish my throwing was and what a long way I had to go before I could begin to call myself a potter, I bitterly regretted the choice I had made at Oxford. What madness had persuaded me to waste those two precious years in the desert of intellectualism? To learn an art properly one ought to begin at the age of fourteen at the very latest. That was now impossible; but instead of being thankful to have discovered my vocation at the mature age of twenty, I had deliberately thrown away those two years, and here I was now, at twenty-two (late, late, much too late) farther than ever from being a competent potter and still not in sight of being able to support myself.

But in Dr Farnell's study I did not see it like that. For one thing, I didn't have much of a clue how I was going to start my potting life. I didn't really fancy the idea of working permanently at Braunton Pottery, and I was unaware that there existed, even at that date, such a thing as a school of art where pottery could be learnt. And, chiefly, I didn't want to leave Oxford. In the previous two years I had got through what I thought of as the 'boring' part of the classics course, consisting of a minute study of classical texts, how they had been transmitted through the ages, the authenticity of the manuscripts and the scribes, errors which had crept into them. From now on I would be studying philosophy; and at the age of twenty the word still had power. I would be dealing with Reality. I wanted to explore it in all its depth – Plato, Aristotle, Spinoza, Kant, Ethics, the Philosophy of History and the Theory of Know-ledge. The prospect intoxicated me: I would find out the meaning of con-sciousness, which even then I dimly guessed might turn out to be the same as the meaning of the universe. Even while I was still a schoolboy I had felt that it was necessary, inevitable and above all supremely desirable that I should go to Oxford to study philosophy. I had never for a moment entertained the thought that I would not go there – still less that I would go there and then drop out half-way through.

Sometimes at Wimbledon if my father was introducing his sons to a visitor, he would say when he came to me, 'And this is the philosopher', and my head would churn with a confusion of pride and feelings of unworthiness. I always envied my school-fellows their mental skill and athletic prowess, but I knew I could not compete. It was true I had a horrid kind of cheap window-dressing talent which enabled me to do well in examinations and to win scholarships, provided the competition was not too severe; but in my heart I was ashamed of this and knew that the real thing I had to do was to confront the sphinx of meaning in the solitude of my skull and to wrestle with the questions which philosophers have the audacity to call absolute.

And here I was, just beginning all these studies for which I thought I was destined. How could I suddenly reject that?

Did I also give any weight to the reflection that for at least four generations some direct ancestor had studied or taught at Oxford, starting in the eighteenth century with the semi-mythical Dr Cornelius Cardew, D.D., of Liskeard and Truro? I think I probably did; even at that age I was inclined to be a kind of natural Confucian, and filial piety was high in my scale of virtues. Perhaps we of our generation were peculiarly in awe of our 'elders and betters'. I know I was. All my rebellions were secret and underground. I never had any moral courage to face unpleasantness.

So I solemnly promised to put pottery aside, like other childish things, and to concentrate on study. But I realize now that my promise was a double-faced one: a 'public' promise to Dr Farnell and a private one to myself – that I would indeed eat, and still have, my cake. What the College authorities required of me was a total renunciation of pottery; but in my private heart I told myself, 'This is simply a two-year bargain. Carrying it out is just a test of my willpower. When the two years are over and I am free again I will return to pottery.' Such was my infatuation that I was easily able to persuade myself that I could faithfully serve two Muses – not simultaneously, it is true; even I had just been forced to see that – but consecutively. In effect I was saying to the first, Divine Philosophy, 'Come live with me and be my love – *for just two years*, until I have taken my degree. Then I shall abandon you and return to my real love, whose earthy and plebeian name is Pottery.'

Did I really think that this willpower would be such a powerful force that I could devote my whole self to philosophy while all the time I had promised myself, body and soul, to pottery as soon as I was 'free'? The fact is that I still retained a fanatical belief in the power of the will, carried over from childhood. When I was a child, and people told horror stories about balloons, how if a member of the ground crew held on to the ropes too long he was carried aloft and later dropped to his death through exhaustion, I used to think to myself, ' *I would never let go*. I'd just tell my arms to hold on till the balloon came down again, and if I told my arms to do that they would have to do it' – an authoritarian view of the human body which always breaks down, usually sooner rather than later.

But in the same spirit I now imposed my own will upon myself. I told myself, 'Of course I can wrestle with that sphinx and penetrate her secrets, if I tell myself this is what I'll do.' During the next two years, however, every time I found myself at grips with the sphinx, all I was left with was the effort of my own will. All my intellectual faculties were tightly held in a kind of cramp, so that the natural resilience of the mind was unable to function freely – intellectual resilience being the one thing that lay beyond my muscle-bound reach.

So as those two years went on my intellectual powers, in spite of all the nourishment that Oxford could give, waned and wasted away instead of growing, because willpower used like that, deliberately and in isolation, acts as a blight. But it was too late to turn back. I clung on desperately, and all through the weeks of the final examinations I dosed myself every night with strong black coffee. All to no avail. I just scraped through with a Third Class Honours degree, and even that was thanks to dogged pedestrian work in the Ancient History papers. In Philosophy alone I would have failed totally – the Muse had detected my duplicity. My father was horribly disappointed; but he soon got over it and began to encourage me in my new career.

After it was all over, some of my Oxford friends told me, 'Well, at least you have been taught to think.' I said to myself, 'Taught to think! What nonsense! The only thing this kind of education teaches you is verbalization, a deliberate evasion of the thinking process.' But what I did learn at Oxford was method, and now at a distance of fifty years or more, I am glad I persevered to the bitter end. That kind of mental discipline helps sometimes in unexpected ways. I had acquired a technique for dealing with my own limitations, and learnt how to tackle unknown and unfamiliar fields; it gave me a clue and a key, so that I did not have to waste time in regretting the gaps in my education or in envying those who were taught subjects which were missed out in my own case. In short, I had learnt how to be capable of going on learning.

During those two years, the dictatorship of the will was fortunately not quite total. I continued to visit the Ashmolean Museum. There was no collection of early Chinese wares in those days. It was the Minoan and Mycenaean and early Mesopotamian pottery which attracted me. I realized that hand-thrown tea cups were indeed a practical possibility, and that the handles on those prehistoric cups (wine cups, I suppose, really) were far more functional than those of our modern china, and had been made by exactly the same bowing process that I had learnt at Braunton. At Braunton I got the blacksmith and the carpenter to make me a kick wheel, with the active support of my father – that is to say, he paid for it. The price as far as I remember was £7. It was a good wheel and went with me to St Ives, then later on to Winchcombe and eventually (in 1967) back to Cornwall again. It is still the same old wheel, now rather like the knife which first had a new blade and then a new handle. At Braunton Pottery also they showed me a tiny paragraph in the trade magazine *Pottery Gazette* which said that an English artist, a Mr Bernard Leach, had learnt in Japan the 'secrets' of Oriental stoneware and had lately returned to Britain to open a pottery at St Ives in Cornwall, in partnership with a Japanese potter, Mr Shōji Hamada. There was also a minute photograph of a strange black artifact described as a beer mug. At that time I paid little attention, but I stored it away at the back of my mind, for possible future use.

I was beginning to wonder how I was going to start my potting life after I was free. That same summer of 1922 I crossed the water in a boat hired at Braunton Hill, in company with two cousins, Ian and Lucy, and revisited what was left of the old Fremington Pottery. There was quite a lot: all the buildings were intact, including the little dwelling house with a glazed galena tile built into the wall on each side of the front door. The biggest surprise was that we found Bill Short, one of the original Fishley team. He was deaf and had a cleft palate and a stammer, so it was difficult to understand what he said; but there was no mistaking his excitement and pleasure at having visitors. When the place had been sold to a big Barnstaple pottery ten years previously he alone had been kept, to carry on with making the traditional cloam ovens.

I told my cousin Ian I would like to get possession of the pottery and make pots here.

IAN: 'But who would do the work?'
ME (indignantly): 'I'd do the work myself.'

I began to realize that from now on I was going to have less and less in common with my cousins and my Oxford friends. I was embarking on a life the validity of which they would not be able to recognize.

My father, always quietly but enthusiastically supporting me in all my projects, inquired whether there was any hope of buying or renting the pottery. Eventually the answer came through that the place was offered for sale at £300, 'on condition that it was not to be used for pottery manufacture'. (Today it has been sold and resold many times; nothing seems to be left of the old buildings.)

One advantage of my forced studies during the last two years at Oxford was that they gave me a good excuse to continue spending my vacations at

St Breward on Bodmin Moor, where, as I absurdly pretended, I could concentrate on my books and studies with no temptations or distractions. I had discovered Cornwall – and St Breward – four years previously at the same stage of adolescence at which I discovered the pleasures of long-distance walking. At an age when most boys, my own brothers included, acquired motor-bikes, I made the discovery that it was a great pleasure, excitement and satisfaction to walk twenty or thirty miles a day. This passion for walking had taken possession of me at the age of sixteen when I was among a party of schoolboys sent to Cumberland to help with the harvest of 1917 (the famine year of the First World War), and it reached its peak during the next two years.

From the top of Saunton Down on a clear day you can see not only Exmoor but the Welsh mountains across the Bristol Channel and even the Preseli hills of Pembroke. To the south, the horizon is the crisp blue line of Dartmoor, even more enticing and a bit more accessible. So at the age of seventeen I set out on foot to go there; and having got there, slept in that terrifying silence and solitude somewhere near Yes Tor. Next day I made my way across to the other side of the moor and lay among the whortleberries gazing westward. There on the horizon was the unexplored country of my ancestors – craggy rocks outlined against the sky and looking like the crust of the Bread of Life itself.

Everything on that first exploring walk into Cornwall was memorable. At Polyphant my unbelieving eyes saw the first Celtic roadside cross. I stopped at Five Lanes and asked a man the name of the next village. The way he said 'Trewint' almost made me jump; the word was out in a flash as if it had been freshly coined that second. I thought to myself: 'This is it; this is where I belong.' As dusk fell I reached the slopes of Brown Willy and slept in a damp cave which next morning I found I was sharing with a goat and her newborn kids.

3

WHAT DO YOU MAKE
OF THAT?

For the next four years I never missed a chance to spend the winter vacations at St Breward, staying at West Rose Farm with Mr and Mrs Raymont and their family, saturating my mind with the set books (chiefly Plato's *Republic* and Aristotle's *Ethics*) and my body with the smoke of the turf fires. One day at the end of 1922 I went into Mr Hawken's shop in St Breward to buy something – candles or a bucket or a pair of boots. They took me down into a sort of basement store, and there all over the floor was an immense hoard of pots: pitchers large and small, washing pans, milk pans, and the humpy shapes of the great cloam ovens. All except the cloam ovens were glazed with the same galena brown and yellow glaze which Mr Fishley used, but it was often discoloured with grey or greenish patches and blotches where the faggot firing (damp furze bushes, as I afterwards discovered) had played on the surface. I found out that they were made at Lake's Pottery in Truro, thirty miles to the west.

It was now the beginning of January, 1923. I immediately went to the village and hired a bicycle so that I could go and see the pottery. I started early in the morning and found the pottery at Chapel Hill in Truro and met Mr Collins, who managed the kiln. He showed me how he dipped the pitchers in galena glaze and set them in the open kiln, and told me about the faggot firing. By the time I had seen everything it was already late in the short midwinter day. I told myself, I will go to the railway station. If there is a train I will go on to St Ives and see that 'Japanese' pottery which I read about in the *Pottery Gazette*. If there's no train I'll go and visit the Chilcotts here in Truro. (The Chilcotts were the only cousins who still lived in Cornwall.)

There was a train. When it reached St Ives the sun had already set. I asked about a pottery. 'You mean Leach's pottery?' They directed me up the Stennack, and there, where the houses came to an end and the open country began, I found a shed and a gate and a signboard with a curly inscription just legible in the dusk, 'The Leach Pottery'. Inside the gate I met a short, stocky man, George Dunn, and asked him if Mr Leach was in. No, but he would call Mr Hamada. Then Mr Hamada came out and I began to explain myself to him, asking whether he thought there would be any chance for me to work here after I had left Oxford, which would be in July.

Hamada was all alone in the pottery and slept in a tiny bedroom at the far end of the workshop. He said he thought there might be a chance for me, since he himself would be returning to Japan towards the end of the year and Mr Leach might be glad to have a helper. So he volunteered to take me over to Mr Leach's house, nearly two miles away at Carbis Bay. We walked up Trenwith Lane in the dark and then by footpath to the Cornish Arms. Down in a sort of valley below us there seemed to be a large town with many small lights twinkling. It was the herring season: the 'valley' was the sea, and the lights were those of the St Ives fishing fleet out in the bay.

At last we reached the old Count House where the Leach family lived. (A Count House was where the tinners used to meet at regular intervals to share the pay-out of the mine.) I met Mrs Leach, a warm and charming person who looked rather like someone out of a Japanese colour print. I also met the five children – David, the eldest, was a boy of about twelve. The house seemed vast, cold and empty. There were only a few pots to be seen, and they looked very strange and austere to me. Hamada explained in Japanese the reason for our visit. Leach listened to what he said, turned to me and said, 'All right; but first of all let's find out what your ideas are.' And he went to the shelf, picked up a curious deep bowl with incised fluting on the outside, put it right into my hands and said, 'What do you make of that? Probably eleventh century.' It was a very strange pot to me, made from a cane-coloured clay. It had a turned, unglazed foot, and was coated with something which looked like a white slip but which might perhaps be called a kind of dusty matt glaze. My good angel protected me and made me hold my tongue. Of course I could make nothing of it, having never seen anything like it before.

In England at that time Chinese stoneware of the Sung period was practically unknown, or only beginning to be known by a few *cognoscenti*. (America, I think, was more enlightened in this respect.) I was just able to connect this bowl with the Tz'u-chou ware which I had seen and handled at Gerald Reitlinger's[1] house in Gloucester Road. What had struck me about those was that they revealed a bridge between the things I thought of as real pots, and the late Chinese porcelain in my father's house in Wimbledon. They were rather similar in shape to the porcelain vases, with high shoulders and tight waists. But on the other hand they had the unmistakable marks of having been thrown on the wheel. They also had deeply undercut feet, unglazed, revealing that the material they were made of, though not red like that of the pots I knew, was

---

[1] Gerald Reitlinger was a friend from Oxford days. – S.C.

still recognizably a sort of clay. Like the porcelain, these Tz'u-chou pots were covered with painted decoration; but instead of blue and white it was a beautiful sepia-brown on an ivory or cream ground. Reitlinger's elder brother, to whom they belonged, pointed out to me that the drawing was much more lively, much less conventional, than that of the later blue and white. To me the strangest thing about them – as with this bowl of Mr Leach's – was the deeply turned foot-ring, something I had never met before. But this bowl he had put into my hands was doubly difficult. There was no painted decoration, only this delicate fluting; and its glaze was more like parchment than any glaze I had ever seen before.

It was a sort of initiation ceremony, and I don't think I really passed – at any rate not on that first occasion. The fact is that however much, like others of my generation, I venerated Chinese civilization, Oriental stoneware did not at first appeal to me. But at this moment I was taking the first step in a process of integrating all pottery from soft earthenware to porcelain, towards a state of feeling where you could appreciate them all as pots, though some might be easier and attract you more than others. It was a long process which began now when I first came into contact with Leach, and it has continued all through my potting life, until eventually I have reached a more or less enlightened state where the treatment of a Chinese porcelain plate or bowl speaks of clay, and of the needs, functions and expression of human users and makers in the same language as a European earthenware pitcher or a West African water pot.

That first meeting with Bernard Leach was a decisive one. As time went on it gradually began to dawn on me as a possibility that what I naturally liked or thought I admired was not necessarily the last word, and that many kinds of pot which, like this fluted bowl, were at first inaccessible to me had qualities which I would be able to learn about if I tried.

Nevertheless, honesty compels to admit that I never loved stoneware by my own natural inclination. By temperament I am a simple-minded earthenware man. But the logic of technique has always increasingly compelled me to recognize the serious limitations of earthenware: technical shortcomings where the technique is primitive, as in European peasant wares; and aesthetic barrenness when the technique has been forcibly upgraded, as in the so-called 'fine' earthenware of industry. Gradually I came to realize that the greater contains the lesser: you can, if you want to, do many things in stoneware which are very like earthenware – but are nearly always better. Examples are the sgraffito slipware of some Chinese peasant stonewares, and the long tradition of painted Tz'u-chou ware. There are even some kinds which are fired at stoneware temperature with stoneware glazes, yet are logically and strictly 'earthenware', since the body is still porous.

But all that lay in the distant future. On this particular winter evening in January 1923, what saved me was the fact that Leach was not only the prophet of early Chinese and Korean wares but was also excited about the English slipware tradition; and so my enthusiasm for Truro and Fremington must have told him that perhaps something could be made of me, and that I could be useful.

My own impression of that evening is that it was all arranged there and then that I should come and work at St Ives as soon as I was through with Oxford; but Muriel Leach assured me later that it was by no means so quickly settled in my favour. Anyhow, from my point of view, the important thing was that it was eventually so settled, and the course was set for my first serious steps towards becoming a potter.

It must have been about now that I had my first introduction to the world of post-Victorian arts and crafts. An architect uncle, hearing that I was interested in pottery, sent me along to meet Sydney Greenslade and other members of a society which had been founded by William Morris himself some time in the 1880s. Sydney Greenslade was an architect, and had rooms in Gray's Inn in London. I liked him but I was rather intimidated by other members of the society who were there; they seemed to me to be academic and somehow puritanical. They were all great enthusiasts for Martin ware, which I now heard about for the first time. The last survivor of the four brothers was even present – he was the one who used to make the grotesque modelled heads and faces; but at this date he was a very old man, whose discourse was only of rheumatism and of how it prevented him from doing his work. I was shown innumerable fine specimens of Martin ware and was obliged to be polite about them.

Sydney Greenslade and his friends were kind and encouraging, but stern. They took care to impress upon me that the society maintained very high standards of craftsmanship and that to be admitted to membership would be a privilege not easily to be achieved. But I did not perceive any compelling necessity to strive to achieve it.

I also went along to a shop or gallery in Conduit Street where arts and crafts were sold, and asked if they had any pottery by Bernard Leach. They had a few small pieces, products of the earliest firings at St Ives. Of course I found them strange and difficult, and also expensive. While I was looking at them and trying to understand them, the proprietor of the gallery was called to the telephone, evidently by a craftsman who was undertaking some special order.

'What price should you charge? Well, the more you ask the better they will think it is.'

I was deeply shocked. I decided that arts and crafts – or at least their selling side – emitted a stink; what exactly of, I was not quite sure, but it seemed to be of something old and stuffy, over-upholstered and decaying; cobwebby, sticky and contaminating.

4

THE LEACH POTTERY, ST IVES

I spent nearly three years (1923 to 1926) at the Leach Pottery, the most important part of my education as a potter. So it is disappointing that I can remember so little from that time. What I learnt there I certainly learnt profoundly; but also painlessly, almost unconsciously, as if in spite of myself. It may perhaps seem odd to some potters that in those three years I never acquired a whole-hearted or deep devotion to Japanese pottery. It is true that Bernard lent me his copy of Kakuzo Okakura's *The Book of Tea*, and I read it with enthusiasm. I loved the idea behind the tea ceremony; only the objects, the things themselves, left me cold or indifferent. He once tried to tell me about hand-modelled tea bowls and their points; but the seed fell on stony ground. In those days, the discussions at the pottery were mostly about Chinese and Korean work, and about the practical methods used in Japanese potteries. Or is it simply that this was the aspect of Leach's teaching which at that time I was most ready to absorb?

But in the perspective of years later it is clear to me, whichever way I look at it, that the landing of Bernard Leach and Shōji Hamada on the island of Britain in 1920 was for craftsmen potters the most significant event of the twentieth century. I don't mean that it was the cause of all those waves of enthusiasm for craft pottery which arrived during the following decades and which have been continually increasing in momentum ever since. The waves of enthusiasm would probably have come anyhow. Nor is the importance of the event to be measured merely by statistics – the number of students and pupils whom Bernard Leach has influenced. I think it is rather a matter of depth than of extension and lies not so much in the numbers of his followers as in the power and influence of the ideas which he imparted.

He taught us two things. The first was that the best pots of the Far East were not the technically perfect productions of the Ming and Ching dynasties but the works of earlier periods, which have more life and make a more significant statement; and that 'provincial' porcelain of later date, made for the people themselves, has more to say to us than all those masses of export wares which went to Europe in the seventeenth, eighteenth and nineteenth centuries. This was a simple extension into our own times of that necessary process of learning from the Far East which has been going on all through our Western ceramic history.

The second part of his teaching was related to the first. It was he who first brought to potters in the West the ideas and ideals of the best and most enlightened of the early Japanese tea masters: the doctrine that technical accomplishment counts for little beside inner life, that plain things made for the use of humble people have more *mana* or power than articles of luxury; that irregularities in craftsmanship and accidents of firing do not necessarily impair the beauty of a pot but may even enhance it – provided they are not added deliberately or contrived self-consciously.

Every touch by the potter is *physiognomic* – that is, it is an infallible guide to his real character, to the state of his mind (or his soul). All his meanness and all his egoisms will inevitably be betrayed. On the other hand, if he is, in Jacques Maritain's phrase, 'fundamentally rectified and lifted up along the lines of beauty',[1] then nothing can stop the healthy character of what he makes from becoming visible. 'How can a man conceal his character?'[2]

Thus Hamada always used to speak of clay 'bodies' as if they were human bodies ('a good healthy body') and his highest praise for a pot would be to call it 'kind' – which is Anglo-Saxon for what we now call 'humane'. He also used to throw away pots which showed too much of what he called 'tail' – the ineradicable marks of aesthetic falsity in the potter. But how a man can learn to see and recognize his own 'tail' was a thing he never explained to me.

These were the ideas which now gradually began to penetrate into me (sometimes against my conscious will), and I found I was taking the first steps towards realizing that there was much more in pottery than merely becoming a proficient producer. It went without saying that pots had to be of a professional standard, acceptable for their purposes. But also, whatever you made would have its own indelible character, good or bad; and this character was the most important part of a pot, and necessarily came straight out of 'the real you'.

Thus there were no clear lines between techniques, aesthetics and ethics. You would only be able to make good pots if you were in some sort of sense 'good' yourself. Not that moral beauty necessarily produces artistic beauty – it obviously doesn't; or rather, the connecting links are too complicated for one to be called the cause of the other. What you had to do was dig a bit deeper,

---

[1] *'foncièrement rectifiées et exaltées dans la ligne de la beauté'*, Jacques Maritain, *Art et Scolastique*, Paris, 1927 edition.
[2] Confucius, *Analects*, book 2, chapter 10.

down to the common taproot which nourishes both. And the only way to set about that with any hope of ultimate success was by hard work. 'Without unceasing practice, nothing can be done. Practice is Art. If you leave off you are Lost,' as Blake said in 'Laocoön'. You must make pots unceasingly even if they betray – as they almost certainly will – the worst as well as the best in you.

The day I arrived to start work at St Ives – it must have been in July, 1923 – I was surprised to find quite a crowd at the pottery. Besides Leach and Hamada and George Dunn, there was Edgar Skinner, elderly, retired and benevolent, who was helping with the business side of the pottery; Mr Bassett, an old St Ives fisherman who was a 'tight friend' of Hamada; and Sydney Greenslade, down on a short visit from London. There was also a man called William Staite Murray, whom I now briefly met for the first time. Sydney Greenslade led me aside to tell me how pleased he was that I was starting with this group who were 'so full of enthusiasm'.

As far as I remember, by the next day all the visitors were gone, and there remained Leach, Hamada, Edgar Skinner, George Dunn and myself. Hamada was busy and preoccupied, working for an exhibition to be held before he left for home in the late autumn. He was throwing tall Tz'u-chou type jars, using a very small and (as it seemed to me) very inefficient and inadequate kick wheel of the English type, the shortcomings of which did not seem to trouble him in the least. He used the same wheel for trimming his pots, and for this he perched them on a leather-hard clay chuck – a totally new and unfamiliar process to me.

The only other wheel at that time was Bernard's Japanese hand-wheel, a beautiful piece of nicely balanced wood spinning on a porcelain cup-bearing which turned on a long spike of hardened wood or bamboo. To spin it, you held a sort of drumstick by its knob, inserting its point into one of several holes in the circumference of the big wheel-head, and these holes were set at a slight angle so that you could only turn the wheel in the traditional Japanese direction – that is, clockwise. As a result, all the processes of throwing as I had learnt them at Braunton had to be reversed; and so, since Hamada was using his wheel all the time, I had to learn how to throw on this wheel, when Bernard himself wasn't using it.

Besides the use of the Japanese wheel, and the new technique of trimming the pots by the turning process, there were plenty of other new things to learn, two of which were especially exciting: the Japanese 'spiral' method of kneading, and the art of throwing 'off the hump'. Both of these were difficult at first. For the kneading I deliberately adopted a system: every morning I practised it for ten or fifteen minutes before breakfast, and after a fortnight of this I began to acquire the knack.

I soon discovered that if you did it with the right rhythm and tempo, using the weight of your body rather than the muscles of your arm, you could knead for a long time without becoming tired: and that the few minutes spent in kneading, far from being time lost, were valuable because the process not only made the clay fit for throwing but also polarized your mind and gave you time to think about the pots you were proposing to make. I found it to be one of those seemingly mindless or automatic hand processes which give a craftsman an unforeseen bonus, and I still think it would be unwise to cut out clay-kneading in favour of a de-airing pugmill.

This was the first time I realized that there might be a fallacy in the gospel of labour-saving devices. People always seemed to be saying that it would be a good thing to eliminate 'all the donkey-work', as they called it. Certainly some donkey-work is fit only for machines. But every process has to be judged on its merits, and this was one which passed with honours.

Throwing from the hump meant cutting each pot from a big lump of spinning clay with a short piece of twisted thread held by one end only, instead of the European system of making up separate balls of clay and cutting each pot from the wheel-head with a wire. It took longer to learn this, and even now I have a beginner's tendency to allow the thread to make a sloping instead of a level cut.

In return, I was able to demonstrate the Devon method of 'bowing' or handle-making, and can claim to have introduced this technique at the Leach Pottery and thereby to a much wider circle of potters. The method, though almost universal among traditional potters in the West, was apparently not used – or not generally used – in the Far East.

Bernard now proposed that he and I should go over to Saunton to see the Fishley pots about which I never stopped talking. I forget how we made the journey: he had not yet acquired his celebrated motor-bike and sidecar, and I never used anything but my feet. I suppose we went by train. When Bernard saw the Fishley pots – mostly green-glazed pitchers, bowls, plates and flower vases – he was polite; but he soon quietly disappeared into the kitchen and came back with some of the comb-decorated oven dishes and plain water pitchers. His enthusiasm for these opened my eyes to something I had never thought about before. 'These are the things', he said, 'which would interest my friends in Japan. Fishley was evidently the last of the peasant potters of England.' It did not take me long to move over to seeing the Fremington pots in the way he saw them: the green-glazed 'decorative' ware as a modern deviation and the plain kitchenware as the authentic channel of expression.

Some time after we got back to St Ives, an unexpected diversion occurred: a proposal from Gerald Reitlinger that I should accompany him on a long

Mediterranean cruise. He was to have gone with his brother, but Henry had now dropped out for some reason, and so there was this spare first-class ticket asking to be used. Would I like to come? I had to make up my wavering mind in a hurry. I told myself, 'I've already lost two precious years at Oxford. My father is desperately hard-up, and my mother seriously ill. It is obvious that I must try to become self-supporting as quickly as possible, seeing that so much money has already been wasted on my education.'

But everybody – father, mother, friends, even Leach himself – told me I should go, and it did not take much to convince me. It was clearly the opportunity of a lifetime; in those days Mediterranean travel was not often available to younger sons of large, hard-up, middle-class families.

Never having left Britain before, I busily got myself a passport; and my father, always aiding and abetting me, gave me (in spite of being so hard-up) some extra money 'so that you will be able to buy that wonderful pot if you see it'. His favourite maxim was 'You never regret your extravagances; you usually regret your economies.'

It was to be a wonderful round trip; Venice–Egypt–Istanbul–Greece–Venice; with stops of about a week in Venice, Cairo, Istanbul and Athens. Travel is wasted on the very young: and yet youth is the time when one is most able to enjoy it. I suppose it is just another case of '*Si jeunesse savait, si vieillesse pouvait*' – the young have strength but no sense: the old have sense but no strength. In retrospect my main regret is that though I spent several weeks idling on Italian ships, I failed to learn the most beautiful of all European languages, imagining that since I knew Latin there was no need to take any trouble with Italian – an elementary fallacy which even at that age I should have had enough sense to avoid.

The biggest pottery experience was picking over the dry rubbish heaps at the old potters' quarter of Fostat outside Cairo, and occasionally finding fragments from the period of the medieval caliphate – shards of painted faience and brown and yellow galena-glazed slipware. Gerald Reitlinger even picked out a fragment of Chinese celadon imported in the Sung or Yuan period. I discovered that shards like these, with their broken-off bits of drawing, are in some way more exciting than entire pots. But I also spent hours in the Egyptian Museum, absorbing the series of magnificent black-painted terracotta pots from Predynastic to Roman times.

At Tripoli in Lebanon there was a pottery where the clay slip was run out to stiffen in plain trenches dug in the porous soil. Here the potter was throwing on a kick wheel which was tilted at an angle away from him. This enabled him to get a better view of the shape he was making; but if he stopped the wheel, the pot would heel over and lose its shape. These tall, two-handled, high-shouldered amphoras were being made in two stages: first, a shape something between a deep bowl and a flower pot was thrown; and when these had stiffened slightly, another potter made a series of roughly thrown rings of wet clay. Each ring was tapped on to the top of the lower half, and the thrower then completed the shape by centring and raising the new piece.

Towards the end of October we saw Venice again, rising from the northern horizon, gilded and fragile in the autumn sunshine. By this time the idleness of travelling first class had begun to give me what Ernest Hemingway (in *A Moveable Feast*) calls 'the death loneliness that comes at the end of every day that is wasted in your life'. I was also coolly aware that the Mediterranean was not my place, and was hankering for the open-endedness of the Atlantic.

At the beginning of November I was back in England, dizzy with sun. Hamada and Leach were both in London holding exhibitions. The last two firings had more or less burnt out the old kiln which they had built in 1920; but the pots were spectacular. Hamada's exhibition created a sensation and became a landmark for years afterwards. Everything was sold, including the best and most expensive ones, which he had hoped to take back with him to Japan.

Here at Paterson's Gallery in Old Bond Street Bernard introduced me to Katharine Pleydell-Bouverie, who was coming to work at the pottery for a year. She seemed to me very beautiful and also very big, with a large frame like a French peasant's; and yet at the same time somehow petite, because her features were so curiously fine.

Leach told me that there was now a second Japanese potter at St Ives, Tsuranosuke Matsubayashi, who was already hard at work pulling down the remains of the old kiln and getting ready to build a new one. After a few days Bernard said, 'What are you doing now?' and I realized he meant, 'For God's sake, get back to work at St Ives.' So I went.

George Dunn, who could neither read nor write and who had in consequence an infallible ear, always called Tsuranosuke Matsubayashi 'Mister MacByash', which I suspect was a good deal closer to the right pronunciation than any of us ever got, tied down as we were by the insuperable handicap of literacy, and thinking only of the way the name was spelt. Mr Matsubayashi was a man of about twenty-seven or twenty-eight: an absolutely typical Japanese young gentleman, Bernard assured me. He was totally conventional and sometimes frighteningly correct in his manners, but most of the time managed to be charming, humorous and sympathetic. He claimed to represent the thirty-ninth generation in the unbroken succession of the Asahi Pottery. When you came to think about that, it seemed to mean that the Asahi Pottery must have been founded in the seventh century A.D., and ever since then had continued in the same family, thus making our eighteenth-century dynasties of potters seem like *nouveaux riches*.[3]

Besides having these thirty-nine generations of potters at his back, he was (I think) a graduate of the Kyoto Porcelain School and knew as much about the theoretical basis of ceramics as any Western ceramist of that time (probably more than most of them), and yet was also what used to be called among English tradesmen and artisans – and the description implied the highest praise – 'a thoroughly practical man'.

By the time I got back to St Ives he had already torn down the remains of the old kiln and had built a temporary one for firing special bricks for the new kiln. He immediately put me on to help him make firebricks, hammering the stiff crude local kaolin rock into wooden moulds. It was my first introduction to the unwelcome fact that about four-fifths of a potter's work is hard labour on what seem at first to be intrinsically dull jobs. As one becomes a little less dull oneself, one often finds that those jobs are not quite so dull as one thought at first.

I was now allowed, greatly to my pleasure, to occupy Hamada's old bedroom at the back of the pottery and to sleep in the bed he had made for himself after a Scandinavian model. Matsubayashi occupied proper conventional lodgings in the town.

Besides being an amusing companion and making me work extremely hard at the brickmaking, he became my mentor and tutor during the following months, teaching me many useful if elementary things about pottery. He told me that if you want to make the most of the plasticity – 'the prasty', as he called it – of a clay or a clay-mix, you should make it into as watery a slip as possible and then stiffen it slowly. About the souring or ageing of clay, he said it should be put away in the clay cellar at exactly the right consistency for throwing and left there as long as possible – for months or even years. In this way, he said, something which he mysteriously called the Alkali Permutation 'would be going on so nicely'. I think he was talking about base-exchange: but he made it sound like some kind of transmutation of the elements.

He had a habit of introducing his information with the formula, spoken in slow, careful English, 'At my father's pottery – ah – having in Japan, we are – ah – having – ah – very nice arrangement for cray-making . . .' Alas, the arrangements for clay-making at the Leach Pottery in those early days were far from 'very nice'. They were chaotic, and always inadequate for our needs.

He told me about a way of de-watering slip by freezing, as used in Japanese

---

[3] My friend Mr Kim Schuefftan informs me that the records of the Asahi Pottery cannot be traced back further than the sixteenth century.

potteries: in frosty weather let your clay slurry freeze thoroughly, and then, when the thaw comes, the needles of clear ice will melt and the surplus water will have been effectively separated, so that the clay will soon be in a fit state for wedging and kneading. 'But be careful', he told me with a grin, 'that there are no needles of ice left in the clay-mass to cut your hands.'

He also gave me two very useful rough rules. For most clays, he said, a slip is about half water, half clay; and a plastic clay body is about one-third water and two-thirds clay. If you have to mix two clays together, one of which is plastic and the other non-plastic (for example, ball clay and kaolin), don't slice them up and try to knead them together until mixed; in this way the plasticity is lost. They should both be turned into slips and then mixed, and this will make the most of the plasticity of the mixture. He told me many things of this kind, now so long built into my daily practice that I am no longer conscious of how I acquired them.

Later on, he announced that he was going to give us evening lectures on the theory of ceramics, and we all sat round the eating-table in the main part of the pottery, armed with notebooks and pencils.

It was sometimes rather difficult to make out what he was telling us, since none of us had any scientific training for this kind of thing. On top of that, his English, especially his pronunciation, made him difficult to follow. Thus he was continually speaking of an element which he called 'karium'. I discovered later that this meant potassium. In addition to the Alkali Permutation there was also a mysterious thing called thinter-point. Every ceramic substance, he said (I am not sure if he excepted quartz from this rule), had not only a melting point but also a 'thinter' point. This puzzled us all, but I realize now that he was speaking of the Tammann Temperature (0.55 to 0.6 of the Absolute Temperature of Fusion) at which particulate solids become sintered together without the help of a liquid phase.[4]

I regret to say that all this wealth was completely wasted on me at the time. And Bernard was almost as bad; he was always interrupting with philosophical questionings, such as whether all this theoretical stuff was really relevant to the quality of what you produced. Matsubayashi had an imperturbable self-confidence derived from his thirty-nine generations of potting ancestors and was sublimely unaware of something which the rest of us could not help noticing: that in spite of his mastery of the theory of ceramics, his incomparable technical training and his centuries of unbroken tradition, he was totally unable to make a good pot. Bernard never lost an opportunity of telling him that he did not begin to know what a good pot was, or how to make one; but

---

[4] See Michael Cardew, *Pioneer Pottery*, Longmans, London, 1969, chapter 6.

Matsubayashi's armour was impenetrable and he always remained serenely immune to all this.

On one occasion, however, he saw – and took – his opportunity for an innocent revenge. We were discussing a particular pot, a modern Chinese ginger jar with a beautiful turquoise-green glaze, and wondering how it was done. 'What a pity', said Leach, with characteristic generosity and enthusiasm, 'that we can't all go to China and find the place where it was made and ask them what they do. I feel sure it is something absolutely simple.'

Smiling his Japanese smile and sucking gleefully through his teeth, Matsubayashi quietly replied, 'I think – ah – rather complicated.'

At that time I imagined that the scientific background of pottery was unimportant; and though I dutifully kept my notebook in front of me, it was filled with nothing but doodles – drawings of beer mugs and fat pitchers. The only person who kept full and conscientious notes was Katharine Bouverie. More than twenty years later, when I was struggling with unknown ceramic troubles in West Africa, I realized what a fool I had been and deplored my former idleness. In the winter of 1944–5, when I was home on vacation from West Africa, I went over to visit Katharine at Coleshill. Luckily for me she had kept all her old notes and I humbly and obediently copied them out into my own notebook.

One day at St Ives, Mr Arnold-Forster, a painter friend of Bernard's, came into the pottery and showed us a big oblong moulded dish he had just acquired: old slipware from Staffordshire with black and yellow stripes slip-trailed and 'feathered'. It was glazed on one side only, and the unglazed outside of the dish had turned black with use, like old leather; but underneath this you could see that it was made of a kind of buff fireclay. He recommended it to me as the sort of thing a modern potter ought to be aiming at. Its great merit, he pointed out, was that it did not look like something artificially made but was more like a natural phenomenon, something that had just grown, with the inevitability of a fruit or a vegetable-marrow. It was a magnificent specimen, and this was the first time I had seen one of these things. Yet I remember saying to myself, 'But this is a *moulded* dish; I want to be a *thrower*.' Perhaps I also thought I wanted to make something a bit more 'personal'. I was not quite ready for the 'natural phenomenon' theory.

I still prefer thrown to moulded pots, but now I entirely agree with Arnold-Forster's proposition – that good pots, like that dish, have an impersonal, classical quality, humane but not personal in an individual sense. At that stage I was still slightly under the illusion that an artist potter should consciously try to inject his personality into what he makes. It seems to be a stage which one has got to live through. Normally, it should be only a stage; but in the craft pottery world today this Narcissus-dream, which ought to be just a temporary phase in the evolution of a craftsman, seems to have become a fixation, elevated into an ideal or an orthodoxy.

The theory seems to be that the more personality you can inject into your work, the better it will be: that is, people will be able to say more about it. Talk becomes the main thing. Instead of enjoying things in a natural organic way, we want to be always discussing, assessing, dissecting and scoring up 'points'. If you want to talk, let's talk; but if you want to make pots, cut out the talk and concentrate on the work – that is, do some practical thinking, and leave the discussions for another time, or a future age.

Arnold-Forster also produced a huge celadon dish of the Ming period, and that was another stage in my education. Up to then I had been unable to like celadons; but in fact most of the ones I had seen were nineteenth-century Chinese troughs or *cache-pots*, with embossed moulded decoration: they reminded me of the dreary imitations, made in Europe, in which landladies used to grow their aspidistras. Leach had shown me one or two early Sung celadons, and I had (of course) failed to appreciate them. The glaze was semi-matt and so cloudy as to be almost opaque, so that you could not see the underlying clay; and the colour was so subtle that to my uneducated eye it was not a colour at all, just a dim grey. This Ming dish on the other hand, had a bright, almost transparent glaze and the colour was unmistakably green. I liked it immediately.

Later on, Leach patiently tried to make me see that the earlier celadons had more reserve, more reticence as he called it; they might be more difficult to appreciate at first, but if I went on trying, I would find that they were really better. All my life I have *believed* this; but when I try to *feel* it I realize that even now I am not really a saved soul. I know Bernard is right but I can't help it, I still like the Ming celadons better.

When Bernard returned from London after seeing Hamada off on his travels back towards Japan, I was still trying to master the Japanese wheel. He found me making cups or mugs 'off the hump'; looked at them for several minutes, and then turned to me and said, 'I can see you are still having difficulty controlling the material, but *I like your forms.*' It was one of the best things I had ever heard – as if he had said to me, 'You'll do.'

Soon after that I got my own kick wheel brought from Braunton. At first I set it up out of doors, but later on, when that got too cold, a place was found for it in the little wooden shed where Hamada used to work. I was now able to get down properly to the business of throwing, and I was disgusted when I discovered what a long way I had to go before I could call myself any sort of thrower. The truth was that at Braunton Pottery I had never seriously tackled the difficulties of throwing 'in series', and I now realized that unless you can do this, you are not a thrower, only an improviser. I had an order for two dozen beer mugs from a friend in Oxford. I knew more or less what shape I wanted to make but I was amazed and appalled by the difficulty of getting them to come even roughly the same size and shape, and with rims which were tolerably level. It seemed to be several months before I had made a set which satisfied me, though it can't really have been as long as that.

Most of the throwing I did at that time was for *raku*. The Leach Pottery was having a continual struggle to keep its nose above water financially, and so we had to make a lot of highly coloured *raku*, because that was the only thing that was easy to sell. I made dozens of large bowls and the kind of Japanese beaker called *unomi*, and Bernard decorated them with coloured slips. Our *raku* body was about equal parts of ball clay and kaolin, with plenty of coarse grog added. After firing it was a dead-white, fat, cold, chalky body; but at least it was responsive on the wheel, quick and easy to throw (unlike the yellow slipware clay).

Bernard also got me to make a series of big thrown plates for slipware, using the same incongruous chalk-white body. I learnt a lot about throwing big plates and above all found that shape is just as vital for them as it is for pitchers or any other kind of pottery. I permanently discarded the fallacy that 'plates are easy' (as one of the apprentices at Braunton Pottery had once said to me).

Bernard decorated them with slip-trailed designs – the Mermaid of Zennor; a rampant dragon; a running hare, and many others. We biscuit-fired them, and then dipped them in galena glaze and fired them at 1000°C, set face downwards in a small updraught kiln built for the purpose.[5]

When Matsubayashi had finished building the new three-chamber kiln, on which we all worked as his supporting labourers, we got ready for the first firing – stoneware in the first chamber, slipware in the second, and biscuit ware in the third. The kiln had an enormous firebox in front, with special firebars which Matsubayashi had made for it from the saggar clay mix. All went well up to about 1150°C and then the kiln stuck; in spite of all our sweaty labours down in the pit where the stoke-hole was, the temperature refused to go up. (Our mistake was probably that we had been stoking too fast, and had over-stuffed the firebox.) At last, in the middle of the night, Matsubayashi said, 'Give me the poker.'

He went down into the pit, took off the fire-shield, and began a furious campaign of poking and shaking, grinning all the time against the scorching white heat of the fire. He went on, and on, and on, until we thought he must

---

[5] See Bernard Leach, *A Potter's Book*, Faber, London, 1940, page 180.

melt; but it worked: enough air got in at last and the temperature began to go up again.

When the finishing temperature was nearly reached, Matsubayashi looked into the spy-hole of the first chamber and began to emit curious warning hoots: 'Ho, ho, ho, ho hey! Awful zings happen!' The bungs of saggars had partly slumped and were leaning over and blocking the fireway.[6]

On the day of unpacking we found that the stoneware was badly ashed in places, and smoked or discoloured by all that over-stuffing we had done around 1150°C. The slipware in the second chamber was an unrelieved disaster. Owing to the dampness of the new kiln, all the lead had volatilized from the galena, leaving the pots 'dry', with just an occasional tantalizing square centimetre of brown and yellow glaze. In the general consternation I was tactless enough to quote an eighteenth-century proverb, 'Experience keeps a hard school but fools will learn in no other.' Bernard immediately retorted, 'Experience may be a hard school, but anyone who *expects* to learn in any other would be a fool.'

Firewood was always a problem in those days. In West Penwith, that ultimate peninsula of Britain, the stuff hardly exists; certainly not on the scale needed for a pottery. Once we were obliged to use old railway-sleepers; the result was a disaster because of the 'pickle' in the wood.

It was not until several years after I left St Ives that the Leach Pottery gave up wood firing and went over to oil. I happened to be down at St Ives on a visit at the time of one of the first oil firings. The stink, the noise, and all the attendant mechanization were enough to convince me that wood was the only fuel for me, and that I must be careful never to build a kiln in a country where it was scarce.

[6] See Bernard Leach, *A Potter's Book*, page 217.

5

DIVERSIONS

Life at St Ives was not all pottery. We each had to take it in turns to cook for a week. This frightened me at first, since cooking was one of the many important branches of knowledge lacking in my education. However, the others took pity and helped me, partly no doubt in self-defence. Edgar Skinner introduced me to the pottery garden, a strip of ground beside the main road where the showroom now stands. He showed me how to pick and cook the spinach which seemed to be the main or the only crop. Matsubayashi taught me the proper Japanese way to cook rice, and George Dunn showed me how to 'scrowl' a mackerel. Besides mackerel, rice and spinach, there was some-times an improvised version of *gu-na-be*. Instead of a charcoal brazier we put the gas-ring on the table and boiled spinach leaves in it with slices of steak, each of us picking out his share with chopsticks while the pan was simmering.

We ate our rice from little Chinese bowls of Tz'u-chou type. They were quite modern. Bernard told us that on the voyage home in 1920 he was leaning over the ship's rail in Shanghai or Hong Kong, and saw a group of coolies eating out of these bowls. He asked to buy them, and that was how he acquired them – for about a penny each, he said. Since I very seldom had any pennies at all at that time, their cheapness made a big impression on me. They were of the ordinary classical Chinese shape, with rather straight sides. The sepia decor-ation was simple and completely right: plain banding with a few dashes placed with the utmost restraint and economy of means. I have never succeeded in making any bowls as nice as these, though to be fair I have never tried to imitate them directly. If I had, the result would probably not have been good – 'How can a man conceal his character?' But the memory of those bowls (I wonder whether any of them still survive) tells me continually about the kind of beauty which is proper in pots, and about what they say to us: in short, what the potter's art is about.

That autumn I began to learn the Cornish language. Robert Morton Nance was giving evening classes once a week at the Old Cornwall Society down in the town. I had been wanting to learn the language for a long time, chiefly I think because it fed two of my ruling emotions – romanticism and a passion for words. The idea of it tantalized me: there was this ancient language, idiomatic and idiosyncratic, which yet possessed an almost Roman dignity. It seemed as if it had only just disappeared over the western horizon, taking with it all sorts of echoes of our ancient British and Romano-British ancestors. Surely something could be recaptured, if one only acted quickly enough and took the trouble to relearn it. Much of its vocabulary and many of its idioms seemed in a way already familiar: to learn one only had to remember.

The loss had been our own fault, or the fault of our recent forefathers, who in their haste to be assimilated with English civilization had done nothing to keep it alive. Even its memory was not treated with proper respect. In the early eighteenth century there had been a small band of devoted people who cared for it and tried to gather up its remains. But in the nineteenth century it became fashionable to sneer at it, or at least to patronize it as a curious fossil, as if Cornish people were masochistically castigating themselves for having consented to be robbed of their birthright.

We were a small class of five or six people, one of whom was Richard John Noall, an elderly recluse, extremely Cornish, who lived just up the road at Hellesvean. He used to teach me simple greetings like *Fatel yu genough-why?* (How do you do?) as we walked home, speaking with the Cornish intonation which was natural to him. I felt I was listening to the authentic sounds of the language which had been pronounced extinct for the past hundred years.

At weekends, my chief entertainment was exploring the Penwith peninsula alone, walking out towards Zennor and beyond. There is something about the air in west Cornwall which magnifies things, especially on those early spring days in February or March when the sun is suspended in a light haze and the universe is giving one of its continually repeated lessons about the reality of time, saying 'Here comes a new-minted season, which you in common with all other living things on earth have never experienced before, and will never experience again.' Carn Galva on such mornings used to look like an enormous mountain, the ultimate western rampart.

Once Bernard and I were lucky enough to be invited to go 'round the land' after pilchards, on a St Ives fishing boat. Going 'round the land' meant you sailed out from St Ives, rounded the Land's End inside the Longships, then went far out to sea to shoot the nets, and would come back next day to Newlyn on the south coast to sell the fish. Our boat was called the *White Heather*. She was a small sailing boat with an auxiliary motor and a crew of about eight.

Going 'round the land' was quite an experience. All the tides of the North Atlantic seem to meet there in a head-on battle, and the *White Heather*'s jumping was remarkable; she did everything except sink. In the second half of the night we were allowed to help with the hard work of pulling in the nets.

This kept us warm and interested – the nets were full of pilchards and mackerel. We felt we were becoming useful passengers at last, and began to forget our sea-sickness. When all the nets were in the crew took some of the mackerel and boiled them in sea-water: the best food you ever ate.

When the time came for Matsubayashi to go home, he led me aside and said, 'I hope you will stay here with Mr Leach, and always help him with the work, because – ah – I think – ah – Mr Leach – ah – rather poetical.' I assured him that he was 'telling me my own dream', as the Greeks used to say; that I had no plans to leave the pottery, and hoped to work here for many years. This was true: I had as yet no idea of starting a pottery of my own. I thought I would stay at St Ives, doing some of the supporting work for the stoneware, making the thrown *raku* ware and, mainly, producing the slipware which was my special passion.

Matsubayashi left soon after this, not before he had provided Katharine Bouverie with plans for her first stoneware kiln at Coleshill in Wiltshire. He wrote charming letters from home, telling us he was intending to marry 'the most beautiful woman in Japan'. But something went wrong: the marriage never took place, and we heard later the sad news that he was dead.

All through the winter of 1923–4 the Leach Pottery faced a continual struggle for survival, and Bernard tried to think of ways to keep it going. One of these schemes was to take part in a kind of local exhibition which was to be held in the Drill Hall, a large, draughty, forbidding building down in the town. We were to give daily demonstrations there to try to interest and entertain the public. I was to do the throwing, while the others staged *raku* firings.

During this winter at St Ives I had been living a hard life, very close to the ground. I enjoyed all these self-imposed hardships, and made a cult of them. There was of course no bath at the pottery, and no source of hot water, except the kettle, and I thought that was fine. I had always hated indoor baths and indoor sanitation – they were depressing and somehow sordid. Besides, I told myself, if you were accustomed to a cold bath out of doors, in winter as well as summer, you would be better able to survive when the day came – as it surely would – when from one cause or another all the comforts of civilization were suddenly removed. A small stream, known as the Stennack River (though it was only a trickle) ran through the pottery yard; so I hollowed out a little pool and used to jump into it every morning. But I soon discovered that west Cornwall, which is supposed to enjoy a mild climate, can in winter be a very cold place; and that one of the coldest spots in all of west Cornwall is where the pottery stands at the top of the Stennack – a funnel perfectly designed to catch the full blast of the north-east wind. And the coldest place in the pottery was my bedroom, with its one window facing north-east.

Towards the end of March one of those strong persistent winds set in. The great event down in the Drill Hall was now due and we worked hard to get everything ready. On the first morning I went down early to prepare the clay and set up the wheel. When I reached the hall it was still locked, and I had to wait around shivering in the wind until the doors were opened. I don't remember much about that day's work because towards the end of it I was seized with a curious pain in the chest.

In the evening I got back to the pottery feeling hot and weak, and decided the best thing for me would be a nice cold bath in the pottery stream; I tried it, but it didn't seem to do any good. Next morning when Leach arrived he quickly had me taken to the St Ives cottage hospital in an ambulance, and I lay there for the next six weeks with pneumonia.

There were no antibiotics in those days. All they could do for pneumonia was to wrap the patient's chest in a cotton-wool waistcoat and hope for the best.

At the bottom of a deep pit in the ground you are every minute about to be buried alive by the cold mud which is continually seeping in all round you and collapsing on to you from above, threatening to drown you. Your only hope is to keep on shovelling it away and struggling to get out. But the harder you work at this the worse it gets, and the more difficult it becomes to breathe, because of the unbearable pain in your chest. You have to snatch short, sharp breaths of air, because if you try to take a deep breath this heavy log of wood – that's what it must be, a great log of wood stuck down there – will kill you.

Was it two or three days, or a week, or only one night? At last I knew where I was, in a hospital bed, wrapped in this cotton-wool waistcoat; and it was still intolerably painful to breathe. When I eventually began to get better, I was able to read. Bernard used to bring me books, the most beautiful I had ever seen: early Chinese paintings of landscapes – towering rocks; waterfalls; Taoist sages sitting in contemplation; the roofs of a village lying in the valley. Every picture was decorated with inscriptions in Chinese characters, and these seemed to me even more wonderful than the paintings themselves.

It was long past the middle of April now; I was missing the spring, and the wood anemones would be in flower. But Katharine Bouverie brought bunches of them to put beside my bed. The first day I was allowed to get up and go outside it was already early May. I stood in the hospital garden looking across the bay at the distant cliffs and Godrevy lighthouse. They were clear-cut and seemed far removed and out of reach. I felt I would never again enjoy my old intimacy with the landscape. From now on it would never be anything more than a spectacle to be gazed at. I would no longer be identified with it as in the past. I had lost my youth.

6

DISTRACTIONS

When I told Matsubayashi that I intended to stay on at the Leach Pottery 'for ever', I had been perfectly sincere; but within about a year something happened which changed all that.

One day in early 1925 I was kneading clay in the pottery when two preternaturally beautiful beings walked in. One of them had short auburn hair which curled tightly all over her head, making her look like the Hermes of Praxiteles; the other had dark hair cut in the style they used to call 'bobbed', giving her the look of one of those grave and serenely beautiful page-boys who appear sometimes in fifteenth-century Italian paintings. They were the two most beautiful people I had ever seen in my life. They just came in, watched me for a few minutes, said nothing, and left again.

This vision was a consequence of the plan Bernard had been talking about for some time: to get other craftsmen or women – weavers, for instance – to come to St Ives and establish workshops there, so that the pottery and all it stood for would not be quite so isolated. Both he and Hamada had visited Ethel Mairet's weaving shop in Ditchling in Sussex and were enthusiastic admirers of her hand-spinning, weaving and vegetable dyeing. Bernard had probably spoken to her about this idea and perhaps had asked whether she could recommend one or two of her pupils who would be ready to start their own workshop and would like to settle in St Ives.

As soon as I got the chance I asked him about the two visitors, and was intensely disappointed to hear that they had already left St Ives. I asked particularly about the 'fifteenth-century page' and Bernard was able (thank God) to tell me that she lived in Ditchling and that her beautiful name was Luned Jacobs. From that day my life entered a new mode, directed entirely towards the time when I should see her again. But I had no idea when that would be. Making pots now became, temporarily, nothing but a régime that had to occupy all my energies, a means of relieving the tensions of what was evidently going to be a long period of waiting.

Eventually Bernard told me the bad news that Luned and her Praxitelean friend had decided against setting up their workshop in St Ives. But two other weavers, Leo and Eileen Baker, came down from Ditchling during that spring, and stayed at the Count House with the Leach family. They knew Luned quite well, and told me a lot more about her and her family. She was the second of three daughters of W. W. Jacobs, the celebrated author of *The Night Watchman* and other stories of London seafaring life. They also said that Luned's mother had been a prominent activist in the Women's Suffrage Movement in the years before the First World War. Father and mother were now separated.

All this made me more than ever determined that I must somehow make my way to Ditchling and see Luned again. Meanwhile there was nothing to be done but to go on waiting, working harder than before. I had absolutely no money for travelling, and hitch-hiking had not yet been invented. Hitching lifts by sea was my substitute, for any journeys for which walking was not practical. I asked George Dunn whether he knew of any cargo boats going up the south coast; he told me boats sometimes left Newlyn with roadstone from Penlee quarry.

I was suffering from boils at that time, an affliction probably induced by too much hard work. George Dunn had his own simple prescription for this painful condition. In his crude and direct way he confidently told me that the best cure was for me to 'get a nice woman and she would take all this bad white stuff out of me'. But his well-meant advice was wasted: I didn't want any of his nice women, I wanted Luned.

So I took myself and my boils over to Newlyn and hung around the quay looking for a likely boat. There was an ancient schooner in the harbour, and I eventually found its skipper in a pub. He was quite willing to take me, but he didn't know when he would be sailing, and had no place on board where I could sleep. When I explained that I could not afford to sleep in lodgings he at last showed me a small hatch on the deck, saying that I would be quite welcome to try sleeping down there if I really insisted.

When night came I let myself down into this small black hole and settled down to sleep on a heap of old sails and burlap. All was well for the first hour or so, but I woke suddenly with a strange itching all over my body. Turning on my electric flashlight I found, not dozens, but many hundreds of enormous and very hungry fleas all over me. I succeeded in killing a few and tried to sleep again; but after some hours of this, I realized that it was a losing battle – their reinforcements were inexhaustible. At last, towards the end of the short summer night, I climbed out of my hole, bitten all over, and finding a nice coil of rope on deck lay down on it to get some sleep.

The next thing I knew, the sun was shining and there was an elderly weather-beaten face looking at me – not the skipper of the previous evening.

He asked me what I thought I was doing there, so I explained. He said I was making a mistake trying to sail in this ship. The skipper, according to him, was a habitual drunk, there was very little prospect of his getting a cargo or sailing soon, and the schooner was anyway scarcely seaworthy. So I gratefully attached myself to him and he took me along to the jetty which served Penlee quarry.

As we went, he asked me what I did for a living. When I told him I was a potter he was evidently baffled, but went on asking questions about what it involved, and whether it was possible to earn a living at that occupation. He also told me about himself. His name was Hoare – his first name was, as I discovered later, Abednego. He had been a Scilly Islands pilot all his life, and was now retired or semi-retired. He was a great enthusiast for the Bible, and assured me earnestly that, all things considered, it was 'a very useful Book, well calculated to enable a young man to get on in the world'. I was not very keen on the Bible, having been compelled, at school and at Oxford, to read large parts of it; but this was the first time I had heard it recommended as a young man's guide to worldly success. Perhaps he meant to imply that a study of the Bible would have kept me away from the pub and the acquaintance of the drunken skipper, and even possibly saved me from the absurd ambition to become a potter.

But I was thinking of something quite different – the surprising discovery that all my boils had suddenly and miraculously been cured; the fleas had done more for me than George Dunn's nice women.

At the jetty there was a small steamer loading roadstone. Mr Hoare took me along to the captain and helped me to get a free passage on her. She was a Glasgow boat bound for Littlehampton, a small port on the coast of Sussex not very far from Brighton.

Next morning Mr Hoare came down to see us off. He had been thinking over the puzzle of my being a potter. 'I think I see now what it is: *it's a fad*, that's what it must be.' I thought to myself yes, I suppose he is about right. He is a pilot, and that's an *occupation*. The world could not get on without pilots and lots of other necessary occupations. But is a potter, the kind of potter I am – or want to be – really necessary? In the view of Mr Hoare and the human race generally, obviously not! 'It's a fad.' Anyway, I told myself, even if it is considered only a fad, I intend to stick to it.

There was a westerly gale blowing and the voyage to Littlehampton was rough and wet. The boat was heavily loaded and rode deep in the water, but, as one of the crew explained, the hatches were well battened down and there was not much chance of sinking. The weather being so bad, I took refuge in the galley, where I found most of the crew sitting round a table, all talking in a strange Glasgow dialect which sounded like the bubbling of a huge pot of porridge – I understood less than one word in ten.

At last we slid into Littlehampton haven. I left the ship and made my way to Brighton and over the South Downs to Ditchling. When I called at the house, Luned was out and her elder sister Barbara opened the door. I left some kind of message for Luned, and Barbara told her that 'a commonish young man was here, asking for you'. Later on, Luned explained to me that in Ditchling language 'commonish' meant 'looking as if he had come from the Common'. There were, in fact, two Ditchlings: the village, which had once been an ordinary Sussex village but was now largely inhabited by an immi-grant population of artistic people from London and other large towns; and Ditchling Common, a mile or two to the north, where the sculptor Eric Gill and a small group of other Catholic converts had built a community of craftsmen called the Guild of Saint Joseph and Saint Dominic. Gill himself, with his family and a few followers, among them David Jones, had recently moved on again to the deeper retreat of Capel-y-Ffyn in the Black Mountains of Wales. Of those who remained on Ditchling Common, Hilary Pepler was the leading spirit. He was a writer and printer and ran St Dominic's Press with a few assistants. There were also one or two weavers, a furniture-maker and a wood-carver.

The faithful who worked at the Common viewed the urban immigrants of Ditchling village with a severe eye, as dabblers and escapers without any serious foundation of religious faith. But in the mind of people like Luned's sister Barbara, dwellers on the Common were weird, fanatical and *farouche*, wore beards, and generally looked untidy and unwashed. Except for the detail of the beard the description fitted me near enough.

Luned later took me up to the Common, and we visited St Dominic's Press. I bought two of their smaller publications, *Libellus Lapidum* and *Aspidistras* – two little collections of satirical rhymes by Hilary Pepler himself. There were other, more substantial books there which I eyed longingly: Eric Gill's *Sculpture: an Essay on Stonecutting* (printed in 1923) and an English translation of Jacques Maritain's *Art et Scolastique*; but though they were not at all expensive at that time, I had no money to buy them. (A few years later I acquired both these books, read them carefully from cover to cover, and was greatly influenced by them.) Hilary Pepler very kindly *gave* me a bound volume of some issues of *The Game*, a monthly magazine very largely written by himself, printed on beautiful thick handmade paper and illustrated with austere woodcuts by Eric Gill.

I read it all carefully. It seemed very odd stuff to me, and half the time I scarcely knew what they were talking about. I was repelled by the pervading religious dogmatism and the insistence on the monastic virtues of poverty, obedience and chastity. I wasn't afraid of poverty; in so far as it meant making one's style of living as simple as possible, it was obviously necessary if I was going to devote myself to pottery. But if I could achieve it by working hard and without compromising things which I certainly thought more important, I intended to get rich as soon as I could – though what I meant by 'rich' was nothing more ambitious than what the eighteenth century would have called 'an humble competence'.

Obedience? Frankly, no! I intended to go my own way.

As for chastity, I was ready to endure it when necessary as a means to some other purpose; but as a thing to be aimed at for its own sake, I could see no point in it.

But even though the tone seemed to me so puritanical I could not help being impressed by some of the things they said. It was the first time I had been made aware of the great impetus which the Catholic Neo-Thomists brought to all the old arguments of John Ruskin and William Morris in favour of craftsmanship and against the industrial system. These Neo-Thomists were concerned not so much with questions of art and beauty, as with attending first to fundamentals. 'What alternative is there,' they asked, 'except to begin again and reduce life to its simplest terms?' My desire to make pots had begun as an aesthetic revulsion against industrial pottery: I wanted 'kinder' pots. Theirs seemed to be an ethical revulsion. They saw the 'ugliness' of industrial products as a natural and inevitable consequence of the ethical unsoundness of the social system that produced them, and they insisted that the ethical unsoundness – and the capitalist system itself – were the natural consequences of turning away from the true religion.

I don't know how much of all this I took in at the time, but at least it fortified my conviction that wanting to be a potter was something more than just a fad.

Some time later, Pepler wrote me a postcard, on which he asked 'Have you a soul?' I remember thinking this was a rather unnecessary question. Since he was a Catholic, he surely believed I must have one, and I couldn't see why he should be asking me about it. I realize now that it was a sort of invitation, meaning, 'Are you converted, or likely to be converted? If so, why don't you come and join us here?' Did I ever reply? I doubt it.

All went well at first between Luned and me. W.W. Jacobs seemed to be fatalistically resigned to all his daughters' affairs, however peculiar, and he treated me with a sort of amused and benign indifference. Luned took me to the weaving shop to visit Ethel Mairet, and we met her brother and sister as well. They had been born and brought up in Barnstaple, north Devon, and had known my parents and also Edwin Fishley; Ethel Mairet was still using many of Mr Fishley's pots. I realized that before the First World War and her second marriage to Philippe Mairet, she had been the wife of Ananda Coomaraswami and had in fact built a house quite close to ours at Saunton; and that when I was still a child, I had seen some of her early textiles there, dyed with colours she obtained from various plants growing on Braunton Burrows.

Luned and I visited Burgess Hill Pottery, where they were hand-throwing flower pots with amazing speed and efficiency, using the clay in a very soft and sloppy condition. I 'borrowed' one of their wheels and made a fat pitcher with the sloppy-plastic clay, but was scolded by the foreman for using 'time which belonged to the Company'.

We also went up to London to see the British Empire Exhibition at Wembley, then (1925) in its second year. There we unexpectedly came across a large slipware pitcher which I had made at St Ives. I had no idea that Bernard had sent it to the Exhibition. Already at this early stage he was an enthusiastic promoter of his pupil's work. But instead of being grateful and flattered I was indignant to find my bad pot displayed in a glass case and marked with what seemed the shockingly excessive price of 2 guineas (£2.10).

I went back to St Ives, and Luned soon came down too, staying at the Count House with the Leach family; she had already dropped the idea of setting up a partnership with her friend. She was a vegetarian of the strictest persuasion, and insisted that I conform, as of course I did, a willing sacrifice on the altar of love. She indoctrinated me in the theory of the Dominance of Woman, began to undertake my re-education by making me read Bernard Shaw's *Man and Superman* and *Back to Methuselah*, and succeeded in convincing me that marriages were made by women, not by men. We also went for long walks together to Zennor and beyond, gathering crottal (lichens) on the rocks, to use in dyeing her yarns. We were always in each other's company, and eventually Muriel Leach (who was keen on the conventions) insisted that we ought to get properly 'engaged'. That suited me all right, but Luned was probably wondering whether she really wanted to marry this enthusiastic young man, and if she did, what were we going to use for money?

We went on like this for a few weeks or months, but in the end her mother arrived, a formidable feminist whom I now met for the first (and only) time. I became aware that things were not going the way I wanted, and soon after she left, Luned broke the news: she did not intend to marry me; on the contrary she was in love with and proposed marrying Kenneth Hamilton-Jenkin, the historian of Cornish mining. As rivals for Luned there was no possible competition between him and me; my position was evidently hopeless. He was not only a man who had his secure place in the established world – he was already working on his first (and best) book, *The Cornish Miner* – he also had a proper income, and even owned a car. Besides all this he was strikingly handsome, and possessed all the virtues and recommendations that were so deplorably lacking in me.

But the main thing wrong with me, I decided, was that I had no money. So I began to be furiously exercised over the problem of how I was ever to put myself into a position where I could earn enough to get married (supposing I ever again wanted to). Anything I earned at St Ives would obviously have to depend on the profitability of the pottery, and the prospects of increasing this by hard work did not seem to be good. I thought stoneware was extremely difficult to make because it was so hard to get a high enough temperature. It was certainly difficult to sell it in those days – it was thought to be too expensive, and unattractive in colour. Yet stoneware was the main thing at St Ives; slipware was only a sideshow. What I wanted was to concentrate on making slipware and to do it on a generous scale so that I could sell it cheap. But there was clearly no prospect of doing this at St Ives, where there was no space or equipment for serious slipware production.

Meanwhile I tried to dismiss Luned from my mind, but could not. I endured the emotional torments of the damned, cut off absolutely from The Good, raging in a hell of impotent despair in which all that I desired was fatally, inexorably and irreversibly removed out of my reach. One evening, when this infernal turmoil was assailing me more furiously than usual, the emotional squeeze suddenly made me aware that somewhere down inside my body, a kind of centre existed, but it was so very small that it was powerless to help me. At this thought I squeezed myself tighter still, and the small centre became even smaller – a minute speck which hardly seemed to exist at all. But soon, all this squeezing turned the tiny speck into a kind of spark; the tighter I squeezed the brighter the spark became. It was still powerless, but it refused to be extinguished. I thought, perhaps this is what people like Hilary Pepler mean when they say 'Have you a soul?' But how very curious it is – so powerless, and yet somehow it feels invincible. It has no size at all, no dimensions, no mass – just a subatomic focus of energy, which behaves as if it was inextinguishable. I suppose that must be what made Plato affirm so confidently that the soul could not die.

Probably this kind of experience – this Intimation of Mortality – occurs quite commonly to people in their mid-twenties. Before that, your sheer physical exuberance occupies all your attention, and no other voice is heard; you think, or rather you are sure, that you can do everything. Then, about these middle twenties, you suddenly realize that you are not a universal genius and, moreover, that you are getting nowhere; your life has no shape. A potter has one precious advantage – that he is already to some extent in the business of shaping; and I clung to this one asset for dear life.

7

LOOKING FOR A POTTERY

There were two consolations in store, for all these agonies of disappointed rage. The first was that I now at last began to appreciate Norah Braden. She had already been working in the pottery for several months, but at first she had seemed to me a prickly and absurd person. Perhaps that was merely my reaction to the fanfare of praises and the high key of expectations which had preceded her arrival. Professor Sir William Rothenstein, head of the Royal College of Art, had written to Bernard extolling her as some kind of genius – I suppose the currency of letters of recommendation was already a bit inflated, even at that time. In build, appearance, and even in character, she was more like a guinea-hen than any other creature. I did not see this at the time; but years later when I went to West Africa and saw wild guinea-fowl in the Bush – so much more handsome than the domesticated bird – I realized that the reason I liked them so much was that they reminded me of Norah Braden.

She was a compact ball of concentrated integrity. Her look was kind and her voice was gentle – the compact ball seemed to be quite soft; but sometimes it turned out to be a rolled-up hedgehog. She had the gift of the *enfant terrible*, liable at any time to say something apparently naïve, yet containing a concealed barb which might perhaps pass as unintended – but you could never be quite sure. She was a compulsive deflater, with an infallible eye, ear or nose for any kind of mental or emotional unsoundness, sentimentality, sloppiness, pretentiousness or self-importance. Since we were all suffering from a normal or more than normal share of these spiritual warts, she had a great time exercising her tonic and healing gifts. They were certainly gifts, certainly healing, but as with any tonic, the first application made one wince, like iodine lotion on a fresh cut.

You could observe quite clearly the invigorating effect of this treatment on Bernard, who was still to a great extent living in a dream-world of his pre-1914 coterie of Japanese artists. She flapped this dream away deftly, neatly and quickly, like a kind but firm nurse removing a bandage long overdue to be changed. I gasped at her courage: previously none of us had presumed to interfere in this area – we just accepted it as an unavoidable patch of absurdity in Bernard's make-up. But what she did was not from conscious courage, still less from a callous ruthlessness. It was a natural Cassandra-like gift: she had to do it. Any relationship other than one of complete honesty and sincerity was impossible for her. I was shocked by the way she talked to Bernard, but the effect on us – and on him – was like magic.

My turn came too. My pots and I had to submit continually to her almost invisibly fine shafts. If I worked the clay too long, till the pot became all fat and no bones, and took it from the wheel thinking it was a fine full-bellied thing, she would just say, 'It looks as if it needed a pin stuck into it to let out some of the air.' A little later you began to think that it wasn't only the inflation of the pot that she was puncturing. I was now able to make big fat pitchers with long necks, and was very proud of them. Norah looked at them and said, 'They are like proud, strutting peacocks. Why do you have to make such proud peacocks?' She didn't say 'What have you got to be so proud about?' But I had an uneasy feeling that that was what she had consciously or unconsciously meant.

She had certainly realized that something was missing in my relations with Luned. But now that the 'engagement' was suddenly cut short, I began to feel the warmth which lay below the prickles. One day my friend William Lloyd came over from Zennor, bringing the Mozart sonatas for two unaccompanied flutes, and he and I played the slow movement from one of them, I taking the second flute part on the clarinet. This inspired Norah Braden to bring out her violin – among her many other accomplishments she was a good amateur violinist. She introduced me to the great Handel Sonata in G minor for two violins and bass, and she and I used to practise the two solo parts together, she playing the first violin and I the second on the clarinet, over and over until I knew every note.

This new friendship was my first consolation. The second was a totally unforeseen legacy of £300 from my Aunt Ella.

Before the 1914 war, when we were children, we sometimes used to be taken by train to stay with our grandmother at Liss in Hampshire. 'Big Granny' lived here in a big early Victorian house with her two middle-aged unmarried daughters, Aunt Ada and Aunt Ella, both of whom we adored because they spoilt us. We were a bit afraid of Big Granny, but she was not really frightening. She had a sister who lived in London, our Great-aunt Gussie. Aunt Gussie in her youth had been in love with Edward Lear. He loved her too and wanted to marry her, but because he was middle-aged and poor and suffered from epilepsy he never had the courage to propose. The house at Liss contained a large collection of Edward Lear watercolours. The *Nonsense* books were there too: early editions, tattered and falling to pieces from the attentions of generations of children. We in our turn devoured and maltreated them, it being tacitly understood that Edward Lear 'belonged' to us in some special way and was in fact practically a sort of relation – as indeed he would have been, if only he had married Aunt Gussie.

But Aunt Ada died in 1912; and when Big Granny herself died in 1916, the estate was sold and Aunt Ella, whose whole life had been enclosed in that house, revolving round her mother, her almost innumerable nephews and nieces and the Girls' Friendly Society, was now out in the cold world alone, rather pathetic and bewildered. She did not survive this uprooting for many years, and now in her will she had left these considerable legacies to all her nephews and nieces.

So I suddenly found I had some capital, and I was free to look for some place where I could embark on my plan to make slipware on a serious scale, in (I hoped) a traditional country pottery. If I could find such a place it would also have the short-term advantage of taking me away from St Ives, where the proximity of Luned and her impending marriage were a continuing cause of emotional embarrassment to me. Here was my chance to escape from this situation and to work out my own salvation, ploughing my own furrows in a new place and in my own way.

Bernard had made a plan with the furniture-maker Gordon Russell to put on a grand demonstration of the country crafts at the Russell workshops at Broadway in Worcestershire. This was to last for a whole week during Easter 1926.

Bernard and I set out from St Ives on his motor-bike. The sidecar was full of our tools and gear, and I rode behind on the carrier. It was a three-day journey. We buzzed eastwards in a thick moist blanket of sea-mist; nothing could be seen but the hedges between which we went, the mist condensing on our faces and eyelashes, a curiously refreshing sensation. We didn't see much of the country, but, as Bernard remarked, we got a more intimate feeling of its character. We got as far as St Blazey, and there the motor-bike broke down.

Next day we managed to reach Cullompton in Devon, and on the third day we made better progress, over the Mendips and along the ridge of the Cotswolds. Towards the end of our journey we passed through Winchcombe, a small but handsome town all built of severe dark grey Cotswold stones.

At Broadway, a kick wheel had been set up and they provided some blue-grey clay which had been found when they were digging foundations for a new building. This clay was extremely plastic, and much nicer on the wheel than anything I had used at St Ives. It's funny, what a lot the clay itself contributes to the character of what you are making, imposing its own individuality so that the shapes you throw are slightly different, even though it is the same you that is shaping it. Using this clay I was surprised by what I could do with it – the lightness of the pots and the ease with which I could lift them from the wheel. They kept their shape with refreshing elasticity.

Gordon Russell had an architect friend staying, a keen member of the Design and Industry Association, and in the evenings the four of us used to have great arguments about handcraft and manufacture, Gordon Russell and his friend advocating the use of machinery to do the bulk of the heavy work. They spoke from the point of view of an architect and a furniture-maker. Gordon Russell was planning this type of production for his workshops, maintaining that good design, plus machines, plus hand-finishing could produce work as fine in its own way as that of the past, and more appropriate to the twentieth century, avoiding the self-consciously mannered style – and the high prices – of the Arts and Crafts Movement. Bernard and I spoke as potters, both of us insisting that in clay-work – or at least in making pots – it was necessary for the human hand to have control at every stage. We forgot to mention pugmills, blungers, crushers and ball mills.

Sometimes we discussed my own plans. Gordon Russell and his father were both eager to see a pottery established in the neighbourhood and were extremely helpful to me. Old Mr Russell told me about the pottery which used to be working at Greet, just outside Winchcombe six or seven miles to the south, and he took me over to see it.

Greet Pottery had been started early in the nineteenth century by a family named Beckett. Sometimes it was called Becketts' Pottery; and the road has always been (and still is) called Becketts' Lane. They produced only the ordinary range of 'redware', as it was called: unglazed flower pots, chimney pots, land drains – hand-thrown in those days; and also milk pans, cream pans and the enormous straight-sided open pans which everyone in country districts used for their washing. The last three types were galena-glazed on the inside, but not outside. They had never, as far as I could find out, made any pitchers. Winchcombe was too close to Birmingham and its galvanized buckets for any tradition of pitcher-making to have survived.

We were told that the last Beckett to run the pottery had died when he was still quite a young man, leaving a widow and three young children. Mrs Beckett had tried at first to keep the pottery in production, employing one thrower, Elijah Comfort, and a boy to turn the wheel for him; but early in the 1914 war she gave up the attempt. The pottery had thus been lying idle for eleven or twelve years when I first saw it; but Elijah Comfort still lived in Winchcombe, working as an agricultural labourer.

Mrs Beckett had eventually sold the place as a smallholding. There was a brick dwelling house, plenty of outbuildings, a large barn, cart sheds, an orchard and a field or two. It had been bought by Mr and Mrs Butler, a retired farmer and his wife, as a home for their working retirement – Mr Butler was keeping one or two cows and a pig, and Mrs Butler raised poultry. The long building which had once been the pottery was not used at all, except that Mrs Butler had found that the old kiln was ideal as a nice, quiet, cool place for broody hens.

Exploring the pottery building, I found a beautiful big kick wheel still more or less in working order, a bevel-gear boy wheel on which the big pans had been made, and the remains of a second kick wheel; all three with lovely mahogany wheel-heads, 18 inches (45 cm) in diameter. In the workshop there were two flues for drying out the pots, long *kangs* (as I called them from the Chinese word for a fire-heated bed). They had a fireplace at one end and a chimney at the other; and big red tiles along their whole length near which the ware boards used to be set. All the ware boards were gone, of course, but the uprights for them were still in place, with holes 6 inches (15 cm) apart for the pegs on which the boards rested; just the same arrangement as that used at the Fremington and Truro potteries.

The kiln itself was impressive, a great updraught structure with a chamber of 10 feet (3 metres) diameter inside, 18 inch (45 cm) thick walls, and all the iron bandings still in position. There were four fire-mouths, as at Fremington and Truro. At the top of the updraught chamber there was a dome, with holes spaced for the flames to pass into what we afterwards called the 'hovel', a second updraught chamber tapering into the chimney. This went through the roof, and at the top there was a damper which could be lowered on to the chimney by means of a chain. The chain was hooked on a nail in the trunk of an apple tree, already in blossom though it was still only the month of April.

Looking at the chimney, the damper, the chain and the apple tree, I suddenly had the sensation called *déjà vu* – 'You have been here before.' Maybe it was only an unconscious memory of what I had seen at Fremington; but what I really think is that the kiln was telling me, 'This is where you are going to be.'

The whole pottery gave out a feeling of generosity and of good old-fashioned country ways of working. But there was also an alternative prospect on my horizon. Someone, probably Katharine Bouverie, had told me about the pottery at Verwood in Dorset, on the western fringe of the New Forest, and I went to see that as well.

Verwood must have been one of the most primitive potteries to survive into the twentieth century. At the time I saw it, it belonged to a local timber merchant, for whom its chief merit was as a place where his offcuts, otherwise useless, could be used as fuel. There was no pugmill, all the clay being tempered by a boy with bare feet treading it out on a stone or cement floor. There were two or three kick wheels of the English or cranked type, and when they had to make big pots they undid the treadle arrangement and tied a stick to the crank of the spindle. A boy (the same boy who trod out the clay) sat on a stool in front of the wheel and turned it by alternately pushing and pulling the stick – a process which is not such hard work as it sounds, because the flywheel keeps the wheel going and the turner only has to give a push at the right moment of each revolution – the flywheel does the rest.

The pottery was manned by two or three throwers with a boy and an older man called Meshek who managed the kiln. The kiln was perhaps the most remarkable feature of this pottery: enormous, partly below ground level, and loaded from the top. It looked as if it was the direct descendant of the Romano-British kilns which have been uncovered in the New Forest area. When it was full, a temporary covering was made, consisting of old broken pots and pieces of tile. There was only one fire-mouth and it was fired with wood only, whereas at Truro – and even I think at Fremington – coal was burnt in the earlier stages of firing.

Here they made the usual flower pots and washing pans and also – this was its special recommendation in my eyes – pitchers of a very fine shape, much fatter than the Truro and Fremington pitchers but, like them, free and generous in feeling. They were glazed with galena and fired at a very low temperature, nearer 900°C than 1000°C.[1]

All these traditional pots were set in the open kiln without any saggars or other supports, but I thought perhaps I could make some arrangement with the owner and the potters, letting me work there and share the kiln, making saggars to occupy part of the kiln space. But even I could see that such an arrangement – imposing myself as a sort of cuckoo in this ancient nest – would be rather difficult.

I went back to St Ives to think about it. Bernard was in no hurry for me to leave. I don't think he had any other pupils in immediate view at that time – difficult though that is to imagine in these later years. At St Ives I reflected that it was all very well for me to dream of working in a traditional pottery, but I had no first-hand experience of firing an updraught kiln. So I went to the pottery at Truro and proposed to Mr Collins that I should come up and help with one of their firings.

In Truro I stayed with my cousins the Chilcotts; their two sons were already out in the world, but the daughters were still living at home. At the pottery, all

[1] For a description of Verwood Pottery, see the *Pottery Quarterly*, no. 24 (1959), pages 127–31.

was being got ready for a firing. The old kiln had a hovel like that at Greet Pottery, but instead of a dome to separate the two chambers there was a sort of circular balcony looking inwards to the main chamber; you could safely walk round it and look down on the pots just below. Mr Collins used to do most of the setting from the wicket of the main chamber, and when this lower part was full the wicket was built and closed, and Mr Collins would complete the setting from the top, leaning over from this gallery. He even used to walk round it during the early stages of the firing, enveloped in a cloud of coal smoke, to check whether the pots were evenly distributed. If he saw a place where a chimney was likely to develop, he would close it to equalize the draught. 'The smoke hasn't affected my puff, so far,' he told me. He was about sixty at that time, and had probably been doing this all his working life.

When I reported for duty at the pottery, coal fires had already been lighted the night before, in all four of the fire-eyes. These fires were increased during the next day until the inside of the kiln was red-hot; and then a great ritual began. Four blunt-pointed pitchforks ('pikes') were produced, and the huge faggots of furze were carried in and untied. Next, the embers of coal were allowed to subside and the heavy iron firebars were pulled out on a shovel and taken outside to cool. Each fire-eye was now just a glowing ashpit full of red-hot coals.

You took your pike, separated a branch or two of the furze bushes (you couldn't use your hands, because of the prickles) and poked them into the fire, where they immediately burst into a furious blaze, sparks of embers and ashes flying up through the setting. You had to keep on pushing in new branches, because each one only blazed for a few seconds. Thus there were four men all busily and continuously stoking the furze, and the whole place was full of smoke, flying ashes and the hot smell of the blazing bushes.

This went on for about forty minutes, until your firebox was three-quarters full of glowing embers and it became increasingly difficult to poke the next one in. Then Mr Collins gave the signal; we all stopped stoking, a long fire-rake was brought and one of the men raked out all the embers; others shovelled them into an iron pan, and two men carried them away, tipping the embers out on to the floor of the drying shed, where they continued to glow, helping to dry the damp pots on the shelves above. This raking-out process took about twenty minutes; by the time it was finished all four fires had died down, and it seemed to me at first that the temperature inside the kiln must have dropped dangerously low. But in fact this was not so; the effect of the twenty-minute pause was simply that the heat was given a chance to rise from the lower part of the setting to the pots higher up.

Then the signal was given to begin stoking again, and the whole cycle was repeated, hour after hour, all of us stokers becoming hotter and dustier. I began to wonder how many hours this was going to continue, and how long it would be before I dropped dead from heat and exhaustion. At last Mr Collins went up to the spy-hole in the hovel to try his test-piece. He used to put a small pot with glaze on it where it could be seen from the spy-hole, and he simply held the tip of his poker close to this to observe whether the glaze was properly melted: if it was, it reflected the iron tip like a mirror. Long before it got to that stage the test-piece would shine and reflect the poker – the skill lay in recognizing the exact degree of mirror-bright reflection which meant that the glaze was properly matured. Then there would be one more hour of 'easy' stoking to eliminate possible patches of under-firing, and the kiln was finished. The final temperature was about 950°C, and thanks to the system of intermittent stoking and cooling-off at regular intervals, the heat was evenly distributed with no serious over-firing at the bottom and no under-firing at the top; and (if the setting was properly done) no serious horizontal differences in temperature.

We clammed up the fires, and I went back to the Chilcotts' house to have a bath. The whole firing was only a little more than twenty-four hours, which included about eight hours of the faggot stoking.

Next day Gilbert Chilcott took the two girls and me in a rowing boat down the tidal Truro River as far as Malpas (pronounced Mopas) where it joins up with the Tresillian River. Coming back we had to row against the tide. I had never found rowing so hard before and thought, 'Shall we ever make it back to Truro?' I had to drive my arms to keep going, and wondered, 'Why am I suddenly so feeble?'

I went along to the pottery and found Mr Collins there. 'You see,' he said, 'it's a foolish idea for someone like you to try to be a potter. It isn't work for a gentleman. Now look at me; I've already got over *my tired*; but you still haven't got over *your tired*. We are used to this kind of work, but folks like you will never get used to it. It's too hard for a gentleman.' I accepted his words meekly, seeing well that it would be difficult to explain that I didn't want to be a gentleman. If he said I was one, then that was merely my misfortune and I was determined to overcome that handicap. Nothing was going to frighten me away from being a potter.

I returned to St Ives and at last came to the conclusion that Greet Pottery, Winchcombe, was the obvious place. So I wrote to Mr Butler agreeing to rent the pottery building from him for 10s.(50p) a week, and began to make preparations to leave St Ives.

8

WINCHCOMBE

What I wanted from life in 1926 was, first, to teach myself to become a good thrower; and secondly (as a natural consequence of that), to make myself economically self-supporting, so that I would be in a position (if that was what destiny decided for me) to marry a wife and raise a family. The first of these ambitions was, I have always felt, realized only in a very imperfect way. The second ambition was indeed realized, but again in a flawed way – that is to say, I did at last meet Mariel; we did eventually get married; we had three children and we were happy. But the hard work of bringing them up and giving them a respectable education fell entirely on her.

However, those first years of Winchcombe Pottery do have a certain general interest for potters and for those who are curious about the evolution of craft pottery. The commentators (usually more numerous and far more articulate than those who actually produce the stuff about which the comments can be made) say that I was trying to 'revive' the English Slipware Tradition. But I don't think I was conscious of any such aim. What interested me was to make pots which could be used for the purposes of daily life, and to make them cheap enough for ordinary people, as I mentally called them – that is, obscure middle-class people like me and my friends and relations – to be able to use them and not mind too much when they got broken. I also wanted to make them in a modern style, though by this I did not mean using modern manufacturing techniques. It was only the style that was to be modern, but if you had asked me what I meant by that I could not have given a coherent answer.

It obviously meant that I had to work in a proper workshop on the same scale as the old country potteries, not in a small one-man studio. And the ware had to be simple, not too elaborate or too difficult to make. I wanted the pots to be warm and direct and above all natural, like those made at the old potteries in north Devon, which looked as if they had occurred naturally, by a common consent between the potters and the environment in which they lived.

I planned to use local red earthenware clay and to raw-glaze with the clean fresh yellows and browns of galena glazes. This was what the Winchcombe kiln was designed for and, above all, it was what I liked best. I soon discovered that this slipware has its own special difficulties. Galena (which is lead sulphide) is the natural ore of lead and only needs to be ground and mixed with clay and a little quartz to make a glaze which fires brown on red clay and yellow over a white slip. It has the advantage of being practically insoluble in dilute hydrochloric acid, which means that it is safe for the potter himself (though not necessarily for his customers, as I subsequently discovered).

I had already learnt at St Ives that it has to be open-fired – that is, the combustion gases must be free to circulate round it, so that all the sulphur can escape; otherwise it will be entrapped in the glaze, producing a surface as rough as coarse sandpaper, with a very unpleasant mustard-like colour. If the fuel, or the kiln, or even the pots themselves are at all damp, the same sort of thing will happen: the lead volatilizes, leaving an unmelted 'dry' surface instead of a proper glaze.

The Winchcombe years, so far as I can distinguish them, divide themselves roughly into three groups: early struggles; early successes; and family life. During the first period I made all the mistakes that a young potter can possibly make when he starts a workshop of his own. You learn much more quickly that way and you never forget those lessons, but all your experiences have to be paid for on a strictly cash basis.

After putting up a camp bed in a far corner of the vast loft, and an eating-table down below, beside the smaller of the two *kangs*, the first thing I did was to explore and clean out the kiln. I removed the relics of Mrs Butler's broody hens – feathers, hay, old eggshells and occasional clutches of ancient evil-smelling addled eggs long ago abandoned by the sitters; and eventually got down to the true floor and the symmetrically spaced holes coming up from the flues. The dome which separated the main chamber from the hovel and chimney seemed to be very flat, sagging alarmingly on one side. I never ventured to tread on that part and even when working underneath it I always felt nervous. But I thought it might last a few years.

Finding Elijah Comfort was not difficult. He was living in North Street, Winchcombe, a short, grizzled, late-middle-aged man who was almost com-pletely deaf. He agreed to come back to the pottery as a thrower for the same wages he was getting as an agricultural labourer – something like £2 a week. He also found a boy to turn the big wheel for him. The first boy only lasted a few weeks; then he found Sidney Tustin, who had just left school, aged fourteen. Sid didn't like turning the wheel for Elijah and at the end of each week always said he would leave. But after I got a power-driven wheel for Mr Comfort (it was driven by a spluttering, apoplectic petrol engine), he taught himself to throw on the second kick wheel and gradually became reconciled to a potter's life. There must have been something he liked in it, for he continued to work at Winchcombe Pottery until he reached retirement age.

The plan was that Elijah Comfort would make the flower pots and the great washing pans which had always been the chief production in the Becketts' time. The washing pans were to be set in the first circle of the kiln, their rims resting on the pan-rings of which there were many hundreds stacked round the kiln – another valuable legacy from Becketts' Pottery. That would leave the central part of the kiln – about half of the total capacity – for bungs of saggars containing the glazed ware which I was going to make.

But first I had to make the saggars; and before I could begin to employ Mr Comfort, I had got to ensure an adequate supply of clay for both of us. For the saggar-making I bought a truckload of fireclay from a firm in Stourbridge. It came in pulverized or granulated form, a grey, granular material which seemed to contain the right amount of grog. All you had to do was to slake it in water and then add enough of the dry clay to make it fit to knead. The surprising thing about this material was its plasticity – much greater than that of the mix of kaolin, grog and ball clay we had used at St Ives. As a refractory material for high-temperature use it would have left much to be desired, but it was adequate for earthenware temperature, it was nice for throwing and the saggars lasted well in use.

I knew that galena would not work in closed saggars, so I decided to make holes in the saggar walls and take the risk that fly-ash from the faggot stoking might get in through these 'windows' and spoil the glaze.

Getting enough clay for Elijah and myself was a more difficult proposition than I expected. Out in the middle of Mrs Butler's orchard there was a large marsh-like hollow which in the Becketts' day had been the sun-pan or settling and stiffening pit for the washed clay, the yellow, silty-sandy flood-plain clay from just below the orchard grass. This had all been used up now, except for one small patch of ground at the far end. The sun-pan itself was entirely grown over with sedges and bullrushes, and had become the home of moorhens and frogs. At its head was the old mixing-pond, now a grass-grown circular hollow. Around it there had been a circular brick-paved track where a horse used to walk round and round dragging a sort of rake or harrow which churned up the water and clay. When the slip was thick enough they used to open a little 'gate' and run it out into the sun-pan through a grid. The grid was still there in the ground, overgrown with grass. The water supply came from a pipe which brought it from an intake further upstream in the little River Isborne.

I gazed at all this, and my courage failed at the thought of all that would be involved in bringing it back into working order. I thought I had already bitten off quite as much as I could possibly chew in taking over this huge pottery with its enormous, 600 cubic foot (17 cubic metre) capacity kiln. Mr and Mrs Butler had only rented the pottery building to me on a yearly tenancy, and if I were to propose now to mess up a great area of their lovely orchard as well it would land me in difficulties not only with them but with my bank account too.

At Braunton Pottery and at Truro they did not have to wash the clay. It came from Fremington in the as-dug condition and they simply weathered it and pugged it, picking out occasional stones or roots by hand. So I wrote to Willie Holland's brother, who used to dig it, and got him to send me a truckload by rail.

Up the road in Greet village there was a small tile- and brickworks. Some of the clay-workers there had formerly worked in Becketts' Pottery and the manager was friendly, so I was able to arrange with him that the Fremington clay should be taken there for weathering and pugging and then sent down to the pottery. A message came that the clay had now arrived, and where should they put it for weathering? Instead of going there and selecting a place, I simply answered that anywhere would do, wherever it suited their convenience. They happened to dump it where a heap of small coal had been lying. When the pugged clay arrived at the pottery it was full of little pieces of coal, which we only noticed during throwing. We dug out the worst bits with a sharp bamboo, but after firing, the pots were pitted all over by the pieces which had been missed. Pots from the first firing of the Winchcombe kiln – if any have survived – can be recognized by these 'coal-blows'.

Next, I bought from the brickworks two loads of the local dark grey tile clay. The first load was satisfactory, but the second had come from a different part of the pit and was full of limestone fragments, too small to pick out, so small indeed that you did not even notice them while throwing. After firing, this clay seemed good at first; but a few days later I made acquaintance with something which is well known and feared by brickmakers and potters, and is called 'lime-blowing'. The fragments of limestone had all turned into quicklime in the kiln, and now they were slaking and blowing – that is, they expanded and chucked off the clay and glaze between them and the surface of the pot, leaving nasty pits all over it with a small lump of slaked lime at the bottom of each pit. If the walls were thin they blew both ways and left holes.

In the end I had to go back to washing the clay. After a year or two of trying different expedients I acquired a petrol engine to pump the water from the stream and built a small brick-lined sun-pan where the washed clay could gradually stiffen until it was ready for pugging. In this way I was able to wash

Edwin Beer Fishley, Fremington Pottery,
Devon, *c.* 1909.

2 LEFT An earthenware pot covered with black slip with white slip-trailed decoration, under a transparent green galena glaze. Width 4¼ in (11 cm). Made by Bernard Leach at St Ives, *c.* 1925–8. CENTRE A salt-glazed stoneware bottle covered with white slip over wax resist decoration, under a dark galena glaze. Height 7½ in (19 cm). Made by Michael Cardew at St Ives, *c.* 1928. RIGHT A stoneware jug in a light buff body with wax resist decoration, under a mustard glaze. Height 4 in (10 cm). Made by Shōji Hamada at St Ives, *c.* 1923. *University College of Wales, Aberystwyth.*

3 A slipware jug with a Cornish inscription: "Do today and God will bless." Height 6¼ in (16 cm). Made by Michael Cardew at St Ives, *c.* 1925–6. *Collection of Edward Bawden.*

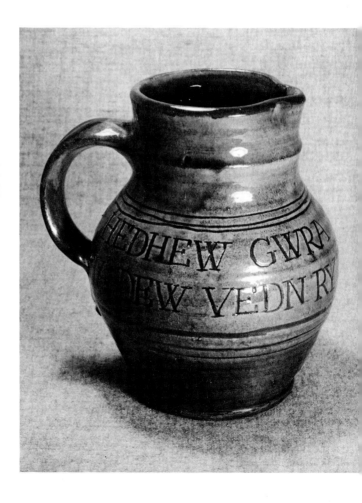

4 Pots waiting to be fired in the loft at
  Winchcombe, late 1930s.

5 Elijah Comfort, Charles Tustin, Cardew
  and Sidney Tustin beside the horse-drawn
  pugmill at Winchcombe, 1934.

6 Cardew shaping the neck of a pot at Winchcombe, c. 1930.

Mariel and Michael Cardew at Winchcombe, 1934.

8 Mariel with Seth, Ennis and Cornelius at Wenford Bridge, 1942.

9

10

A tall three-handled earthenware jar with white
slip-trailing on a red body, covered with an
iron-green galena glaze. Height 13¾ in
(35 cm). Made at Winchcombe, c. 1931.
Collection of Simon Fox. Photograph by Stephen Brayne.

11   A black slipware cider jar with sgraffito
decoration under a galena glaze. Height 16½ in
(42 cm). Made at Winchcombe, 1936. *Craft Study
Centre, Holburne of Menstrie Museum, Bath. Photograph by
Colin Wilson.*

An earthenware bread crock with sgraffito
decoration under a galena glaze. Height 18 in
(46 cm). Made at Winchcombe, 1929. *Craft
Study Centre, Holburne of Menstrie Museum,
Bath. Photograph by Colin Wilson.*

12 An earthenware rose bowl with white slip-
trailing over black slip under a galena glaze.
Height 6½ in (17 cm), diameter 10½ in
(27 cm). Made at Winchcombe, *c.* 1935.
Collection of Simon Fox. Photograph by Stephen Brayne.

13 An earthenware rose bowl with a fountain
design in trailed yellow-green slip on cream slip,
under a red-brown glaze. Height 9 in (23 cm),
diameter 15 in (38 cm). Made at Winchcombe,
c. 1938. *City of Bristol Museum and Art Gallery.*

all that was left of the spoilt Fremington clay, and when that came to an end we used the local clay from the brickworks in the same way.

At last we were ready to fire. Elijah Comfort had made vast quantities of flower pots of all sizes from the big 12 inch (30 cm) pots down to little 3 inch (7.5 cm) thumb-pots, and a few hundred washing pans of the largest size – about 24 inches (60 cm) across – glazed inside but not on the rim or outside. Now he began setting them, while Sidney handed the pan-rings to him. I watched with growing admiration, while pan after pan was put in, its rim resting on the step of the pan-rings, each pan fitting close over the previous one without touching it. He built them up to a height of about 6 feet (1.8 metres), each bung containing twenty or more pans; and when the circle of bungs was complete he topped it off with inverted flower pots and flower pot saucers. This topping-off had the effect of spreading the draught so that when the kiln was firing it would not develop chimneys.

Then it was my turn. I built up my bungs of filled saggars, putting a wad of sanded clay on each rim – Sidney rolled the wads for me. I levelled off the bungs and then followed Elijah's example by adding a topping-off of inverted shallow saggars, each covering a small dish, plate or saucer, until the setting nearly touched the dome. The whole operation took several days of slow, careful work. Then we built up the doorway, pulled up the chimney damper and lit the fires.

I had bought a truckload of 'cannel' coal, which produces a long flame and turns to an ash with hardly any clinker (the name 'cannel' is a dialect for 'candle', and the coal is so called because it 'burns like a candle') and a large supply of larch faggots, enough to fill the whole woodshed, from one of the big estates in the hills which surround the Winchcombe valley. When the coal-firing stage was well advanced and we were looking for the first signs of colour inside the chamber, we noticed that the whole kiln seemed to be steaming; little spouts of vapour were puffing out from every crack, between every brick – you could almost hear the sizzling of all the water we were driving out of the structure; the kiln looked like the boiler of an old-fashioned steam laundry. This was all the damp which had accumulated during the twelve years that the kiln had been standing idle.

Nevertheless the faggot stoking went well. We followed the same system as the Truro pottery, stoking for forty minutes, then raking out the embers and carrying them away before starting again. The larch faggots were much easier to handle than furze bushes, yet they produced the same dramatic flare of sparks. At the end of the firing the test-rings looked quite good.

When we unpacked the kiln we found that the accumulated damp had done its fatal work: nearly all the pots were 'dry', having lost the lead content of their glaze. But there were a few which had escaped this, and their colours were exciting, with a play of light and shade, yellow and iron green, brown and tawny gold such as I had never seen in galena glazes before. Raw-glazing, a big kiln and the faggots were together doing their thing; this was evidently the right way – the only way – to fire slipware.

The combined effects of the damp and the bits of coal in the clay meant that there was very little from the first firing that could be sold; but the few good pots told me to press on as quickly as possible. Meanwhile Aunt Ella's £300 was soon gone and I had nothing coming in. My father had to help me with a few pounds from time to time. But by this time I think he really began to see light at the end of the long tunnel of my education. (My three surviving brothers had long ago become self-supporting.)

It took about two years to recover from the effects of the coal-blows and lime-blows of the first few firings. These were just as disastrous for Elijah Comfort's washing pans and even for the unglazed flower pots – nothing was fit to sell. The year 1928 was the first turning-point. For one thing, some time in that year I began to feel a new self-confidence in throwing. Leach and Hamada and Matsubayashi had all told me that in Japan it is an accepted rule that it takes seven years to become a thrower. My first struggles at the wheel had been just seven years ago; and some time in the summer of that year, in the middle of throwing some pitchers I found myself thinking 'What's this? *I can throw!*' – that is, the shape was at last 'coming of its own accord' and I was not having to struggle so hard. The shapes came quickly and spontaneously, and yet they were still quite good. At last, I thought, I am beginning to get there – to a place where all your practising and training should lead, where you can allow the wheel, the clay and your own reflexes to take over and with their help you can produce shapes which begin to make sense.

There was another, less happy event which made 1928 memorable – the pottery fire. We had just finished a firing; everyone had gone home and I was sitting beside the *kang* downstairs practising the clarinet, when I heard bangs and crashes overhead. I went to investigate, and found the roof-timbers blazing. Fortunately the Butler family had already seen the flames from outside. I seized a bucket of water and ran up into the loft, to find that molten lead from the roof was running down the outside walls of the kiln. I emptied the bucket in the direction of the fire – and missed it. The water fell uselessly on to the kiln chimney, where it instantly turned into blinding steam, leaving me with nothing in my hands but an empty bucket, the roof still blazing as before. Mrs Butler's daughter now handed up a second bucket, and this time I was more careful. Desperate emergency is evidently the mother of improvisation: I seized an egg-baker – a little bowl only a few centimetres across – and kept filling it from the bucket and throwing its puny contents at the fire. Sometimes now the water even landed where it was needed; and it was astonishing to see how little of it was really necessary. The fire was put out quite quickly, but we had been only just in time.

The fire had been caused by a small crack in the brickwork of the chimney just where it passed through the roof. Even this would probably not have led to a fire if I had not been in the habit of closing the damper at the top of the chimney as soon as the firing was finished. This was like imprisoning a tiger. So long as the heat is travelling up and escaping through the chimney there is not much danger; but the case is different if you immediately shut up all that heat in a cage.

Soon after the fire I had to have the whole chimney rebuilt, the bricks having spalled quite badly on the inside. It was a major operation, involving the erection of an elaborate framework of boards against which the bricks were laid. The flat and sagging dome was another problem which had to be dealt with. I had become more and more nervous that it might fall on us while we were setting the kiln; or, worse, collapse in the middle of a firing. I consulted the Winchcombe builders, and they said that a strong wooden platform would have to be built, and that the bricks themselves must have a special two-way taper to ensure the correct curve. Elijah Comfort, on the other hand, told me that when the old dome was built, the work was all done by a single bricklayer during a single night (so that nobody should find out the 'secret' of how it had been done) and that Alan Beckett had come next morning and found that the job was already completed.

Eventually I heard of a kiln-builder in South Wales who knew how to build domes. His name was Garvin; his terms were surprisingly moderate; and there was no nonsense about any secret process. All he needed was a supply of plain firebricks, a good fireclay mortar, and a boy to hand him the bricks. His first step was to dismantle the old dome. I expected it to collapse suddenly, more or less at a touch, but was surprised to see that he had to take it down brick by brick. Next he built himself a platform on which to stand. Then he complained that the new firebricks I had provided were wet, so we hastily found dry ones for him. Standing now on his platform he took time to prepare a good surface – a smooth circle, sloping at 45 degrees – from which to 'spring' the dome.

He then proceeded to lay the first two bricks lying side by side on this 45 degree slope. To my surprise, they stayed there, and did not slide or fall. He went on, laying brick after brick until the first circular course was complete, cutting the last brick to fit tight into its space and ramming it home like the keystone of an arch. The whole circular course of bricks was now firmly locked in position, and he immediately went on to the second, the third and all the other courses, which he laid in exactly the same way. (He had built so many domes that his eye was trained and he was able to dispense altogether with the trammel or guide-stick described in *Pioneer Pottery*.) He provided for the holes at regular intervals by laying one brick 'dry' – without mortar – standing up a few centimetres above the others; when the dome was complete he went inside with a hammer and knocked out the dry-set bricks to leave holes. As the work progressed towards the centre the angle of the bricks became more nearly vertical, but since the circles were now smaller they locked each other more securely. For the last few circles he left his platform and worked from the top, standing on his own uncompleted dome; for the last circle of all he had to cut most of the bricks to a tapering wedge shape, leaving at last a central hole about 9 inches (23 cm) across.

Early in 1928 I had a pugmill made. The Winchcombe blacksmith, Mr Bayliss, gave me the address of an engineering works where the foreman agreed to follow my directions, and when finished, the pugmill was installed in the area behind the pottery, firmly fixed in the centre of a round concrete pavement. The mill was to be driven by a horse which walked round the central shaft, but when everything was set the pugmill didn't work. The clay went round and round inside the cylinder but didn't come out where it was supposed to. I had omitted to explain to the makers that the bottom blade has to be shaped so as to act as an ejector. I kept poking at that exit-hole, telling myself that once it starts to come out it will continue to do so. At last, in desperation, I put my fingers too far in, and only just escaped losing the last joint of my index finger. By the time Sidney could get the horse to stand still, my finger was in a very mashed-up condition.

That was the end of our first day's pugging. I cleaned up my finger as well as I could and, in the evening, went up to Winchcombe to take part in a performance of Purcell's *King Arthur* by the local Choral Society. Not only was I due to be singing in the choruses, but Katharine Bouverie and Norah Braden were coming over from Coleshill in Wiltshire to hear this work. When they learnt about my finger, they insisted on taking me back to Coleshill after the concert. There I stayed for five days, getting treatment for the wound. Less than a fortnight later the new blades had been fixed, Christmas, the horse, was hired again, and the pugmill was working well.

1928 was also the year when I had a wooden hut built, so that I could move out from the pottery and no longer had to eat in the semi-darkness beside the *kang*. The hut was put up behind the pottery, in the orchard, and it is still standing on the same spot. It was a good home for Mariel and me during the earlier years of our married life, and two of our three children were born in it.

In the autumn of 1928 I had my first one-man show in London, at the New Handworkers Gallery which Philippe Mairet had lately opened in Percy Street, off Tottenham Court Road. Not many people came on the opening day; but two or three days later Charles Marriott, art critic of *The Times,* walked in, having perhaps been prompted by Bernard Leach, who was in London for his own exhibition at Paterson's Gallery in Bond Street. In *The Times* next morning, at the end of his longer piece about the pottery of Bernard Leach and William Staite Murray, there was a brief but glowing notice of my pots. The effect was instantaneous; suddenly the New Handworkers Gallery was quite crowded. Sydney Greenslade came in and bought an immense number – the nucleus of a collection of Winchcombe pots which he subsequently gave to the University College of Wales, Aberystwyth.

Leach and Murray both had shows on in West End galleries at the same time as my humble display on the fringes of Bloomsbury, and this was when I discovered Murray's work for the first time – up to then I had not had the opportunity of seeing it, and I had only met him once, in 1923, on my first day at the Leach Pottery. Seeing his work now was an exciting experience: pots decorated with bright red iron pigment in designs that were like fountains, waterfalls or palm branches. Murray, who was always friendly and generous to me, suggested that if I would like one of his pots we could make an exchange. I am sure, now, that what he meant was one pot of his for one pot of mine; but at that time my attitudes were so *petit bourgeois* that I imagined he must mean an exchange by value. The prices of his pots, already at that date, went up from about 20 guineas (£21), and the prices of mine ranged from 2*s*.6*d*. (12½p) to 15*s*. (75p); I quailed at the idea of having to send him a small truckload of Winchcombe pots in exchange for one pot of his, however desirable. I did nothing about it, and have regretted it ever since, especially as 1928 was a particularly good year for Murray's pots. Later on, in the 1930s, he became famous for his monumental works of ceramic art; but I never liked the shapes of those enormous pots so much as those of his earlier manner.

On the day that Charles Marriott walked into the New Handworkers Gallery he asked me what I thought of the other pot shows in town. I was still simmering with enthusiasm for Murray's work and, never reflecting that this is one of the ways art critics get their ideas – by asking artists about other artists – I launched into an enthusiastic appreciation of the Murray show. This story seems to have got around, acquiring no doubt various overtones in transmission, and there were imputed to me some odious comparisons between the work of the two great rivals, Leach and Murray.

Some time later a group of potters which included Leach, Murray, Charles Vyse, Katharine Bouverie and Norah Braden had a joint exhibition at

Colnaghi's Gallery in Bond Street. I went up to see it, and at the gallery Katharine took me aside and began to rebuke me severely: *What* had I been saying to *The Times* art critic? Didn't I have sense enough to know that if I praised Murray and said nothing about Leach (Yes! That was exactly what I *had* done!) Charles Marriott would be sure to say in *The Times* something which meant that he thought Murray was a much better potter than Leach? What had become of my sense of obligation to Bernard, or of the proper duty of a disciple?

I was appalled at my gaffe. I wanted to hide my head and cry – but where in Colnaghi's Gallery could I do that? Not only had I betrayed the Master but (far worse, in my scheme of things) it seemed I had lost the esteem of my friend as well. Worst of all, it wounded my ego and I felt a fool. I got away, still sorrowing and thinking bitterly how much harm a fatuous idiot like myself can do without even realizing it. I climbed on to the top of a bus, to take me right out of this, to visit a friend in Hampstead. As I sat down on the hard seat, I looked round and saw Norah Braden sitting down beside me – she had followed me out unseen and was now busily consoling me, applying balm to my shattered self-esteem, telling me that Katharine didn't really mean all that and assuring me that no real harm had been done.

If someone were to ask me now, who was the better potter, Murray or Leach, I would answer, how can I know? I only know that comparisons between artists are a waste of time. Some of Murray's pots may date; but I remember Hamada's verdict, 'I like his charactair' – by which I think he meant that there was always something big about the things he made, even when they were only small bowls. His work was explicitly art for art's sake. Some of us at that time might have objected to describing our own work in those terms, but I think we would have been wrong; it would have been better to proclaim candidly, as Murray did, that it was a true description. If we refuse to pronounce the formula on the ground that it has become unacceptable through its association with cultural élitism, and insist on using instead a facile platitude like 'art for life's sake', this is mere rhetoric. What is this 'life' – only the good old 'God' who was the cause and the subject of medieval and indeed of all earlier art. Katharine Bouverie, a great admirer of Murray's pots, says in a letter that his pots do not have 'the effortless serenity of the best things made with another end in view than fine art' – pots for storing corn or wine or oil; or, more generally, 'things (a picture, a mosque or a cathedral) to help in the worship of a god'. In all these cases the purpose, or the use, is what occupies the conscious mind of the maker, and somehow this beguiles his mental activity, so that it does not interfere, and can allow the unconscious to take care of that aspect of the work which concerns, not uses or purposes or technical procedures and expedients but the expression, the significance beyond that of being merely a good container for liquids or (like the medieval cathedrals) a daring and innovative work of constructional engineering. Only the unconscious *can* take care of this other thing, which we call meaning. Intellectual activity always seems to be irrelevant, getting in the way, and getting it wrong – proposing for instance some elaborate allegorical or emblematic content. But the content *is* the content, the work itself. It does not need a key with which to unlock it; if it did, it would not be a work of art but a treatise expounding a thesis.

But when a stage is reached where whole classes of useful things are made redundant by some new process or material, or when a particular form of religion loses its hold, we have a perfectly correct instinct to cling to our art, because it is all we have. So we produce art for art's sake. There is nothing in this to invalidate what we make, if what we make is good.

But is our modern work good? We don't know. What we do know is that we have to believe in it, and go on making it. Certainly William Staite Murray believed in his, with the conviction and weight that belonged to his character; he was a natural potter, though his pronouncements on pottery seemed to some of us to be bordering on the pretentious. Even when the shapes he made looked as if he was stretching his art beyond its natural scope or the control of his craftsmanship, they always meant something, and the meaning was not necessarily identical with, or invalidated by the poetical titles ('Persian Garden', 'Indus', 'Ra', 'Cadence', 'Vortex' . . .) which he gave to many of his best pots.

Artists at that time (and I suppose the situation is still more or less the same) depended for their market chiefly on people called collectors. In the 1920s and 1930s there were very few; most of them collected ancient Oriental ceramics, and only bought the work of contemporary artist potters as a curious footnote to their collections. The greatest of all these collectors was George Eumorfopoulos, who afterwards bequeathed his vast stores of early Chinese pottery and porcelain to the Victoria and Albert Museum. In the eyes of collectors there were at this time only three potters who counted: Murray, Leach and Vyse. Charles Vyse had come to the London art-ceramic scene from Stoke-on-Trent, where he had made a reputation as an accomplished creator of genre figures in coloured porcelain. By this time he had gone on from that to making stoneware and porcelain in the style of the classical Chinese wares of the Sung period. His technical mastery was complete and comprehensive; the celadons and *tenmokus* were perfect reproductions of their Oriental archetypes, his draughtsmanship and craftsmanship were impeccable. But somehow the pots were too perfect; you longed for some saving touch of the unpredictable, for some sign of native clumsiness or even of native bad taste. In my scale of values these technically accomplished works were not for a moment to be classed with those of Murray or Leach. They were not *saying* anything, only catering for a certain market (though I realized of course that it was a very, very high-class market).

One Sunday afternoon sometime in the thirties a friend took me along to Cheyne Row to see the Eumorfopoulos Collection. Mr and Mrs Eumor-fopoulos were charming to us, gave us tea and spent a long time showing us the collection. Looking at cabinet after cabinet of T'zu-chou pots I felt like the little boy who was found in tears at a village Sunday School Treat. When they asked him what was upsetting him he at last answered, 'They told me I could eat as much as I wanted to, *but I can't.*' We came back to the drawing room, which was bright with flowers – in vases by Charles Vyse. Mrs Eumorfopoulos explained what a fine potter he was, what a *benefactor*. 'I can't possibly use our ancient pots for flowers in the house for fear of their getting broken. But Vyse's pots are splendid – and they cost practically nothing: not more than a few guineas each.' But I was thinking: I suppose she will never understand; and I too shall never understand.

If Charles Vyse's pots cost practically nothing, mine at that time must have cost less than nothing. A quotation I made in 1928 for a complete dinner and tea service, forty-five pieces in all, adds up to a total of £6 9s. 6d. (£6.48). My 'throwing-diary' for that year has accidentally survived, and tells me that I made a monthly average of 350 pots or between four and five thousand pots in a year: large, medium and small; but no very big ones. The total value of these for the twelve months was £293 12s. 6d. (£293.63). That was the value of my personal production without counting Elijah's and Sidney's; so I don't know what my income was.

Yet I do not remember having ever been conscious of being poor in those years; or, rather, the poverty I lived with was of the kind I had always expected and had always (so to speak) counted on. There was no element of morbid deprivation in it: my wants were few, and I usually managed to have just enough money in my pocket for a life which was full of all kinds of simple pleasures. The fact is, I can now see, that a young single man can afford to be 'penniless', if he is living in the lap of a reasonably affluent society and has plenty of good friends and kind relatives: on condition that he is doing something which he strongly believes in, and is working hard at it. There is nothing blameworthy in this kind of innocent economic semi-parasitism, because it is 'parasitic' only if economics is interpreted in the most narrow way. He himself is independent in the one and only way that can ever make independence admirable: he provides his own motivation. But an artist during his years of adversity and struggle – which are apt to occupy most if not all of his lifetime – needs the friends who can give him not only occasional food, drink and transport but, chiefly, a continuing moral support for what he is doing.

I certainly had good friends. My fragmentary diaries are full of records of diversions. On Saturdays and Sundays I would usually bicycle over to Chipping Campden, ten or twelve miles away, where Leo and Eileen Baker had set up their weaving workshop. If they were out I could still visit their friends, who were quickly becoming mine as well: Christopher Whitfield, a poet who on weekdays made iron beds in Birmingham and at weekends used to tell me about the inexorable experiments recently made by a certain Russian scientist called Pavlov, demonstrating incontrovertibly that men were dogs; or Charles Blakeman, who by family, birth and upbringing belonged integrally to the old village life of Campden and had an instinctive, organic knowledge of all the crafts belonging to that life; or Herbert Finberg, whose father ran the idealistically named Cotswold Gallery (which was situated incongruously in the middle of Soho). Herbert had been my contemporary at Oxford but unlike me had used his time there profitably. He was now setting up a private printing press in Campden, and told me all about typefaces and founts, linotype and monotype machines. He called his venture the Alcuin Press and patiently enlightened my ignorance about who Alcuin was, when he lived and what he did.

John Butler, the son of Mr and Mrs Butler, my landlords, was a lecturer at the University of Wales (later, of Edinburgh) and sometimes spent part of his vacation at Winchcombe. In the summer of 1928 he and I went on a camping holiday through Wessex, visiting all the megalithic monuments and prehistoric earthworks – we had both been reading Nevinson's *Downland Man*. We ended up at the Dolmetsch Festival of ancient music at Haslemere, camping on Linchmere Common and playing recorder consorts with other enthusiasts whom we met there.

Once or twice I rode to the Welsh mountains, which began only about forty miles to the west. In clear weather, from the top of Langley Hill you could see their great ramparts along the western horizon. There in a remote river valley near a place called Gwenddwr, where the meadows were full of pale green Butterfly Orchids, I met a clogger named John Snowden (he claimed to be a first cousin of Philip Snowden, at that time Chancellor of the Exchequer), who carried on his skilled trade with the help of two assistants and a great slicing-knife (sharp as a razor) which was hooked to a bench, cutting hundreds of clog soles from the alder trees which grew by the river. He was from Yorkshire, and used to send truckloads of these clogs by rail to his home town, for the coal miners to wear underground.

Once with my Oxford friend John Lloyd, whose home was in Montgomery, I visited the basket-makers of Pembroke and Cardigan and the coracle fishermen of the River Teifi. On the way there we called on Mr William Rees at Henllan in Carmarthenshire. He was a traditional wood turner and carver; but in his personal appearance there was nothing of the romantic stereotype of an old-time craftsman. A fairly tall and solidly built man, he wore the dark trousers and matching waistcoat of an urban clerk, a striped shirt with a high stiff collar but no tie; on his head an ancient but correct bowler hat. Moving with the sober dignity of a Chinese *literatus*, and speaking the foreign English language carefully and precisely, he invited us to stay for lunch. We sat for hours in his parlour while the meal was being prepared, during which he told us about himself, his art, its ancient traditions and the uses for which his ladles, spoons and bowls were made. At last Mrs Rees, who spoke no English, appeared with food and served the three of us. While we ate, she stood behind her husband's chair to serve her Master and his guests, like an obedient woman of the Far East. We bought many of his beautiful wooden spoons and ladles, for which he used sycamore wood, because it is soft but tough and strong, and has a smooth-wearing grain.

Mr Rees (who died some time in the 1930s) was an artist with the rare gift of an unerring formal sense. He carved with loving attention to the minutest details of execution, yet never lost sight of the simplicity and harmony of the whole. You felt that his ethnic loyalty, his instinct of continuity with the remote past, ensured that he was never betrayed into making a false step. He was by no means the only carver of sycamore spoons in south-west Wales, but I never saw any other work with quite the same economy and purity of form.

In winter, if the frost was so hard that it got into the pottery and destroyed our newly thrown pots, I would go up to London, spending my days in museums or in expeditions to Limehouse, and my evenings making music with my father or with cousins. To go to Limehouse you boarded a bus which took you right away from the smart, sordid streets of the West End, through the canyons of the City, out to the serene spaces of Commercial Road and the East India Dock Road. You got off the bus when it reached the West India Dock Road; already you began to sniff the first faint hints of sea air, and cranes and derricks appeared, behind the rooftops. Down the road, past the lascars' dosshouses, you came at last to all that remained of London's China Town – Pennyfields, Garford Street and Limehouse Causeway. At a shop called San Sam Sing I used to buy bamboo chopsticks, which in those days had hand-cut 'matching' inscriptions or notices, coloured with inlaid green or red; and beautiful plain baskets made of cane and split bamboo. There was soy sauce for sale in large stoneware jars, and pickled bean-sauce in smaller jars. The clay body of these jars was coarse like a saggar clay, and the glaze ranged all the way from a greenish-brown opaque on the easy-fired pots, through a fine black *tenmoku* to an Indian-red *kaki* on the hardest-fired. Choosing one was always a difficult, exciting pleasure. I wished I could buy dozens of them, but what could I do with all that soy? Occasionally they had some of those plain porcelain bowls, ducks'-egg celadon green on the outside, and white inside, which were the urban counterparts of the little T'zu-chou type rice bowls which we had used at St Ives, and sometimes there were plates of the same kind. But my main object in Limehouse was to obtain writing materials: sheets and notebooks of absorbent paper, writing brushes and sticks of Chinese ink.

Painted T'zu-chou ware was always one of my main inspirations; but whenever I attempted to decorate with a brush (Bernard had given me two or three 'Sen Pen Banka' brushes when I left St Ives) I was painfully aware of the handicap of having been brought up in the West, where we are taught to write with a metal point on hard, non-absorbent paper. Even with good brushes, materials and tuition, we can never be on the same terms of ease and familiar mastery in the medium as the potters of the Far East, where writing is simply a specialized, functionally disciplined branch of drawing. Remembering the inscriptions in the margins of early Chinese paintings, in the books Bernard had lent me when I was in the cottage hospital at St Ives, I thought to myself, I must learn to write Chinese characters: that was the best hope. I realized that free calligraphy was beyond my reach because I had not been brought up from childhood to use a brush for all drawing and writing; but perhaps even now if I could teach myself to write with Chinese materials, I might begin to acquire the necessary fluency, without quite so much frustration.

I bought at Kegan Paul's bookshop an elementary Chinese primer, and noting that the 214 radicals are arranged in order of the number of brush-strokes required to draw them, I tried to practise writing them. But I found that the number of strokes apparently needed for a given character often did not correspond with the number stated in the book. This meant that some of the brush-strokes employed must be composite ones, but I could see no way of finding out for myself which those were. Evidently there were limitations to teaching oneself: I needed lessons. I explained my difficulty to the man in the San Sam Sing shop, and when he had understood he agreed to find someone willing to teach me. Unfortunately I only had one lesson, during which my tutor sat beside me in the Tai Tung Lou restaurant, drinking cups of tea. He taught me which strokes were simple and which composite, and in which order the strokes should be drawn; and I told myself I would be able to go on from there. But I was overestimating the strength of my motivation, and I never did acquire the authentic fluency. I ought to have arranged to have a series of lessons instead of only one, and I should have imposed on myself a régime of an hour's practice every day. But that would have been difficult to reconcile with the job of running the pottery at Winchcombe, and with all the other interests which filled my life.

I did get as far as deciding I must transcribe passages from Chinese books – this was how I had taught myself as a boy to read music, by patiently copying and transcribing for the clarinet any composition which I wanted to know, not merely to hear. The question now was which book. I reflected that if I wanted to become familiar with Chinese habits of thought, it must be a book which had been a decisive influence on the whole culture, comparable with our Bible in the West. Obviously Confucius was the one, even though the little I had read about Confucianism did not make much appeal to me. So I bought the Four Books (*Analects, The Great Learning, The Doctrine of the Mean, The Works of Mencius*) with the Chinese text printed above and Dr Legge's English translation and notes underneath; and began by transcribing passages from the *Analects*; I never acquired real calligraphic fluency; I was too busy learning the intricacies of each character, attempting to manage the proportions and architecture of each – trying to run before I would walk. What I did find was a growing affection and respect for the Confucius of the *Analects*.

At this time I was carrying on an intermittent correspondence with Herbert Finberg. He and his friends in Campden maintained the thesis that twentieth-century Western man ought to cultivate the spirituality of the West, and rediscover his own European past rather than go a-whoring after exotic cults from the Far East: Meister Eckhart, St Theresa and Thomas Aquinas have more to teach us than Lao-tzu, Zen Buddhism or the *Bhagavad Gita*, simply because they are more accessible. If we would look a little deeper into our own culture we would find antidotes for our present ills as good as any that can be obtained from the wisdom of the East – better in fact, since we have, or should have, better means of understanding our own philosophers and sages. Yet this line of thinking still strikes me as unadventurous and fundamentally foreign to that other, equally true European tradition which is an eagerness to extend the horizons of the mind by opening its ports and inlets to outside influences, rather than closing them and turning back into ourselves and our own past.

Of all the diversions and excursions of those years, the times when I visited Katharine Bouverie at Coleshill stand out with a special quality. Sometimes she came over in her two-seater open car to the pottery; or we would meet at an agreed rendezvous beside the 'Alpine Pasture', as we called it, where the hill road skirted a green slope high above Winchcombe under Corndean Hill and Humblebee Wood, and we would drive over to Coleshill together. Coleshill

House had been built for her ancestors during the Commonwealth, on gently rising ground in the most northerly part of Wiltshire, looking out towards the flat water-meadows of the upper Thames, where Wiltshire, Berkshire, Oxfordshire and Gloucestershire converge. It was a proud and perfect house built in the Palladian style and conceived on a palatial scale; every time I stepped into the hall and saw the great staircase and gallery, and the niches where the busts of Roman emperors stood (only the virtuous ones, of course), I said to myself, 'You know, you have no business here! This house is designed for the use of princes.' The house looked out over a great park, at the bottom of which, beside the little River Cole, there was an old mill which she had converted into a pottery, and in which she lived and worked, first with 'Peter' Mason (who afterwards died, bequeathing to me her kick wheel) and later with Norah Braden.

Most of Katharine's friends called her Beano. I did the same; but I always had a slight feeling that the name was not quite right for her. Her family, perhaps feeling the same way, had changed it to the more feminine Bina. Even the butler at Coleshill, no doubt echoing Mrs Bouverie herself, always referred to her as Miss Bina. Norah Braden, however, followed neither of these forms but called her Bim, which I really like the best but never learnt to use.

In the evening we used to go up to the house for a bath, and to dine with her mother and her elder sister, Mollie. At bedtime Beano went back to sleep at the mill, and I, having been given a silver bedroom candlestick with a cylindrical glass, went up the stairway to one of the bedrooms on the mansard floor above the great unused saloon. Except for the bathrooms there were no twentieth-century innovations in the house; the vast drawing room and the dining room were lit by large Victorian oil-lamps, each standing on its crystal or mahogany pillar and surmounted by an enormous lampshade, rather like the Quangle Wangle's hat in Edward Lear's poem. Mrs Bouverie and Mollie were the only ones who lived there permanently, but sometimes, especially around Christmas time, the house was full of their relations and friends. Although I must have been in many ways uncouth and uncivilized I never once felt intimidated or out of place in that great house; even the butler never let me feel the inadequacy of my wardrobe. It was accepted that most of Miss Bina's friends were artists of some kind, and were therefore allowed a certain latitude in their clothes and even their manners. After all, she herself belonged to this new and very rare species called potters, who, though obviously not real artists, behaved in some ways as if they were.

9

WHO MAKES THESE WONDERFUL THINGS?

During the summer of 1929 Hamada, who by this time had already established his pottery at Mashiko, came over to England again to have an exhibition in London, and brought with him Sōetsu Yanagi, Leach's philosopher friend. When I went up to London to see the exhibition, Hamada gave me two tea bowls, treasured examples of his earlier Mashiko manner. They were purely Japanese in style and inspiration, very different from the work he had produced during his three years in Cornwall – this had shown strong influences from Chinese, Korean and even European pottery. After the exhibition, Leach, Hamada and Yanagi all came down to Winchcombe, where we had just unpacked a kiln, and I went to meet them at the railway station. On the day before I had made some fairly large bottles on the kick wheel and was particularly pleased with one of them which had 'sailed up' to an unexpected height on the wheel, with ribbing on its sides. I told Hamada I was in doubt how I should decorate it, but when he saw it he said 'Let me try?' He dipped it in white slip, centred it on the wheel and while the slip was still wet gave it two broad, steeply drawn and undulating lines made with two fingers used in the same way as a wooden comb.

Beano invited all three, Bernard, Yanagi and Hamada, to stay with her and her family at Coleshill House, and she included me in the invitation. I remember that one evening Yanagi and Hamada produced a great pile of very fine colour plates of Japanese, Korean, Chinese and Sawankalok pots. We passed the sheets from hand to hand, making admiring noises and comments. We Westerners – Beano and Norah Braden and I – devoured them with a kind of greedy haste, making loud uncompromising comments and giving voice to our instantaneous reactions to all we saw: 'That's marvellous! That's terrific! No, I don't like that one *at all*! Why did the potter have to spoil *this* one, by doing *that* to it?' and so on. During an interval in this flood, Hamada and Yanagi began talking in Japanese with Bernard. They went on for a considerable time, and when at last they came to a pause, Beano asked Leach, 'Can you tell us now what all that was about?', and Bernard replied more or less as follows: 'They are saying that they are surprised to see how different your reactions are from those of Japanese people. You all unhesitatingly give voice to your instantaneous impressions, without ever waiting to find out whether the pot can tell you something to modify those first impressions, whereas the approach of a Japanese would be much quieter, humbler, more grateful and more receptive. When he is shown a pot, he will turn it over gently and reverently in his hands, looking for signs, listening carefully to find out what the pot is saying. During this time he will perhaps be "singing" little comments to himself, which sound to others like wondering hems and haws, sighs and grunts. Only after giving himself a long exposure to the influences coming from the pot, tactile as well as visual and acoustic ("Does it look right? Does it sound healthy? Does it feel kind?") will he venture to make verbal, spoken comments, if indeed he feels called upon to make them at all.'

What they were saying amounted in fact to a potter's version of Ben Nicholson's famous advice to people who are looking at an abstract painting for the first time: 'Let the picture look at you.' Yes; but personally I am a strong believer in instantaneous reactions. Of course they are not infallible, but they have their own incontrovertible validity, and one should always come back to them, though I agree it is better to come back to them *after* you have opened your perceptions to second impressions by giving the pot time to talk to you. First impressions, like children, have an inviolable integrity, an inescapable candour, which is their special value; but that does not mean they cannot be educated.

That summer I began to realize that Elijah Comfort's washing pans and flower pots were not really what is called 'a paying proposition'. Mr Giles, who kept a sort of general store at the north end of North Street in Winchcombe, used to sell them for me. As well as the shop he had a van in which he drove round the countryside, selling kerosene, lamps, brooms, pails and 'Buckley mugs' (earthenware pans) from the borders of North Wales. He himself came from that district and was a charming man with a healthy complexion and a beautiful Celtic lilt in his voice. He had been very pleased when I restarted the old pottery at Greet and he used to sell Elijah's big pans and flower pots around the villages. But he told me that the call for pans was dwindling, and I found that even the flower pots were becoming uneconomic: we could not compete with the big flower pot makers of Reading and Nottingham. There was still a small demand for bread crocks with lids and for big ornamental garden pots, but the requests for these were too intermittent for Elijah's continuous production – they were just an occasional side-line. On the other hand, the demand for the glazed and decorated ware was by this time increasing quite rapidly and we were sending hundreds of them to Barrow's Stores in Birmingham and to other shops as well. The logical thing was, obviously, to persuade Elijah to change over from the big unglazed ware to the smaller things, glazed and decorated, which paid much better.

But that presented a slight problem: Elijah Comfort's tradition did not include such things. He had never done any decorating and was not going to begin now; he probably classed these things in his mind as 'fancy ware', and thought of them with a good deal of contempt. However, I persuaded him to make casseroles with lids, on condition that I did the 'decorating of 'em up', as he expressed it. He also took kindly to the north Devon method of 'ovalling' for pudding dishes and baking dishes of all sizes. (The method is to throw a straight-sided circular dish, and when it has stiffened slightly, a piece is cut out of the bottom, and the sides are then gently squeezed into an oval shape. The bottom is then remade and smoothed by hand with the help of a rib.) I also looked again at the shallow, straight-sided, flat-bottomed saucers which he used to make as stands for flower pots, and saw that they were beautiful. He used to make hundreds of them, in several different sizes and two shapes – deep and shallow. The deeper ones, glazed and decorated, became cereal bowls and the shallow ones a kind of plate; they were among the most popular 'lines' we ever made at Winchcombe.

I got my old Braunton kick wheel back from St Ives where I had left it in 1926. Mr Bayliss, the Winchcombe blacksmith, fitted a heavy iron rim on to the wooden flywheel so that its momentum was immensely improved, and we installed the wheel beside the little window near the smaller of the two *kangs*. The change suited Elijah (he was getting older and was quite glad to leave the heavy work of throwing big ware), and on this wheel he produced board after board of bowls and plates, casseroles, oval pudding dishes and shallow baking dishes, large and small. This arrangement continued all through the 1930s, and that part of the pottery became known to us as 'The Comfortry'.

One effect of this change was that I now had to do all the decorating of these new lines. Some I dipped in white slip and, while they were still wet, comb-decorated in the Fremington way, using a short four-pronged 'comb' cut from an old wooden ruler, or from a piece of soft packing-case wood. Others I did with trailed slip while they were still fairly wet – black slip trailed over white, or white slip over black. In this way, with an unending stream of material to work on, I became proficient and fluent with the slip-trailing tool and (driven by necessity) soon found that the faster I worked, and the simpler the patterns I made, the more pleasing the results became.

We each now (Elijah, Sidney and myself) had a kick wheel to work on. Sid was making mostly egg-bakers, soup pots with lids, and pitchers of all sizes.

The power-wheel was vacant now; and I, having reached the limit of size suited to the kick wheel, felt ready to try making big things. I started with wide-mouthed open jars, in 12 lb (5.5 kg), 15 lb (7 kg) and 18 lb (8 kg) sizes. I did not venture at first to attempt narrow-necked cider jars or jugs in these sizes because, though I knew how to make smaller ones on the kick wheel, I was not sure how difficult it would be to make them in larger sizes. I made the first one on the spur of the moment. It had started as an ordinary wide-necked jar which came up exceptionally well, and I quickly thought why not try? The technique is of course just the same as for smaller bottles: you slightly increase the speed of the wheel and work patiently to narrow the neck without damaging the shape below. This first one (the neck was slightly too long) encouraged me to go on and make more; and all through that year and the years that followed I was mostly working on big pots and jugs or cider jars. I was not quite sure whether there would really be a demand for these cider jars – I did not then realize what a long and respectable ancestry they had, and thought they were something I had invented for myself. I was not sure whether the spigot hole and jar tap would work, and there was a constant fear that many people would turn them down because of their porosity. But I went on making them, fascinated by the completeness of the shape: however large the pot – there were 12 lb (5.5 kg), 18 lb (8 kg) and 24 lb (11 kg), and even a few 30 lb (14 kg) ones – the small neck always seemed to give it a certain neatness and even a kind of elegance which crowned the shape, making its great volume significant rather than merely huge.

The interest in throwing them came from the struggle to make the neck narrow without damaging the form below, and especially without weakening the lines of the shoulder. I did the earlier stages of the throwing as if I were making a very large pitcher, aiming for the same lightness in the lower part and with the same 'athletic' ideal: every part of the pot must be doing its work, with no excess fat anywhere. But whereas if a big pitcher begins to get out of true the form can sometimes be saved by working from the inside, these jugs eventually reach a stage where your hand can no longer get inside. Before that stage is reached the pot must be sufficiently true to be trusted not to get out of control when the slight speeding of the wheel and the necessary pressures on the rim might increase any existing tendency for it to become eccentric. To me, the whole fun of making these jugs was to complete the shape at one throwing, by a sort of magic.

It was often an excruciating kind of fun. On some days pot after pot would go out of control just when I was finishing the neck, and would have to be scrapped. This was doubly painful because I not only had this ideal about shape but was always uneasy about how slow my work was when compared with the apparently effortless productivity of professional or traditional throwers. I did not stop to question whether perhaps the numerous pots made by a professional thrower had as much life in them as some of those I did succeed in making. I felt that it ought to be possible to make many in series without sacrificing any of the vitality. On specially bad days I was reduced to tears of rage and frustration at my want of skill and control, which seemed to be incurable in spite of months of hard work and unrelenting concentration. But there came a day, at last, when I did succeed in making a good series of 24lb (11 kg) cider jars. When I looked and saw that they filled up nearly all the floor space with their voluminous bulk, each with its neat neck, I felt that at last I was getting somewhere. This was more like a proper pottery and more like a true professional standard.

Cider jars were not the only big pots to be made. There were 40 lb (18 kg) bread crocks with ear handles, and lids that were only just large enough to admit loaves of bread in spite of the great bulk of the pot. And one day, a lady who lived in the district asked me to make her a giant teapot, to hold 10 or 12 pints (6 or 7 litres) of tea, for her tennis parties. (In those days you drank tea, not cocktails, at country-house parties.) This presented an interesting functional problem. I knew that Japanese teapots, large as well as small, usually had a cane handle on top; but I had no cane. I was also aware that some Japanese potters made a similar top handle from clay: but I never liked those. For this very big teapot I was not convinced that even a top handle would be adequate: you would need an ordinary handle at the back as well so that you could steer it while pouring. I decided to use both; and for the top handle I went back to the versatile blacksmith, Mr Bayliss. After discussing it with him I persuaded him to make a wrought-iron handle in two halves, wide in the middle (where they were to be joined) and tapered to a round loop at each end. In the wide middle part of each half he made four holes for short screws, finishing the wide ends so nicely that when the two halves were screwed together there was no step at the overlap. I then bound the two tapered ends with raffia, inserted them in the loops provided on the teapot's shoulder, screwed the two halves together and finished the raffia binding after they were joined. I made several of these big teapots, which were popular not only for tennis parties but for other large village gatherings as well.

Their success eventually inspired me to make a really big teapot to hold 3 or 4 gallons (13 or 18 litres). This required some very careful planning, and a further collaboration with Mr Bayliss. First I made a more or less perfectly spherical pot from a 40 lb (18 kg) lump of clay, afterwards trimming the underside to give it a round bottom. My idea was that it should be supported by an iron belt with two knobs which in turn rested on a sort of gun-carriage arrangement, so that the teapot did not have to be lifted at all but could simply be tilted forward by raising a horizontal loop handle placed on the side opposite to the spout. The design of the spout itself required forethought to ensure that when the pot was tilted towards a tea cup it would deliver the tea to the right place, at the right angle and distance and in the right quantity. (This was when I first taught myself how to bend a thrown spout into a sort of swan-neck shape: it has to be done while it is still wet, very gently and lovingly, before it leaves the wheel.) Mr Bayliss even provided the gun carriage with two little wheels and a skid at the back, so that within limits the teapot was mobile. I never found a purchaser for this curiosity, but during the Second World War it went to America, part of a travelling exhibition of craftwork organized by the British Council. I am afraid nobody has ever made tea in it.

In London about this time a new society was formed, called The National Society of Painters, Sculptors, Engravers and Potters, which held exhibitions once a year in the Royal Institute Galleries, in Piccadilly. I think this was the first time the new breed of potters had been admitted to a society devoted to the fine arts. Charles Vyse, who worked in London and had many sculptor and painter friends, was an ardent supporter of this society because it was offering potters such a big step-up in the art world. William Staite Murray was of course a member, and Bernard Leach. The rule was that each potter was allowed to send in up to twelve pieces, and was given a showcase to himself. Since my pots were all very cheap and the subscription to the society was (by my standards) rather high, I was doubtful whether it would make sense for me to join it; but Vyse was insistent that all good potters ought to become members, to help on the business of improving their status and recognition. I didn't know that recognition was supposed to be a problem; my chief problem was how to make more pots. I thought my big earthenware jars would look out of place and uncouth among all that highly respectable stoneware (which was in any case already recognized as 'art'). But in the end Vyse talked me into joining.

At this time (1931) I had recently acquired a very ancient and unreliable motor-cycle with a sidecar. I gathered together twelve of my best and biggest pots, boldly putting prices on them from 7 guineas (£7.35) downwards, packed them carefully into the sidecar, and on the appointed day rode this unwilling vehicle up to London. I parked it outside the gallery and staggered up the marble stairs carrying one pot at a time. I found myself in a large room full of people busily hanging their pictures or putting the finishing touches to their sculptures; so I began unwrapping my pots and putting them out on the floor without paying much attention to the crowd around me. While I was doing that I heard a deep voice behind me asking, 'Who makes these wonderful things?' I turned round, and the owner of the voice introduced himself as Leon Underwood. I said I was the one responsible, and he then began to bring along his friends, all equally enthusiastic. In a short time I became a 'sensation': painters and sculptors were all wanting to buy the pots. By the end of that memorable day nearly all of my twelve pots had been sold before the exhibition had even begun, and there were many requests for more. Charles Marriott in *The Times,* giving, as he always did, special prominence to the pottery exhibits, said: 'What Mr Cardew has done, to put it as simply as possible, is to lift this peasant tradition into the region of conscious art, and still keep its native character and relation to utility. His work is neither "arty" nor affectedly primitive, but "just so" . . .'

I spent a few days in London enjoying the sweet warm sunshine of success. Leon Underwood took me under his wing, introduced me to his contemporaries and friends, and began my education in the art that was modern in 1931. Among the painters I only remember Maresco Pearce, who invited me to lunch at his house in Chelsea. He told me I was a Fauve (but he had to explain what that meant), and said my pots were like Gauguin's painting, the same kind of animal outburst.

Back at Winchcombe, the pottery got more visitors than ever before; and even some old friends who after I left Oxford in 1923 had more or less given me up for lost came to see me again, among them Gerald Reitlinger and David and Tamara Talbot Rice, who were already eminent authorities on Byzantine and Russian art. But they mostly came only once. One view of the solitary and eremitical life I led was usually enough for them. I kept up my membership of the National Society for a year or two, but I didn't see much future for myself in the fine art world. At that time I had not yet heard the Hausa proverb which says that when going on a journey you should not carry calabashes or pots in the same bag as iron tools – meaning, 'If you are poor don't try to consort with the rich.' I saw that this kind of social climbing was not for me: I could not travel in the fine art bag.

So I dropped out of the National Society, in spite of protests from Charles Vyse, who was genuinely concerned but soon had to give me up as hopeless.

10

MARIEL

There was plenty to do in the pottery. There had been a surprising increase in the number of people interested in the kind of things we were making, and our plates, casseroles, bowls and pitchers were being bought as fast as we could make them. I have never been quite able to understand the cause of that sudden expansion. Nobody in those years had any money to spend; perhaps that in itself partly explains the change in their tastes. But more likely, it was simply a coincidence; Depression or no Depression, the pottery was becoming better known as a place where you could buy pots that were useful and not expensive.

At the village of Eastington in the Cotswolds there were three young men who had recently graduated from Magdalen College, Oxford. They were animated by a common conviction that modern industrial civilization was fundamentally inimical to any way of life proper for rational human beings, and they had decided to make the experiment of a completely simple way of living, turning their backs on all the comforts and luxuries which that civilization not merely offered us but was always actively imposing on us, whether we wanted them or not. They bought a small cottage in the village, where the only water supply was a communal outdoor pump and the only sanitary arrangement an outdoor earth closet. Here they were trying to live a life as simple and frugal as possible, supporting themselves as far as they could by working on a farm and in their small garden, and not relying for their support on any income derived from the civilization of the machine.

One of their minor problems in the domestic sphere was to find utensils such as plates, cups and other pottery, which were not the ordinary productions of the factory system. Somehow they heard that there was a potter working at Winchcombe. Of course Winchcombe Pottery was not independent of the factory system: total independence, if it can be realized at all, can only be achieved artificially and at great expense. The pottery was about as simple as a production organization could be at that time: but we depended on a firm in Liverpool for ground galena and on a potter's merchant in Stoke-on-Trent for ground flint.

Alan Griffiths, who was the leading spirit of this trio, walked the fourteen or fifteen miles to Winchcombe, and found the kind of pots, more or less, that he was looking for. It was the first of many visits, during which he and I had long discussions and passionate arguments about literature, philosophy, world history and religion. I learnt much from these encounters; we both had a lot to say, though we seldom agreed. We argued about Chinese philosophy, about the Greeks, and about the Jews. More persuasive than the Newlyn pilot Abednego Hoare had been, he made me read the Bible; also bits of Thomas Aquinas in the original Latin, and Pope Pius XI on Christian marriage. His experiment in living at Eastington was an early stage in the progress by which he came at last to enter the Catholic Church and the Benedictine Priory at Prinknash as Dom Bede Griffiths; a progress which he later described in his book *The Golden String*.[1]

These arguments with Alan Griffiths were almost painfully pertinent for me because they brought me back to a dilemma in my life which was becoming more and more difficult to resolve. I was feeling as if I had led myself into a trap set by my own optimism and wishful thinking. The life to which I was committed seemed (in spite of all my optimism in starting out) to be condemning me to unholy poverty. If I intended to go on making pots in a way which was so different from that of my contemporaries, it would only make sense if I renounced the normal secular life and embraced a kind of solitary monasticism. But unlike Alan Griffiths, who at this time was as yet only setting his feet upon the first steps leading to his goal, I felt no vocation for that life and had no intention of trying to convince myself that I had one. I felt I had somehow cheated myself: I had set forth on a road which I had supposed would lead me to a life of normal domesticity, but now it was threatening instead to take me straight in at Jerusalem's wall, where I did not belong. Surely no younger son of a poor Catholic family can ever have felt such frustration at finding himself being pushed into the priesthood by social pressures. My case was worse, since I knew that the fix I was in was a consequence of my own free choice when I decided to be a potter.

On 1 May 1932, which happened to be Sunday, my brother Philip came down from London in one of his fast cars to visit me for the day. Philip was easily my favourite brother. From his earliest childhood he had been by far the most talented musician in our family, but, greatly to the distress of my father (an amateur violinist who loved Corelli, Haydn and Mozart beyond all other music), he had broken away from the family orthodoxy by acquiring a saxophone and was by now an established jazz-band leader and orchestrator.

---

[1] Dom Bede Griffiths, *The Golden String*, Harvill Press, London, 1954.

In spite of this musical apostasy he never lost his love of classical music and constantly played it with his friends, as a semi-professional. Whenever we two whose lives had gone off into such entirely different directions happened to meet again he was usually willing to play Mozart or Handel with me as in our boyhood. He now lived in London, in a narrow but very grand five-storey Regency house in a back street of Camden Town called Regent's Park Terrace.

He shared this house with two friends, one of whom came down with him. They arrived about one o'clock and we all three had lunch together. Just when we had finished our lunch, the figure of a visitor emerged from the firewood shed at the back of the pottery. I wasn't looking that way, but Philip's friend, Bernard Cook, turned to me, saying, 'I think a gypsy woman has come to visit you.' Assuming that this was one of the many visitors who used to come daily to see the pottery, I thought bother! and said out loud, 'I wonder why these tiresome people should choose Sunday morning to come.' Unfortunately the open hut must have acted as a sort of sound-box, because to my distress our visitor easily overheard both these remarks, and naturally felt extremely embarrassed.

She also felt extremely disappointed. Years later, she told me the reason she had come that day was something David Talbot Rice had said to her, suggesting she go and visit 'a potter who works in Winchcombe, living a very simple life, like you; in fact he is a sort of hermit who lives all alone in a tiny hut in the orchard behind his pottery.' And now she had made this pilgrimage to the hermit's cell, expecting to find a venerable sage with a white beard who would be able to bestow on her some of his ripe wisdom and spiritual advice. But when she reached the hermit's cell all she found were three young men with bad manners who looked like Oxford undergraduates. However, she concealed her disappointment and, being hungry, ignored the rude reception we had given her and sat down to eat the sandwiches she had brought with her, while we three (I hope) tried to make ourselves agreeable.

Mariel at that time was living in Gloucester, working at one of her periodical jobs. She had a well-planned system about these jobs. Some time after leaving Oxford (where she read English Literature and Geography as well as Anthropology under my old Philosophy tutor Dr R.R. Marett, and carried away an impressive collection of degrees and diplomas), she had suddenly decided that her true work was to be a painter. She therefore planned to divide her time in half, free to paint for as long as her money lasted and then taking a job again until she had saved up £100 to enable her to go back to painting. It did not take her long to accumulate £100, because the jobs she took were quite well paid by the standards of those days, and her way of life was, to say the least, frugal. She spent little on food, next to nothing on clothes, and seemingly never felt that cold weather was a hardship. Perhaps this is a good system for painters, though I could not imagine myself potting under such nomadic conditions; but, then, pots are easier to sell than paintings.

The system evidently suited her constitution. She had what Beano later described as the complexion of the goddess Pomona, and she wore her thick, abundant hair in two long plaited pigtails. But her most remarkable feature was a pair of large, intense, deep eyes like those you see in ancient portraits from the Fayyum or from the Catacombs, eyes which attained their apotheosis in early Byzantine frescoes and mosaics representing the Mother of God. In short, she was beautiful; though (as I hastily assured myself) 'not my type'.

I proposed to Philip that we should go and see the little field which I had recently bought for clay-digging. We walked in pairs, Philip and I in front, Mariel and Bernard Cook behind. Philip was talking to me about cowslips and early purple orchids, dog violets, wood sorrel, and so on, and Mariel listened (Bernard Cook's supply of polite conversation being almost non-existent). She had not seen or heard brothers enjoying so much harmony together and began to think that perhaps they were not such bad people after all. While we were in the field, inspecting the fruit tree I had hopefully planted there, a black thundercloud came up, so we quickly returned to the hut, and Philip and his friend left to go back to London. After they were gone the rain and thunderstorm arrived. I gave Mariel tea in the hut and afterwards showed her the pottery.

It was the beginning of an intermittently tempestuous friendship which finally, after nineteen months, led to our getting married. All that summer we met often. She was currently working as the curator of the museum in Gloucester, and lived in two tiny rooms in a back street. When I went to see her in Gloucester we would sit up half of the night talking; sometimes I slept on a sofa in the small living room. Once or twice she came over to Winchcombe, and on one occasion she made tea on the outdoor table in front of the hut, for three or four local children who happened to be around. The way she presided over that tea table made me think, well! she puts on an act of being a rootless bohemian, but what a wonderful old-fashioned mother she would be if she ever had children of her own. Beano used to tease me about my girl-friends, saying that I only considered each of them in the light of the question, 'Will she do?' Very gradually and with much reluctance I began to admit to myself that if anyone were to ask me if Mariel would 'do', the answer would have to be 'Yes'. Our long talks seemed to indicate that (unlike my other girl-friends) she did not mind my being poor and even actively approved of it. All the others had been unattainable in different ways, but in every case I had decided (unwarrantably, I dare say) that the insuperable obstacle was that I had been too poor.

All through 1933 I was pursuing Mariel, trying to make her agree to marry me. During that time I imbibed (under protest) some of the ideas which animated her and her painting friends, and it seemed to me a more promising way of entry into the world of 'art' (as opposed to 'craft'). Until that time I was always a misfit; I did not belong in the fine art world of the National Society, but neither did I feel at home in the arts and crafts world. I found its atmosphere curiously suffocating. The original Arts and Crafts Movement inspired by William Morris certainly had a fine Victorian moral fibre and a no doubt necessary if somewhat pedantic insistence on good workmanship. The trouble was that the products of all this good craftsmanship usually looked laboured and mannered. With Mariel and her friends I could escape from the careful, precious, enclosed world of post-Victorian craftwork. They seemed to be saying, forget all this preoccupation with the means of expression, and instead, *say* the thing which you see needs to be said – the light on the hillside or on the tree, on the cracked ceiling of the tenement you occupy or on the chipped kitchen sink – without fussing so much about all the craftsmanship; *just say it* when you feel it must be said and let the craftsmanship take care of itself and catch up if it can. Even if the craftsmanship can't catch up now, it will eventually, given the will and the compulsion on your part to make your statement while the light is still there.

But I soon found that I had not got the necessary temperament. Sure, if I wanted to make a pot I made it, and found out about how to make it as I went along; but most of the time I failed altogether to *see*, in the way that painters see. I could not see their purple shadows or pink leaves because I looked at the world not with the innocent eye of a child or a painter but with the prosaic intellectual eye of one who had been trained to use his head rather than his senses. I did not begin to understand what made Mariel make a drawing of two or three crusts and a dirty white plate on a table in some seedy café. I only saw them as sordid, deprived of any significance, and moreover very meanly designed. I could see the beauty of the light on a hillside or a tree but failed to respond when it touched the cracked ceiling or the sink. This was evidently another country: all my training had made me indifferent to it or had led me to look the other way.

I saw that my only hope was to stick to the kind of pottery I believed in and to the craftsmanship which I had been so painfully acquiring. But at that time the politically earnest people, all the left wing (and we were all left wing in those early thirties) began to make me feel that my pottery was useless in terms of 'social value'. They said, or I fancied I heard them saying, 'We can use artists of all kinds, to promote the Revolution. They need not do direct propaganda. The mere fact of their art proclaims emancipation and will help to sweep away the rubbish of the past and break the bonds that are confining the people. But yours is merely an art which ministers to the tastes of a small minority, and a backward-looking, reactionary minority at that.' So I was thrown back yet again into my old state of isolation from all the main streams. I didn't agree with what the careful craftsmanship people made, and the free-expression people didn't approve of me: what use was I to society at large? Yet like all my friends I believed in the 'Revolution', and wanted to feel needed.

By the autumn of 1933 I had at last persuaded Mariel to marry me. In that October we went off together to the south-west of Ireland for a twelve- or fourteen-day premarital honeymoon. Excursion tickets in those days were sometimes astonishingly cheap; otherwise we could not possibly have done it. We went by train to Fishguard and then straight to Cork on the night boat. Sitting in a café in Cork we met a very friendly young man, a soldier in the Free State Army, who found us a good cheap lodging for the night. The city of Cork at that moment was seething with unrest – perhaps it always is – and there were to be two great rival political rallies that evening. Our friend told us tales about the Troubles, which then meant the guerilla warfare against the Black-and-Tans, in 1933 still a recent and inflamed memory. When we left him we roamed the crowded streets, sniffing the atmosphere of violence. Mariel, who is half Irish, was all in favour of seeing as much of the fun as possible. But I had caught the eye of one or two partisans spoiling for real trouble, and managed to persuade her back to our lodging and our bed.

Next day we took a bus to Macroom, through a country unlike any I had ever seen. Not that the shape of the landscape was different; it was rather like some part of south-western Britain. But the buildings, and the people we met, were as unlike anything in England as they could be. Every small town we passed through seemed to consist of bare, barrack-like buildings with few windows (most of them boarded up), their walls plastered with inflammatory political slogans. They looked as if they had all been built to withstand a siege or a riot, as indeed they perhaps had. Some of them had apparently been built in the eighteenth century with beautiful, humane proportions: but it was humanity with a hard, brave, battered face.

At Macroom we left the bus and began to walk. At first we walked through cultivated, softly undulating country, then unexpectedly we were on a wild heath which went on for miles; not higher than the surrounding country, but with sudden bare outcrops of rocks through which our road twisted. After a time we found ourselves in cultivated farmland again, though it was bare and heathy and thinly populated. We looked in vain for a suitable haystack or barn where we could spend the night, but eventually we saw an inviting cave on a hillside. There was a sort of hurdle arrangement with a few boards across the mouth of the cave, but that was no obstacle; it was beginning to get dark, and we were soon inside and settling down for the night, keeping our clothes on because it was getting cold. Before long we were aroused by an unearthly hooting and yelling above us on the hillside, followed by a thunderous stamping of hooves and bellowing of cows. We lay low, keeping very quiet, and presently outside our 'door' we heard the heavy breathing and snuffling of many cows nosing around it. We kept silent, hoping they would go away again. Then we heard heavy human footsteps approaching; somebody stopped at the entrance of our cave. It was dark now, but through the chinks you could see a figure moving. This was a moment when we really lay quiet; we hardly dared to breathe. Then there was silence outside; we began to breathe freely again. But a minute or two later, out of the silence, a very gentle voice spoke in English: 'You must be feeling chilly in there. Surely you'd better come up to the house and get warm.' Carrying their packs, the two Babes in the Wood came out of their cave, and after allowing the cows to enter their rightful sleeping-place the farmer took us up to his house.

The farmhouse was wonderful. The young children had just gone to bed and the farmer and his wife with his (or her) father and mother were all sitting round the turf fire. That evening they told us more stories about the time of the Troubles. And the grandfather told us about what life was like now under the Free State Government. 'Sure, there's no money in the country at all, but the cupboards is all full.' (Everyone had enough to eat.) They put us to bed in a nice barn, with loads of hay to keep us warm, and gave us breakfast in the morning.

A couple of days later our walk brought us to a place called Gougane Barra, where there was a lake overhung on all sides but one by steep mountains and precipices. At the lower end, where the land was fairly level, we saw a large building made entirely of timber, with a board saying 'Cronin's Hotel'. It looked empty and rather forbidding; but we knocked, and a very good-looking girl (whose name was Mollie Cronin) came to the door with a large dog. We found that Cronin's Hotel was indeed quite empty (the season being over) and that it was quite cheap. Mollie Cronin led us to a vast pitch-pine bedroom. We unpacked our belongings and came down to the equally enormous pitch-pine dining room below. I got out the recorder and began to play 'My Lodging is on the Cold Ground'; within a minute the door opened and a face appeared – not Mollie this time but her brother, who played the flute. Would we not come into the kitchen? – where almost at once we were made to feel that we were a part of the family.

Night after night, as long as we stayed there, the flute-player and I sat side by side on the kitchen settle, proposing tunes to each other. 'Do you know "The Jaunting Car"?' I didn't, by that name, but I knew the tune when he played it. So we played it together, over and over again until he thought of a new one. 'What about "Smash the Windows"?' So we played that too, and so on, hour after hour. I knew most of them, because when we were boys our father used to play all these Irish jigs and reels and hornpipes on his fiddle. When I was older I learnt to play them too, first on the tin whistle, then on the clarinet, and later on the recorder – there was a book at home of about two hundred of them. We stayed at Cronin's Hotel for several days, until it was time for us to be getting back to Cork to catch the boat. Then we walked fifteen or twenty miles over the mountains to Bantry, where we got the bus for Cork. One day remained before our boat sailed, so I left Mariel (who wanted to spend a day in Cork, drawing and painting) and took a bus along the coast to Youghal where I had heard there was a pottery. This pottery made only flower pots, but it was interesting to see the way they prepared the clay; washing it to a thick slip and then adding dry clay (previously powdered, or rather granulated) to thicken and stiffen the slip until it became plastic. The grains of dry clay acted like a very soft grog, kind to the hands, making the clay easy to throw with, and giving the pots a pleasant granular surface. But the main advantage was that they could be dried more quickly and more safely.

We took the night boat to Fishguard. I returned to Winchcombe, and Mariel went to London to think about getting married. She insisted that we must be married in church, and we agreed there should be no 'social nonsense'. We persuaded Alice Mason to come from Wimbledon to 'give away the bride', acting instead of a father or mother. She had come to my mother as nanny in about 1891, when my sister Pinny was a baby, and she had remained with the family uninterruptedly since then. She had just recently retired from the last of her labours, which was to keep house for my two younger brothers and their friends. Philip consented to act as best man, after protesting vehemently at being made to participate in what he called 'all this black magic'. On 23 December Mariel came down from London and stayed the night with Mrs Butler, together with Alice Mason, with whom she shared a bedroom and who entertained her most of the night with lurid stories about myself in childhood. I slept alone in the hut; or rather, I lay all night on the bed, tormented, as men in that situation commonly are, by horrible doubts, mental wrestlings and agonies. But when at the first light I got up, I was determined that nothing was going to stop me now from doing on this day what I had wanted for so long.

At the church there were already two present, the Vicar of Winchcombe, the Reverend Meurig Davies, and my old Winchcombe friend Ellison Awde, who somehow had received private information of what was being planned. Mariel came up from Greet with Alice Mason and Mrs Butler in a friend's car; and when it was all over Mariel and I walked back together to Mrs Butler's house where she gave us all a wonderful breakfast. Later that morning we set out on foot again to walk to Andoversford and there caught a bus to Burford where her mother lived. She took the news quite calmly when we told her.

INDUSTRIAL
POTTERY

Not very long after we were married Henry Bergen began to make long summer visits to the pottery. During the next five years he became a real friend to both of us.

Henry Bergen was the first American I had ever known. At this time he was in his middle or late fifties, a tall, powerful man with a rather square head and an athletic build. He was by profession a scholar, and most of the year he worked in the British Museum, preparing an edition of *The Troy Book*, an epic poem by the fourteenth-century English poet Lydgate. I do not know how exactly he came to meet Hamada, Bernard Leach and Staite Murray. By the time I knew him they were already his friends.

Bergen was not a potter, but he had worked out in his head, and on paper, two or three (or more) designs for bowls and plates, which he very much wanted to carry out in slipware – hence his visits to Winchcombe. In themselves I liked the designs – I remember chiefly a fawn-like creature with folded limbs, and a running stag or doe. But they were too much like engravings in metal for slipware: stiff and static rather than alive. I would make bowls and big plates for him and hand them over to him when they were ready for slipping and decorating. He made paper cut-outs of the designs and pressed them carefully on to the inner surfaces of the pots so that when they were dipped in slip the paper would act as a screen or 'resist'. He also engraved a complete alphabet of beautifully cut Roman capitals and a series of numerals, using small seal-like chunks of cheese-hard clay. (He was a trained typographer and book designer.) After these letters had been given a soft biscuit-fire he used them as stamps or seals so that by slow, painstaking work and careful spacing he could impress an inscription all round the rim of a dish. These bowls and dishes were then slip-glazed and fired, and most of them came out very well; but I could never approve of them because they looked too much like things that had been thought out intellectually instead of coming naturally out of the inspiration provided by the actual making of the pot.

Mariel, Bergen and I had endless arguments about philosophy and human history. The quality of his mind fascinated me. He always seemed to think in a concrete, material, even materialistic mode rather than in abstract or theoretical terms, and I found this refreshing and satisfying compared with the cloudy and endlessly modulated shadings of meaning which characterized the thought and talk of most of my Oxford friends. The whole way he expressed himself seemed quite different from European ways of thinking. Like many others at that time, he placed all his hopes for the future of the human race in the USSR. If anyone asked him why he was a Communist, he always gave the simple, lapidary answer, 'Because Communism is the only system which is ethically justifiable.' Stalin's 'Treason Trials' of the mid-1930s, in which many of Bergen's heroes, the Old Bolsheviks of the Revolution, perished, shook his faith in the USSR but not his belief in Communism.

He persuaded me to read the works of Karl Marx (or, rather, some parts of them) and I experienced a particular kind of 'conversion' or illumination, which coloured all my thinking at that time and has continued to colour a good deal of it ever since. Repressive régimes all over the world follow an elementary rule of self-preservation when they proscribe the reading of Marx, or discourage it in various more refined ways. He plants in the human mind what the Japanese Fascist governments of that time used quaintly to call 'dangerous thoughts'. Marx fundamentally altered my thinking about history, politics and philosophy, blowing away vapours and clouds, and giving me a new perspective. I saw that Marxism was one of the great disruptive forces of modern times, comparable with Freud's dissolution of the classical psyche, a potent corrosive of the whole infrastructure of European philosophy, religion, political and economic systems, all our civilization and all our culture.

Mariel and I, in our arguments with Bergen, queried whether under a Communist régime a craftsman's work would be tolerated; but Bergen dismissed this doubt, saying that if we lived in Russia we would have a much better chance to do our work. He was probably carried away by all those glowing descriptions in *Soviet News* of how crafts were being actively encouraged. But I suspected that the crafts were being fostered only on the periphery, just as in capitalist societies crafts are tolerated and even encouraged as ornamental adjuncts of the 'real' civilization.

Partly as a result of all these debates, I was beginning to convince myself that anyone who claimed to work as an independent craft potter in an industrial society ought at least to try to contribute something to industrial pottery. But the English pottery industry at that time showed no inclination to make use of a craft potter in the field of design. The only initiatives which had been made up to then had come from another quarter altogether – from architects and others who were aware of existing collaborations of that sort in Scandinavian countries. Their approach however was not from the position of a craft potter; it was essentially a movement from above, being conceived only in terms of designs to be supplied by those who, being educated in what was known as the Theory of Design, would be considered competent to supply them.

By this date I was at last beginning to grow out of my old dislike of bone china and white earthenware. The long and difficult process of getting over my prejudice had first begun in 1930, the year when Stoke was celebrating the bicentenary of Josiah Wedgwood. I would never have heard about those celebrations but for the fact that in the village of Stanton, two or three miles from Winchcombe, there was living an elderly lady named Eliza Wedgwood. She arrived at the pottery one day with a modest request: would I let her 'borrow' Elijah Comfort and his wheel for a day, because she was planning a small celebration of her own in the village, in honour of her great-great-grandfather. She offered to send somebody who would take care of the transportation of Elijah and his wheel, and I of course agreed. I myself did not go to the celebrations, but Elijah thoroughly enjoyed himself and was a great success with Miss Wedgwood and the whole village. Eliza Wedgwood was delighted with the success of her experiment and came over again to the pottery to thank me for my help (as if I had done anything at all, except say yes). She spoke interestingly and charmingly about all the hard pioneering work Josiah Wedgwood had done, and she gave me a little book which had been made for the bicentenary, in which the life and work of Josiah's ancestors were described: how they prepared their clay and how their pots were made and traded in the seventeenth and early eighteenth centuries. At the pottery she also met Henry Bergen, who himself wanted to visit Stoke, so she invited us both to tea with her at her cottage in Stanton, where Bergen made a great impression on her. She gave us introductions to her relatives in Stoke, especially to the reigning Josiah Wedgwood, who was the Chairman of the Directors.

Josiah Wedgwood invited us to lunch with him and other directors in their special room at the works canteen, and we were shown all through the factory, which at that time was still on the site where the original Josiah Wedgwood had founded it, calling the place Etruria in celebration of 'Etruscan' (that is, ancient Greek) vases. Wedgwoods at that time, like a few of the other great pottery firms, was an entirely self-contained organization doing its own grinding and preparation of the materials for the clay bodies, glazes, frits and colours. In addition to all the making and decorating shops, the great up-draught ovens for the bisque firing, the glost kilns, decorating kilns and frit kilns, we saw the great chaser mills for grinding calcined flints and Cornish stone for the clay bodies. These enormous and beautiful pan-grinders had been the standard machines for grinding hard rocks to a fine impalpable slurry before the invention of ball mills or alsing cylinders in the second half of the nineteenth century. They delivered a very good product and were only superseded because they used too much power. (In Cornwall, where water power is plentiful, similar machines for grinding Cornish stone survived a little longer.) Our visit to Stoke was an exciting and stimulating experience: here was a great city almost entirely devoted to potting – a good place for any potter, even one who like myself had been trained in the other school, of Oriental stoneware and porcelain.

By 1938 I had become quite convinced that I, as a craft potter, ought to work in the industry as well as making my own individual pots. Of course I valued my independence, but I felt that my way of life cut me off from the lives of my fellow-citizens in general and from the majority of my fellow-potters in particular. I wanted to find out what working in the pottery industry was like from the inside. If I could get an entry into it, my plan was to use the fine earthenware body for making teapots, coffee pots, milk jugs, sugar bowls, cups, saucers and plates; and perhaps later, whole dinner services. I intended them, not as individual productions but as 'prototypes' (I liked that word) to be reproduced by the methods which were standard at that time: jiggering and jolleying, possibly slipcasting, and of course throwing. I argued that the current shapes of these articles were distantly descended from those made by the working craftsmen of the eighteenth century; who, though they con-formed with the agreed consensus of their period, had still to a great extent been free agents with a lively feeling for clay forms. But in the current production, all the life had been sucked out of their forms because for too many generations the firms had gone on reproducing them through the medium of the design shop and the modelling shop, in which clay was never touched. The time was long overdue, I maintained, for the shapes to be rejuvenated from their original source.

I went up to London to talk to William Staite Murray at the Royal College of Art, hoping that from his influential position as Professor of Ceramics there he might be interested in my idea, and that he might possibly be able to help me with contacts in the industry. But Murray responded to all my earnest ideas only with negations. Pitying no doubt my simple-minded enthusiasm, he patiently told me three things, all of which I see now were true. He said, 'First, you have to understand that a factory is only interested in the design of their products in so far as it serves the one thing they are interested in, the balance sheet. Secondly, if you think you have ideas for teasets and so on which industry could very well use, don't worry! If the industrial people think they are good ideas, they won't come and ask you for them – they will just use them.' Thirdly, when I explained my ambition to make free prototypes on the wheel which could be used for production, he was emphatic and memorable in his condemnation: 'You can't make love by proxy.' He was right, but at that time I could not accept it.

I made up my mind to go up to Stoke and find out for myself whether anyone in the industry was disposed to entertain the idea of employing a craft potter to supply designs or prototypes. I knew that Josiah Wedgwood was a good friend, but decided (mistakenly, as I now think) that the whole style of that firm was too formal to be a suitable place in which to make the experiment. But he, or Gordon Forsyth (who was in charge of the local art school), gave me an introduction to Mr A.E. Hewitt at Copelands. I was admitted to his office and explained my plan. He was not enthusiastic, but I was so warm in my convictions that in the end he relented, and agreed that I could be allowed to work in one of their shops where there was a wheel which was unoccupied.

I found an inexpensive room in Stoke with the help of one of the Copelands employees. Every morning I walked to the factory in Copeland Street at the same time as the other workers, but I did not have to punch the clock, because I was not being paid. I often wonder how I, a married man with, by 1938, three children, managed to finance this whole adventure. The fact is, Winchcombe Pottery was manned by a very efficient team – Ray Finch (who had joined me in 1936), Elijah Comfort, Sidney Tustin and his younger brother Charlie; and their labours supported me for these few weeks.

The shop to which I had been assigned was one of several, which together formed the 'making side' of the factory. It was a long room perhaps about 70 × 20 feet (21 × 6 metres). On each side of a long central aisle there were the machines, each standing in its bay. Each machine was allotted 12 feet (3.5 metres). They were mostly jiggers and jolleys; but at the far end there were two throwing wheels and two (horizontal) potter's lathes. One of these wheels was to be mine; I did not use the unoccupied lathe, but did all my turning or trimming vertically, on the wheel, as at home.

Until then I had not realized to what a great extent industrial pottery at Stoke-on-Trent at that time was still essentially a craft-based industry. Most of the workers were highly skilled men and women; and the main difference between the way of working at Copelands and that of our little group in Winchcombe was not, essentially, the difference between mechanization and handwork; it was rather the difference between a very large, sophisticated organization and a very small and primitive one. Perhaps there were about twenty or twenty-five people working in this shop, and the atmosphere was beautiful. Each jigger operator had a mould runner to keep him supplied.

They were quite young boys (at that time boys began to work in the factory at fourteen, if not younger); I can still hear the joyous, rather Spanish-sounding songs one of them was always singing or whistling. Each jigger had to have an assistant to operate the batter, a flattening-out machine which stood next to the jigger. These assistants were generally women. Many of the jigger workers could also throw if called upon; they used to teach themselves in the evenings at the art school.

Then there was a handsome, short, middle-aged man named William Morris, who looked after all the boards of ware, managed the pugmill and kept everyone supplied with clay. I think he also looked after the steam engine which supplied the power for the endless cotton rope which ran all round the shop at the top of the wall. Half-way along, this rope had a weighted tension-frame to keep it at the correct tension. The rope itself was black and shining with the special graphite rope-dressing which was always used; at each machine it was led down by a pulley to floor level, passed round the driving pulley, sent up again to the top of the room, and so on to the next machine. The arrangement was almost silent and only made a sort of gentle humming as an accompaniment to our work and the singing. At certain regular times, without any signal, one was suddenly aware that the rope was slowing and almost immediately it came to a halt – the tea-break. After about ten or fifteen minutes it started up again without any signal or comment, and everyone resumed work.

When I revisited Stoke several years later I was shown round a brand-new factory which had just been built a few miles out of town. The making was all being done in one vast hall containing perhaps hundreds of machines, each supplied with power from its own electric motor. The place seemed to have lost the friendly, intimate atmosphere of the old making shops; in place of the gentle humming of the rope-drive, here each worker started, stopped and restarted his machine as often as the work required it. No doubt in this way much less power was being used; but the effect was that the whole hall was filled with the restless, intermittent buzzing of electric motors, lacking the organic rhythm of the old rope-drive system. I marvelled at the adaptability of the workers, who all seemed perfectly happy, though I dare say there were some among the older ones who secretly regretted the change. I remembered that this new factory had been planned with the utmost care as an ideal working environment and a model for the future, but wondered what the long-term effect of this restless atmosphere might be on the minds of the workers. Even with the most careful planning and the greatest goodwill something always seems to get lost.

Sometimes I watched the thrower who was making teapots and milk jugs on the wheel across the aisle from me, admiring his speed and accuracy, and also the wonderful collection of potter's ribs on the wall behind him, all made by him out of clay and then hard-fired without glaze. I also watched the turner, shaving the walls of the teapots and other things until they had exactly the right thickness. When he had finished the shaving he reversed the direction of the lathe and began the polishing, a second process which was done to all the pots; then with a sharp tool he neatly released the pot from its horizontal chuck. He, too, was also a thrower in case of need; but mostly he worked as a turner. They told me that a thrower's work was by far the best paid of all; but that the standard of speed and accuracy required was such that by the age of forty, having saved enough money, he would retire and set himself up with a poultry farm.

I had decided that everything I made would have to be turned, because if a pot had any of the accidental (or incidental) marks due to hand-throwing it would be automatically disqualified in my eyes as a 'prototype', nothing being more distressing in an industrially produced pot than any suspicion that it has been as the ghastly phrase is, 'hand-crafted'.

I did not stay there longer than about three or four weeks. I made and turned a number of teasets and arranged to come back a month or two later, to paint them after they had been bisque-fired. I did this in another part of the factory, a quiet, unused corner of one of the decorating shops. I gave all the sets one or other of the two patterns which I used to paint on the teasets which I made at Winchcombe, using a rather severe and limited palette of black and yellow with a green wash in some areas.

Later on, Copelands sent me all the results. I was quite pleased with them myself. To Mariel and others they looked very cold compared with what we made and used at home. But I had known before embarking on this experiment that what I was proposing to do would only be an attempt to treat symptoms, not the real causes. To attack those would have been a much tougher undertaking, hardly to be tackled in one man's lifetime with the prospect of making a dent in what were the established technical procedures of an old and highly successful industry. Progress in any reforms of such a radical nature could only be made in an indirect way, and related to a much longer historical perspective. I had been too often invited to admire the smooth, pure white surfaces of fine earthenware and bone china not to know that the potters in Stoke were not about to be converted to something else.

But I was after all a sort of disciple of Bernard Leach, and ever since the years at St Ives I had been aware of the great gulf separating Western pottery and porcelain from that of the Far East. We were at that time part of a very tiny minority; not many people were aware of that chasm, which was obvious to me if I compared any Chinese bowl or plate (especially if it was of the simplest and most purely utilitarian sort) with a corresponding article produced by the Stoke industry. Neither of those things would normally be classed as a work of art, both being simple, realistic utilities made as cheaply as possible for the common uses of humanity; yet the thing which separates them is almost invariably there and consists of a built-in, fundamental difference in what I had learnt at St Ives to call quality. The Oriental bowl is kinder, more humane, and has a more harmonious relationship with the earth. One can say it is simply a difference in the techniques used, and of course that is perfectly true: the Oriental bowl has been given only a soft biscuit-fire, or none at all; then the body and the high-temperature glaze are matured together, and help each other, being quite close to each other in composition. But this difference of technical procedures is not a superficial thing: it arises from two different ways of feeling about Nature. Oriental thinking, and indeed all pre-industrial thinking, knows that though Nature may seem hard-hearted and her laws inexorable and often cruel, yet she herself is the very raw material you are working with, and of which you yourself are necessarily a part. You therefore always have to treat her as your friend, as someone with whom you must somehow keep on good terms, or else you and your works (even if they succeed) will be no good. She is after all your mother, not an enemy to be subdued, or a slave to be violated.

12

BIG POTS

It can be argued that each moment of your life, every step you take and movement you make will inexorably determine all your future steps and movements; but there are some events which are specially potent. They seem quite trivial at the time, yet they determine the future in a direct, incontestable and unmistakable way; though I did not know it then, one of these took place in 1936.

When in the summer of that year Mariel and I saw a notice that a performance of Purcell's *Dido and Aeneas* was to be given on a certain afternoon at Cheltenham Opera House, we thought 'How wonderful', and immediately decided to go to it. We took both the children, Mariel carrying Cornelius, the new baby, in a sling which she had made from a large piece of hand-spun Assam silk; Seth, being now about eighteen or twenty months old, was able to walk most of the way from the railway station. The performance was planned as part of a conference convened in Cheltenham by something with a name like 'The New Education Fellowship' – a great gathering of education experts from what is vaguely termed 'all over the world', with lectures, concerts and exhibitions of various kinds. However, when we reached the doors of the Opera House we found a notice pinned up saying 'Cancelled'. After a few moments of hesitation, Mariel pronounced the apparently innocuous words 'Never mind; let's go and see the exhibition of children's art at the Winter Garden.' Children's art was at that time a novelty. After wandering through all the main galleries at the Winter Garden we penetrated at last to the farthest recesses of the hall, and came upon a rather sad-looking young man with curly brown hair and intensely blue eyes, who was setting out on display shelves a collection of little animals. They were all made of clay (unfired, I remember) in the most charmingly direct style, using a simple convention of short, pinched out projections for the legs and similar but longer protuberances for the horns where needed. They were lively and completely life-like, the character of each animal instantly recognizable. Some were antelopes, some were rams with curly horns, or goats with straight ones, or cows with spreading ones. When we asked this man about them he told us they were made by children at a village school in what was then known as Basutoland (now Lesotho). We both admired them so much that he went on to tell us more about them, and hearing that I was a potter he brought out one or two African hand-built pots which he had with him. We got on so well that we invited him to come over to Winchcombe if he had time during the next few days; he came, bringing with him one of the pots and a few of those beautiful clay animals. He told us that his name was Meyerowitz, that he was a sculptor, that he had lived in South Africa for many years, and that he had recently been working in Basutoland. I felt we had made a friend, although, realizing that we had only met by chance, I did not seriously expect to see him again. But that fortuitous meeting, though on the surface it was no different from any of dozens of other chance encounters, turned out to be the first small event which set in motion a whole chain in which I at last became inescapably involved, and which took me far away from anything I had ever planned or even imagined.

About this time Bernard Leach, who had returned from his long visit to Japan in 1934–5, wrote to me asking whether I could have Harry Davis in the pottery at Winchcombe. Harry had been at the Leach Pottery for about five years, during which he was the mainspring of production there; all through the year or more that Bernard was away on his travels in Japan it was chiefly Harry who kept the whole place together, David Leach, being, I think, still away at that time, studying at Stoke-on-Trent. But I had to write back saying 'Sorry, we're full up.'

Not long after this I received (surprisingly) a letter from Meyerowitz, who was now in the Gold Coast (Ghana), in charge of the art department at Achimota College. He said that he was planning to start pottery classes at the College and asked me if I knew of any potter who might be willing to go there to teach. I immediately wrote back to say that I had heard Harry Davis was probably leaving the pottery at St Ives and that there could be no harm in asking him.

Harry went to Achimota. I seem to remember a slight feeling of envy when he wrote later to tell me how glad he was that I had spoken; but apart from that I didn't think any more about what appeared to be an episode of no particular concern to myself.

At Winchcombe, Mariel and I were deep in our own occupations: she was looking after the children, and painting whenever she saw the chance; and I was making pots. After the 1931 success of the cider jars, 'garden' teapots and other large things, I was no longer inhibited by the thought that big pots were less profitable than small ones. It was not that I had lost interest in small teapots, tea cups and saucers and plates; but I was beginning to find that slipware was not quite the right medium for them – they tended to chip too easily and the painted slip decoration was inclined to run. On the other hand, slipware seemed quite all right for the range of cooking pots – Elijah's casseroles, round saucers and oval dishes of all sizes; Sid's soup pots and egg-bakers. These I think were always our main support-line; but we now extended that range by making great numbers of press-moulded dishes, mostly small- and medium-sized. For them we mixed a special body with a proportion of Stourbridge fireclay added to the ordinary red clay so as to give them some 'bone', to prevent distortion during the firings. They were glazed on the inside only and fired upside-down, resting on their rims; thus they were very useful during the setting of the kiln when we came to do the topping-off. In this position they caught the full blast of the faggot firing, and often came out with an amazingly beautiful quality. Sometimes local reduction turned the normally yellow glaze to a quite strong iron-green – but usually these were the ones which did go out of shape.

One reason for turning our attention to these press-moulded dishes was that when Ray Finch joined the pottery and we became five throwers, there were not enough wheels for each of us to have one to himself all the time. Rather to my surprise, they were an immediate success. We used to send away hundreds of them to Scandinavia.

I myself tended to monopolize the power-wheel; I wanted to make a lot of big pots and was obsessed with trying to imitate the great black-glazed Tz'u-chou and Martabani wares, as far as the earthenware technique could do that. I used to dip the jars and jugs in black slip, inside and out, hoping that it would vitrify enough on the inside to make them comparatively non-porous. When they were black-hard I dipped or poured them with the standard glaze, and scratched designs through the glaze with a bamboo tool; when they were dry I took care to set them in the hottest part of the updraught kiln – that is to say, at the bottom, immediately over the flues. This attempt to bring slipware closer to stoneware does not seem to me, at this distance, to have been a happy expedient. The lead glaze, even at its best, lacks the 'fat', viscous character of that on the Chinese originals; compared with them it has a thin, rather tinny appearance. Another weakness is that the scratched design does not give a sufficient contrast between the glaze and the exposed red body; here and there the glaze runs over the incised lines, almost obliterating them and betraying the fact that it is a highly liquid glaze, quite different in character from the stony *tenmoku* of the originals.

Porosity, I reflected, would not matter quite so much in the case of large bowls and dishes, which were not primarily intended to hold water; and here I felt free to exploit all the colour which the glazes naturally gave us. I made great numbers of large and medium dishes, fruit bowls and mixing bowls; and eventually in 1938 I began to make what I rather subjectively described as 'rose bowls'. At that time I had not yet found out that the massive, rather high foot-ring which this shape seems to demand can more conveniently be made by adding a coil of clay after the bottom has been trimmed, and then throwing this coil to make the foot-ring. At this time I used to leave a great thickness at the base and then laboriously trim it down with the turning-tool, and so for this size I needed 40 lb (18 kg) of clay. But after I discovered how easy it is to make a thrown foot-ring (and how much better such a foot-ring looks and feels), I found that 30 lb (14 kg) was enough.

I taught myself how to make big garden pots, starting with a plain cylindrical shape thrown from a 40, 50 or 60 lb (18, 23 or 27 kg) lump. After it had stiffened for a day I added coils and then carefully opened out the whole shape until it was like a very large pan; and then, after a further stiffening time, I added a last coil to give it a good, solid rim. For decoration, I used patterns impressed by a notched roller on the four handles and under the rim. Half-way between each pair of handles I applied a pad of clay like a sort of medallion, and pressed on to it a stamp I called 'The Moon's Face'. Once or twice I made the same kind of pot but without holes in the bottom and washed the inside with white slip and green glaze.

The fury for bigger and bigger pots was taking hold of me, and I eventually embarked on making some enormous wine or cider jars about 40 or 45 inches (1 metre or more) tall when fired, starting with a 50 lb (23 kg) lump and adding coils until the whole weight of the unfired pot was 100 lb (45 kg) or more. Little by little I taught myself a technique of throwing, coiling and then throwing again, making many mistakes on the way. These big jars all, except one, came out cracked from the kiln, and the one that survived intact is now in the museum at Montreal. It is decorated with incised figures of Adam, Eve, the Tree and the Serpent – it is the only pot I ever made on which I tried to draw human figures.

Bernard Leach was writing *A Potter's Book*, a great act of faith on his part and on that of his publisher. In order to concentrate on writing it, Bernard handed the St Ives pottery over to his elder son, David, acquired a car and a caravan and went to live in it at Shinner's Bridge near Dartington, with Laurie, his second wife. At a later stage in the writing Bernard used to send pages of the typescript to Henry Bergen at Winchcombe, and he and I and Mariel had a wonderful time reading and criticizing them. Bergen was of course in a sense a sort of writer himself, and also knew about typography, having worked in private printing presses in New York. Bernard's typographical manners and customs were like those of William Blake, with a liberal use of italics and capital letters in all sorts of places where according to modern practice they were inadmissible. Bergen reduced all this to conform with the sobriety of modern publishing practices.

Leach acknowledged his debt to Henry Bergen in his preface. He also wanted Bergen to write a preface for him; but with regard to that there is a rather sad story. Some time in the late 1930s Bergen fell sick, and by the early months of 1939 he was suffering from what must have been some sort of stroke, the effects of which he described to Mariel and me saying, 'I feel as if I had recently been bludgeoned.' And so, early in 1939, he arrived in Winchcombe saying, 'Look here, Michael, Leach wants me to write a preface for his book, to stand beside that of Yanagi; but every time I try to write it I get muddled and a sort of blank descends on me.' I asked him how far he had got with it and he handed me a piece of paper with some rough notes. They were not very coherent; and I came to the conclusion that I had better try to write something to help him. So I sat down to compose the kind of preface which I thought would be proper to a man of Henry Bergen's age and background. I had not written more than about a page when some interruption occurred. Either I had to stop and look after the children, or perhaps Bergen was in a hurry to be leaving – time was up anyway. I handed him the uncompleted manuscript, saying, 'Sorry I haven't been able to do much, but I should think this is the sort of thing to say.' Bergen thanked me and took it, and I thought no more about it until the day, about fifteen months later, when a copy of the book arrived from the publisher, with a note inside from Bernard saying, 'Here it is at last with its faults known and unknown.'

When I looked for Henry Bergen's preface, all I found were the few words I had written for him that day in Winchcombe. It was entitled 'Preface by Michael Cardew', instead of 'Preface by Henry Bergen'; and so it has remained in all subsequent editions and reprints. I felt rather ashamed to think that what I had written in the character and *persona* of Henry Bergen, quite appropriate to an elder statesman like him but rather pompous if it were myself speaking, now appeared over my own name. Bergen must have simply sent it off to Leach, perhaps saying that he had been unable to do it but that this was something Michael had written for him. Whether it was thanks to Bernard or to Henry Bergen, or to both of them, they did me a good turn as it worked out in the end; because in 1945, when copies of the second edition at last began to arrive at Achimota in West Africa for distribution among the pottery apprentices there, the discovery that I had really written a preface, however brief, for the book gave me a good name; all books (and by association anyone who contributes to one, even in the smallest way) being held there in the greatest respect.

13

LOOKING TO CORNWALL

I had always thought of Cornwall as home, and had never given up the hope of going back there. Winchcombe was a very nice place to live, but for me it was never more than 'the work-side' – to borrow a Ghanaian expression. That is to say, it was merely a place to which I had migrated for the sake of the work. Most years I paid a brief visit to Cornwall. Each time I crossed the Tamar and saw again the outline of Bodmin Moor on the horizon, I felt the same exultant aching which had come upon me at my first sight of it when I was a boy of seventeen; and each year I vowed again, 'This is my real home, to which I must, some day, somehow, return.' The more clearly I saw how impracticable and unrealistic the whole idea was – to dig ourselves out of Winchcombe and start life over again in a new place – the more fanatical my determination became. And Mariel encouraged it; we were incurable romantics.

Part of the romanticism was a strong desire to use Cornish clay. The only surviving traditional pottery in Cornwall was the one at Truro, where they used Fremington clay, brought down from Devon by rail. But Mr Collins told me that sometimes they could not get it, and then they had to use St Agnes fireclay instead. When I asked him what it was like, he said, 'All right, apart from the colour'. I inquired; and he answered, with great distaste, 'Smutty white'.

I knew that up to the early years of the nineteenth century there had been several potteries in Cornwall. Truro itself had at least two; there was one at Penzance – Richard John Noall of St Ives had an inscribed pitcher to prove it. There was a fairly well authenticated tradition that there had been potteries at St Germans in east Cornwall and at Calstock in the Tamar valley. Beautiful beer jars had been found at Boscarne and at Little Petherick, dated by the experts to the sixteenth century; so it was tempting to conclude that there had been at least one pottery somewhere in the Camel valley as well.

Assuming that these potteries all used local clay, I spent much effort in trying to find plastic clays in Cornwall. Following all the usual clues, I asked retired tin-miners where they had obtained clay for their candles. From their instructions I found yellow clay at a place called 'The Ducks' Pool', near

Saltash, and took a large sample back to Winchcombe for testing. I also tried some sticky yellow clay from Lower Amble in St Kew, where it was being used to puddle another duck-pond. Both clays were complete failures in the kiln. At St Agnes, Mr Doble, who operated the clay-pits, gave me samples of his clays, but these also were unsatisfactory at earthenware temperatures.

I was probably mistaken in supposing that those early potteries had used local clay. In the days when there were no railways people relied on sea transport. It is well known that loads of finished pottery were sent out in sailing ships from Fremington Creek to all the small ports along the Cornish coast (not to speak of Ireland and Wales); and it must have been easier still to send small shiploads of the clay itself. The unavoidable conclusion seemed to be that the only plastic pottery clays in Cornwall were those to be found in the two small pockets at St Agnes and St Erth. However, the quest had not been entirely in vain, since it caused me to embark on my first serious study of geology and its difficult literature.

In 1936, on one of the last days in December, my father died. I was not with him at the end, but had visited him a week or two before. I found him sitting alone on the hard sofa in the music room of the house in Wimbledon, wearing as usual the bright red waistcoat which had been made for him from wool woven by Ethel Mairet. He had given up playing the violin. We talked, but his memory was already confused. When I got up to go he said, 'I expect I shall go on sitting here until at last the Golden Eagle comes.'

Mariel and I went to London by train for the funeral, but the only thing I remember about it is that Handel's Dead March from Saul (which he had asked for) was so excruciatingly caricatured by the organ in the crematorium chapel that I felt thankful my father was not present to hear it.

When the estate was wound up his second wife was naturally the chief beneficiary, but certain well-loved articles went to the children, and Mariel and I found ourselves in possession of about six pieces of antique oak furniture from the house at Saunton. We also received £550, our share of some money which had belonged to my mother, who had died long ago in 1925. This money gave much more reality to our dream of moving back to Cornwall.

In 1937 and 1938 I began a serious hunt for some place in Cornwall where we could set up a pottery. Cornwall, like the rest of the country, was suffering from the effects of the Great Depression of the 1930s. There were empty cottages, derelict buildings, entire farms, to be had for ridiculously low prices. Even the china-clay industry was in a slump; in the hills above St Austell there were several disused linhays, immense, beautiful buildings with long colonnades of granite pillars, which had been built for drying the china clay. But these were much too big for a pottery. I was chiefly looking for a disused water mill, and there were several of these. But always there was some obstacle: either they were too dilapidated, even for us; or the price was too high.

Then, early in 1939, I decided I must explore the country on the western slopes of Bodmin Moor, where I used to stay in the winter vacations when I was at Oxford. I found myself talking to Willie Crowle, a man I remembered having met in 1921 or 1922, when I was staying at West Rose. He said, 'Why don't you go and look at the Wenford Inn?' He told me it belonged to the St Austell Brewery, but they were giving up the licence and trying to sell the buildings – 'and there are several outbuildings there which you could turn into a pottery.'

I went on down the hill and called at the inn. Mr Armstrong, who had kept the pub until the licence lapsed, confirmed that the brewery was trying to sell it and he very kindly showed me round the house and all the outbuildings, many of which were in an advanced state of decay. There was a brewhouse with a huge solid copper brewing-vat; a malt loft above it; a skittle alley which was rapidly falling down; a blacksmith's shop, which Mr Armstrong (who was a granite-mason) used for trimming his stones; a stable with two stalls, a loose-box and a harness room, and a good loft above it; a pigs' house and a cowshed for four cows – this also was practically in ruins. There was a garden at the back and nearly three acres of meadow bordering the River Camel. On the other side of the road there was another small patch of rough land beside the river.

The place seemed far too big and far too ambitious for us: I had been looking for something much smaller. But when I went to the St Austell Brewery and learnt that they were only asking £550 for the whole place (this being, as it happened, the exact amount of our capital), I no longer hesitated. I went to my elderly cousin Gilbert Chilcott, who was a solicitor in Truro and would therefore know how to get a mortgage, so that we should have a little bit of cash left for starting the pottery. He insisted on an independent valuation – which decided that the property was only worth £350. In the end we got it for £500. I think my cousin was rather scandalized that I paid so much.

In Winchcombe we began making plans for the great migration, which eventually took place in June that year. But in the middle of our preparations, Mariel boldly invited six children to come and stay with us. She belonged to a pacifist group called the Peace Pledge Union, which was just then appealing to its members to help in providing homes, temporary or permanent, for the refugee children who had been evacuated from the Basque Country during the Spanish Civil War. So we squeezed in the six extra children; and to my surprise (but not to Mariel's), the whole enterprise turned out to be a great success. It is an interesting fact (which Mariel evidently knew but I didn't) that if you embark on some apparently crazy but altruistic enterprise, many other people immediately rally round and help you, as if they had only been waiting for someone to make the first move. Neighbours and friends helped us in providing extra beds and bedding, Mrs Butler made puddings and several others provided food on various occasions. The children themselves enjoyed it all. The language problem – neither of us knew any Spanish, still less any Euskara – did not arise at all; after all, love, good food, fun and games are what children need rather than words. When the time approached for them to leave, a great crisis arose. The eldest boy, with tears in his eyes, was deputed by the others to ask if they could stay with us for another week at least. Letters or telegrams or telephone calls were exchanged, and the Refugee Committee agreed to their staying on with us for a week longer. I don't really know, but I think perhaps they enjoyed their time with us more than any of their other experiences in England; it was probably closer to their lives at home than it would have been if we had been living in some nice, comfortable, suburban home.

14

WENFORD BRIDGE

Any sane man could have seen, in May or June 1939, that a second war was on the way; but I was stubbornly determined not to see it. This was not because I had been shutting my eyes to what was happening in international politics. Thanks to Mariel's elder brother, who regularly used to send us Claud Cockburn's news-sheet *The Week*, I thought I could see only too clearly what was going on, and the spectacle induced in me a radical cynicism about Great Britain's part in the drama. I now realize that this cynicism was a rather superficial reaction, fairly typical of those who view public affairs with a logical and ideological eye, forgetting that politics, whether it calls itself Capitalist or Communist, is bound to be a messy and untidy affair – since the raw material it deals with is a messy and untidy animal. In my eyes the betrayal of Ethiopia, the tacit encouragement given to Japanese aggressions in China and Manchuria, the shameless hypocrisy of so-called non-intervention in the Spanish Civil War, the refusal to take a stand beside Russia – all this simply proved that capitalism was rotten and hopeless. I was convinced that Fascism represented the last convulsions whereby capitalism was trying to prolong its life. The British Government was capitalist, and therefore it was inevitable that it would collaborate willingly and actively with the Fascists on all occasions. Everything our Government had done seemed to bear this out and I assumed it would always be so. In my view, the Munich crisis of September 1938 proved that our rulers would prefer any infamy rather than impede the progress of Fascism; and when in the spring of 1939 Mr Chamberlain gave a guarantee to Poland, I took this to be just another fraud, exactly the same in kind as all those previous frauds.

Yet although I thought I was one of the sceptics, the prospect of a Second World War terrified me, when I thought of our three children. I remember standing over Ennis's cradle when we got the news about Munich (he was only about six weeks old at the time), with feelings of deep thankfulness. But a day or two later in Cheltenham I happened to hear a boy outside a butcher's shop whistling 'The British Grenadiers' in a minor key; the effect was startling and rather sinister. And when I was in Stoke-on-Trent soon after, I was astonished by the heat of indignation most of the workers showed. I don't think the working people of England were taken in by the Munich Settlement. The reaction of 'righteous indignation tempered with relief' which Christopher Isherwood describes was felt mostly by the comfortable middle classes, including those who thought themselves to be liberals.

I may have refused to recognize the imminence of a war; but things to come always cast their shadows before them, and there must have been some feeling telling me that time was running short. We reached Wenford on 1 June, and we both worked from dawn to dusk between then and September, in a fever of activity. We enjoyed the confidence and exhilaration which came from knowing that the house, buildings, garden and land, however dilapidated, were ours. It was the first time we had known this experience and it was good to realize that we did not have to ask anyone's permission before we tore down a partition or put up a new fence. After the first few weeks we also had Herbert Higman to help us. He kept the pub at St Breward, and Mariel's mother, who was staying there, somehow persuaded him to come and work for us at odd times. He was a retired navy man and had been Master-at-Arms on a battleship. He knew how to do everything, skilled or unskilled, and notwithstanding his high rank in the navy he was ready to turn his hand to anything that needed to be done, from teaching me how to grow vegetables to building in granite. For that, he had a true Cornish passion; the larger and heavier the blocks, the better pleased he was. He and I rebuilt most of the skittle alley walls, and the St Breward carpenter, Mr Greenaway, made an entirely new roof for it, carefully removing and reusing all the old slates.

Time was not the only thing that was running out; the money was rapidly coming to an end. I bought a truck-load of clay from Fremington and another of cutty clay from Devon, and dumped them in separate bays of the granite-lined clay-pit which had been the first thing I made. Before we left Winchcombe I had designed the new kiln and estimated the quantities of bricks. For the fireboxes and flues, the lining of the chamber itself, the dome and the chimney, I obtained kaolin firebricks from the old kilns at Carbis, near Roche, which at that time was still producing them. For the outer wall of the chamber I bought red bricks made at Whitestone, near Bude.

I dug the foundation for the kiln just outside the blacksmith's shop, in a corner of the field which was a waste of nettles and docks. It was to be much smaller than the Winchcombe kiln, 6 feet (1.8 metres) inside diameter instead of 10 feet (3 metres), and with three fires instead of four, but otherwise similar in design, with a dome at the top of the chamber and a tapering hovel above. The flues leading from the fires into the kiln floor were rather complicated to build – three curved vaults with fire-holes pierced in them leading to the chamber. The plan was to use coal and to finish the firing with faggots, as at Winchcombe. For the three fires I used discarded firebars from Wenford Dries, the big china-clay works just down the railway line from us, less than half a mile away.

The kiln had only reached a few courses above ground level when war was declared, and with winter coming on, I symbolically covered up my work with sacking. Then I began making saggars. The saggar-clay was a fifty-fifty mix of white cutty clay and what we called Stannon sand, the waste quartz from the big kaolin mine at Stannon on the moor – this was the clay-mine which fed the Dries at Wenford. I trod up the cutty clay beside the clay-pit outside – cold work at that time of year – and then wedged it on the granite wedging-table in the brewhouse. It was quite satisfactory clay for saggars, considering it broke all the scientific rules about refractory mixes. (At that time I did not know the rules, so this did not worry me.) The mix was easy to throw with if I used it sufficiently soft, and the saggars performed well in the earthenware firings. Many years later, when I had changed over to stoneware, I went on using the same saggars with good results. The matrix of cutty clay combined with the finer, micaceous part of the Stannon sand, and the large quartz grains enabled the saggars to stand up without any distortion or slumping at high temperature.

Those years were a time of discouragement for potters; nobody was going to want pots while the war was on. I have heard that potters in some countries had to turn to making hand-thrown ceramic cases for grenades. Knowing that if I ever succeeded in finishing the kiln and firing it we should have to begin with a biscuit-firing (because you can't fire galena in a newly built kiln), I made some unglazed pans and big pots for storing materials in the pottery. I also made hundreds of 3 inch (7.5 cm) flower pots for Alec Masters at Lower Lank up the hill – he had glasshouses for raising tomatoes and needed the pots for his seedlings.

But it seemed to make better sense to cultivate the land (everyone has to eat), rather than make pots which were not wanted. With the help of Herb Higman I enclosed a small strip of the meadow just outside the garden hedge – the meadow there was mostly nettles and other weeds. In this strip (which we called the orchard) we planted a few apple and other fruit trees, and I dug up the ground and planted potatoes there in the following spring. We also started keeping poultry and ducks in the old pig-house.

Our house, which we still sometimes called the Wenford Inn, was even for that date astonishingly deficient in all the minor conveniences of life. There was no piped water, and therefore no bathroom or lavatory or hot-water system. We used to go across the road and dip our buckets or pitchers in the

stream which came down from Lower Lank, and we obtained our drinking
water from a little spring. When we first moved in, there was not even a sink in
the house. Since there was no tap, it was hardly necessary. But Herb Higman
and I installed an old stoneware sink and a pipe through the wall to carry the
waste outside, where, rather surprisingly, there was a quite efficient drain. If
hot water was needed for washing up or for a bath, it came from a big black
kettle which hung over the wood fire in the main room, and you had your bath
in a round tin tub in front of the fire: very cosy, but a lot of trouble for Mariel,
who bathed the boys every evening. But most days she and I went down to the
River Camel and plunged into its cold water.

When the spring of 1940 at last came, I dug the garden and planted the
potatoes, and then went back to building the kiln. Gradually the circular wall
began to rise above the apron of massive granite which acted in place of an iron
band at the base. I was a self-taught bricklayer, working single-handed,
stopping from time to time to mix a fresh batch of mortar. The only spirit-
level I had was a tiny one I bought at Woolworth's for 6*d*. (2½p). As it was
only about 4 inches (10 cm) long, I found it hard to lay level
courses. Fortunately a friend arrived for a brief visit – Michael Leach,
Bernard's second son. He noticed the cumulative error in the levels of
successive courses, and spent a day or two with me, helping to correct them.

At last I reached the planned height where the dome had to be built.
Following my memory of what Mr Garvin had done at Winchcombe I
carefully laid two springer courses sloping at 45 degrees, and began to build
the dome – it was the first of many that I was to build. I used the sticky cutty
clay for mortar; and was surprised to find how easy the whole operation was:
even the holes for the fire to pass through were not difficult to manage. The
next stage was to build the hovel and chimney. The work went more quickly
now, since the wall here was only 9 inches (23 cm) thick. I levelled the top of
the dome so that I could stand on it, and worked from the inside, gradually
narrowing the radius.

While the kiln was slowly rising, the shooting war had started, and every
day the news was worse. Hitler had conquered France, and Britain was
waiting for him to invade. Concrete pillboxes were built at every suitable
place to cover the main roads and railways; all the signposts were taken down
and stored. The Home Guard was formed. One day a stranger asked if we
knew of a good place to camp on the moor. A few nights later the Home
Guard caught him trying to signal to aircraft with a flashlight. He was a British
Fascist, and was detained.

Another day I was perched as usual on top of the dome, building the hovel,
when I noticed two strangers standing in the garden below. They asked my

name and said they wanted a few words with me, so I said, 'Right! Come on up.' But they said, 'Better come down to us,' and I came. They were plain-clothes police, investigating rumours that I was an enemy agent. They said there was much talk in the parish that we were 'up to no good' at Wenford. Why had we come to settle there, just a few months before the war began? Was it true that we had a secret radio transmitter hidden up the chimney? Some good friend had given us an old *receiver* (from which we heard all our news, and on which we also listened to some of Churchill's famous speeches – the one about fighting on the beaches, and the beautiful one he made on the occasion of Italy's entering the war). The external design of this radio, however, was so painful, and it looked so out of place among our other possessions, that we had decided to put it into one of the cupboards built into the wall beside the fireplace so that we would not have to look at it. Was it true that we had had 'a foreign gentleman' staying with us? Well, yes, but we had never thought of Henry Bergen as 'foreign'. In the end it was agreed that there was nothing sinister about him. Was it true that I received every week a paper called the *New Statesman*? Alas, yes, it was true, thanks to my youngest brother who used to send it on to us when he had finished reading it. However, the officer took a lenient view of this; he said he supposed 'dozens of people read the *New Statesman*'. (In fact, I disapproved strongly of the *New Statesman* at that time, because of its support for the war.)

The two policemen decided we were harmless, and departed. But Damaris Magor, a distant cousin who lived with her father and mother at Lamellen nearby, told us that they continued to 'keep us under observation', an easy thing to do since the house, buildings, garden and meadow, all in the same hollow, were surrounded on three sides by roads, so that it was not possible to go anywhere or do anything, even to visit the earth closet in the garden, without all the world being able to observe us if they so wished.

We were blameless; but the sense of the St Breward people was correct, in a way. True, I was not an enemy agent, but neither was I, in my heart or in their eyes, a loyal citizen. I had made no secret of my opinions, especially at the meetings of the local branch of the Workers' Educational Association. But Percy Coggin, the manager of the local quarry and a keen supporter of the WEA, testified on our behalf in the village, and so did my friend Mr Leese, the headmaster of Camelford Grammar School. I think Herb Higman also helped to allay the local suspicions, since by this time he knew us quite well and constantly had tea with us and the children. So I was able to finish building the kiln without interruption, although we continued to expect a German invasion through most of the summer of 1940.

The kiln was built, and I began to make preparations for the first firing. But

I had been beaten in the race against time: the money was finished, and there was no prospect of being able to sell pots even if we could fire them. I had raised a little additional capital by surrendering an old insurance policy dating from the 1920s; but the bank manager with a cold eye indicated that there was no more to be squeezed out. I taught for two weeks in a small preparatory school, standing in for a master who had broken his arm. But my two weeks' wages as a 'teacher' did not last long. Then a friend of Mariel lent me £50, a kind act which it took me several decades to repay (if I ever did; I rather think she eventually opted for pots instead).

I was still trying to get ready for the first firing, when a welcome diversion occurred: Harry and May Davis came to visit us. He was on leave from Achimota College, and was travelling through Devon and Cornwall studying ceramic raw materials, not only clays but rocks as well – ball clays, china clay and Cornish stone – comparing our local raw materials (which were 'standard' in the industrial sense) with the materials available in Ghana. He described his visit to the aplite quarry at Meldon on Dartmoor. All this revived feelings which I had begun to have about stoneware during the later years at Winchcombe, and made me think again that perhaps after all some day I could make stoneware instead of earthenware.

I envied Harry the exciting work he was doing, especially when I reflected that he was earning a regular salary. Harry with his usual generosity offered to lend me £30, which I gratefully accepted, though here again it was many years before I was able to pay it back.

This enabled me to continue potting for a month or two longer. Then, quite unexpectedly, an interesting and unusual visitor arrived, a Scotsman whom Mariel had met during her painting days in London. His name was Lindsay Lutette, a short, energetic man, with a venerable grey beard (he looked in fact very like the ideal, bearded hermit whom Mariel had expected to meet when she first visited Winchcombe Pottery in 1932). He used to travel through Britain on foot, staying wherever he found receptive or deserving people who appeared to be in need of any kind of help. Usually he would offer to dig the garden, or help to build an outhouse, or put up a fence where one was needed, or repair an existing one. He stayed a long time with us, sometimes helping with bathing the children or cooking the dinner.

Lindsay Lutette had been an officer in the Royal Engineers during the First World War, but at some point he suddenly woke up to a realization of the total wickedness of war, went to his superior officers, and told them he could no longer carry out his duties. His case went up to the Major, who passed it along to the Colonel, and so on, right up through the entire hierarchy of the army. He carried the documentation of all this in his wallet. At one stage, the

Adjutant wrote 'Lieut. Lutette appears to be suffering from some form of religious mania . . .' Eventually the authorities, unable to make any headway against his calm resolution, gave him his discharge and (surprisingly) allowed him to return to private life. Since that time he had become a wanderer, walking through the world and preaching his gospel of non-resistance to any who would receive it.

By this time Mariel was becoming anxious about the future – not our own, but that of our three boys. Seth was now nearly six, and Cornelius four, and she was beginning to worry about their education. I was no help. In so far as I had thought about it at all I had decided that since I had no money, the best education for them would be to attend the village school and then to become apprentices in the pottery – unless any of them turned out to be particularly clever at school, in which case they would be able to win a scholarship to Camelford Grammar School.

But Mariel, unlike me, had no intention of leaving the boys' education to chance. She systematically began to dig out all her manifold academic qualifications, to obtain letters of recommendation from her former teachers in Oxford, and to apply for a teaching job. She found a girls' school in the Chilterns which was willing for her to bring at least one boy with her. She arranged to take Seth, and to leave Cornelius, who was still too young to go to the school, with friends of hers who were living on Dartmoor. Ennis, now aged two, remained with me at Wenford; I used to put him to bed every night and sing to him till he slept.

'Economic reality' had overtaken us, and our family began to show the first signs of falling apart. Only one memory remains with me now from those dark times when our life together was suddenly dimmed by a continuing sense of my own helpless financial inferiority and economic incompetence: we were riding our heavily loaded bicycles to Bodmin Road Station to send Mariel and the two boys off; they squeezed themselves, in the dark, into a blacked-out train which was many hours late and overloaded with soldiers, sailors and civilian passengers. This must have been at the end of the Christmas holidays; it felt like the end of the world.

That autumn (1940) Harry Davis had to go back to Achimota. In those days everybody went by boat – there was no question of flying. But submarine warfare had made the sea voyage hazardous. There were very few remaining boats – most of them had been torpedoed – and berths were limited to 'officers of the Colonial Service resuming duty'. May Davis had always worked as hard as Harry in the pottery at Achimota but was never paid, still less appointed to any official post. Officially, therefore, she was simply an officer's wife; and wives had to wait indefinitely before being given a passage to rejoin their husbands. So May suggested that while she was waiting to join Harry she should come to Wenford to help me look after Ennis. She not only took care of Ennis but also found time to do a whole lot of useful work in the pottery, especially making saggars, of which I still did not have enough. She made hundreds of small plate saggars, and she showed me a much quicker and more efficient way of fixing and levelling the bats on the wheel. At last, after months of waiting in vain for a berth, she left Wenford and went to help her sister in Scotland, and I did not meet her again until many years after the war had ended.

Early in 1941 I received a letter from a total stranger, who said he had a small kiln and wanted to make experiments with glazes; but since he himself was not a thrower he wondered whether I knew of any potter who could come for a few weeks – wages, railway fares, and free living-quarters all provided – to make pots for him. His name was Robert Dewar Finlay, the owner of a brickworks at Hamilton, Lanarkshire. I wrote back to say I would come myself.

I spent five or six weeks at Hamilton, including the whole of May 1941. I had been to Scotland once or twice before, but never to Glasgow, and I was struck more than ever by how different Scotland is from England: even the shapes of the hills change as soon as you cross the Border. And Robert Finlay was not like anyone I had ever known in the south: more dashing, more generous, and displaying a carefree, uninhibited egoism. It showed even in the way he drove his very smart car. I thought perhaps it just came from being rich; but I had met one or two rich men in England, and they had seemed very sober and restrained, compared with him. Before the war, he had for several years run a large and successful plant in Malaya, making stoneware drainpipes with local material and Chinese workmen. Now he had returned to Scotland and was making bricks from waste thrown out by a nearby coal mine.

In his house at Uddingston I felt like a distinguished guest of himself and Mrs Finlay, and occupied two nice self-contained rooms over the garage. He had for years been a great admirer of the work of William Staite Murray, and was aware that I had once had some reputation as a potter. My room was furnished with a collection of pottery books and in the evenings I had a wonderful time devouring some of his technical books and making copious notes. There was a copy of Hainbach's *Pottery Decoration*, full of fascinating information about colours, frits, and the design of frit-kilns, and several issues of the *Bulletin* of the American Ceramic Society, among which I found translated extracts from one of the classic Chinese books on porcelain-making, with beautiful drawings reproduced from the original.

Part of the garage under my room had been turned into a pottery, with a small electric wheel, clays, tubs of glazes and slips and an impressive assembly of pigments and other materials. The kiln was about four miles away, at his brickworks in Hamilton, fired with gas or oil and connected to the main chimney of the brick kiln. He mostly wanted small pots, because the kiln itself was very small; but he left the shapes and designs entirely to me. I made hundreds of pots, jugs, bowls, cups and saucers on the electric wheel, using the stoneware body which he got from the big Govancroft Pottery not far away. Like all the stoneware bodies I had met, it was easy to throw with, provided you did not try to make the pots too thin. It slumped very quickly on the wheel and everything I made needed to be turned afterwards.

Remembering my experience in Stoke-on-Trent, I several times tried to persuade Robert Finlay to embark on making pottery on an industrial scale, training some of the employees at the brickworks. But he refused, saying that his employees 'would never be able to do that'.

Robert Finlay had built a very solid air-raid shelter, in the garden, using quantities of his own bricks, which were good hard engineering-type bricks, so that it really looked very convincing, capable of standing up to anything but a spot-on direct hit by any of Hitler's bombs. So when the inevitable air-raids came, we all trooped into this cave, and sat listening to the bombs exploding on Glasgow. The way bombs explode, in groups of several, brings home the horribly vindictive character of this kind of frightfulness. They were falling on working-class districts as if someone was using a vast lash, and saying to his victims, 'That will teach you, once and for all, to dare to be there.' There was a disgusting element of personal punishment in the performance. The raids never got really close to Uddingston: but they were the nearest I ever came to the horrors of the Second World War.

Coming back to England, with, for the first time for years, good money in my pocket, I stopped briefly with Mariel at her school, and then hitch-hiked to Devon and visited Cornelius at the Tavistock Hospital, where he was supposed to be suffering from tuberculosis. I knew that was unlikely, and sure enough I found him bright and lively and very pleased to see his father. I brought him a huge bag of strawberries. Ennis, the youngest, who was not yet three, had had to be sent away to stay with friends when I went up to Scotland. Of all the things I did in that unhappy and chaotic period, this is the one that I have most regretted, and most wished had never been done, and could be undone. It is terrible to be rejected like that, at such an age.

That autumn I received a totally unexpected letter. It came from the Colonial Office, saying that Achimota College in the Gold Coast was expecting to lose its 'ceramist', just at a time when the College was planning an important enlargement of its pottery department. The ceramist, Mr H.L. Davis, had given in his resignation, and he would soon be leaving in order to join his wife in South America. Mr Davis (the letter continued) had originally, it appeared, been recruited as a result of a suggestion from myself; and seeing that his work there had been outstandingly successful, it was hoped that I would be able to recommend some other similarly qualified potter, who would be competent to take his place. I replied that I unfortunately did not know of any potter capable of taking Mr Davis's place (my words were more true than I knew); but that I myself would be willing to come instead.[1]

---

[1] My father's text gives no explanation for his readiness to take up the post in West Africa. However, from the context it appears likely that his motivation at the outset was for the most part financial. Quite simply, the job offered a regular salary. – S.C.

15

TO A FOREIGN SHORE

Linque tuas sedes, alienaque litora quaere
O juvenis, major rerum tibi nascitur ordo.

Young man, leave home and seek a foreign shore,
A greater destiny is in store for you.

Petronius

Christopher Cox sat at his desk at 2 Park Street, London, surrounded by the usual paraphernalia of a civil servant's office. The most striking ornament of the desk was a rack for ten or a dozen pipes, which he chain-smoked. He had taken a First in Greats at Oxford in the same year that I had scraped through with a Third, and now he was Education Adviser to the Colonial Office. We found each other easy to get on with, and he was friendly and helpful.

He asked what my family commitments were ('At the moment it is rather difficult for wives and children to accompany their husbands to West Africa, but in normal times...'). He asked about the pottery at Wenford, in particular how much it would cost to restart when I returned there after the war, and made a note of my reply. It was a new experience for me to be treated as a person of consequence.

He then went on to tell me about recent developments at Achimota College. The pottery department which had been started by Meyerowitz and Davis two years before the war began was now being greatly enlarged to meet urgent demands caused by the war situation. Indeed, it was proposed to establish a ceramic industry that would supply the whole of West Africa, including the occupying British army. Harry Davis had made such a success of the brick- and tilemaking at Achimota that Meyerowitz had been able to persuade the Gold Coast Government to finance a proper tileworks. This had been built at a place called Alajo, between Achimota and Accra, and it was now to be further enlarged so that its production could be doubled. The small pottery at the College had been producing substantial numbers of unglazed water-coolers, but had so far produced glazed pottery on a pilot scale only.

Now a much larger pottery to produce glazed ware was to be set up beside the tileworks. Detailed plans for this large new pottery had already been drawn up by Davis, but he was now about to leave, so the Colonial Office needed to recruit a new ceramist to set up and run the pottery. This was the job for which I had volunteered myself. They were also looking for an assistant ceramist, to take care of the engineering work – which meant, in fact, the task of improvising pottery equipment from local scrap-iron. Some potter's wheels and other machines were to be ordered from England, but these had to be kept to an absolute minimum – very little iron and steel could be spared from the war effort, and, as well, shipping space was severely limited. Thus for many of its needs the new factory would have to rely on improvisation and on an ingenious adaptation of any materials that could be found locally. I immediately thought of Dicon Nance, whom I had known since I was at the Leach Pottery in the early 1920s. He had been working there for years, not as a potter but as a sort of maintenance engineer. It was he who, among other things, made the prototypes of the kick wheel which is still produced and marketed as the 'Leach' wheel. Like his friend Harry Davis, he was an inspired improviser.

For myself, I was intoxicated by what I was told of these plans for the pottery at Achimota. A dream seemed to be coming true. Here was the larger workshop I had imagined, raised to the scale of a small factory, but still based on each thrower's individual skill and craftsmanship. Of course, as in all dreams, there was a catch: the enlarged scale of operations was being imposed from the start, instead of being the result of a gradual building-up from small beginnings. But this was obviously unavoidable, because it was imposed by the war; and I was now a firm believer in the necessity of making some contribution to winning that war. I had suddenly found work which was connected with the war, work which I was able and eager to do, and this was a wonderful release after three years of semi-frustration. It was out of the question to allow such an opportunity to pass. But there were various difficulties and hold-ups, and it was to be several months before I left England for Africa.

Meanwhile, in April 1942, Meyerowitz arrived in England to promote the setting up of an ambitious scheme, of which the new pottery and tileworks were to be just one part. The full title was to be the 'West African Institute of Arts, Industries and Social Sciences'. The first proposals for such an Institute had originally been drawn up by Meyerowitz and others at the time when he first went to Achimota; but he now saw the emergency of the war as a wonderful opportunity to persuade the British Government to authorize it. In many respects the moment was propitious. The war had been going very badly for us, but these reverses had incidentally emphasized the underlying weakness of colonial economies. The colonies had been expected to subsist solely on the export of their primary raw materials and crops, and they had practically nothing in the way of local manufactures. Now they were trying to stay alive with almost no imports and no exports, and in this situation the new idea of Colonial Development had suddenly acquired respectability. Ever since the collapse of France, British West Africa, long one of the more obscure and least eventful parts of the Colonial Empire, had been moving, if not exactly into the centre of events, yet near enough to them to be vulnerable, since it was now surrounded by territories controlled by the potentially hostile Vichy régime. It had also become strategically important: the West African colonies were being used as a base for supplying the campaign in North Africa. Half of Achimota College had been taken over as General Headquarters, West Africa, and a large force, European and African, was stationed there.

Thanks to his personality and charm, his background and upbringing, Meyerowitz was able to move with confidence and assurance in the world of politicians, generals and top civil servants. In London, he was persuasive in pressing the case for his proposals.

Since Meyerowitz was to be the ruling genius of my life for the next few years, I must pause to give a brief account of what brought him to Achimota, and from there to London.

Herbert Vladimir Meyerowitz was born in St Petersburg on 28 September 1900, and was thus less than a year older than me. His father was a German businessman who emigrated to St Petersburg, where he became a millionaire, and met and married Vladimir's mother, Ljuba Smetanina. She was a brilliant young pianist who had been a star pupil of Rubinstein and had already given concert recitals by the age of eighteen. But when she married her millionaire she had to give up this career in music and devote herself to being a society hostess.

At the time of the 1905 revolution the family emigrated to Switzerland to save their millions, and young Vladimir was sent to be educated at the first Pestalozzi school there. Later on they moved to England, but the climate disagreed with their mother and she returned to Russia. The three children, Martha, Vladimir and Victor, were kept at school in England and used to spend their holidays alternately in England and in Russia. Pre-1914 Europe was a wonderful club to belong to, provided you could afford to be a member of it.

When war broke out in 1914, the Meyerowitz children happened to be spending the holiday in Russia; since their father had never given up his German nationality and the children were technically Germans, they were interned at Ekaterinburg in the Urals. He told me that it was here he was first taught wood-carving, by a local peasant.

In 1916 Germany and Russia agreed to make an exchange of civilian internees, and the three children were dumped in Berlin. Vladimir had to find himself work now, in a series of temporary jobs, until in May 1918 he was drafted into the army and sent to the Western Front. The war was nearly over; Vladimir scarcely saw any actual fighting, and he used to make a joke of his 1918 war service. In 1940 when he joined the Home Guard in the Gold Coast, he had to fill out various forms, and under the heading 'Previous military experience' he took delight in being able to put the name of his old artillery regiment, 'a salutary lesson in history for parochial Achimota'.

After the war he went back to Berlin, where he attended a school of arts and crafts. It was here that he first met his future wife, Eva. They shared a great enthusiasm for African art, especially the art of West Africa, and used to devour together all the books about it that they could find. Then Vladimir moved on to study wood-carving at a place called the Kunstgewerbeschule, where the training was strict and thorough, in the old tradition of German craftsmanship. In 1925, his long training at last completed, he married Eva, and they almost immediately moved to South Africa. It was not the part of Africa that interested them most, but it was at least Africa, and it seemed likely that they would be able to make a good living there. This indeed proved to be the case. In South Africa Meyerowitz gained a high reputation as a sculptor in wood, and carried out many commissions for work on public buildings. He also taught for about five years at Cape Town University, and then opened his own school of art.

Early in 1935 he spent three months in Lesotho (then Basutoland), to study and report on the crafts there. It was soon after this that he was invited to organize and arrange an exhibition of African Arts and Crafts which was to be part of something called an 'Interterritorial Educational Conference' in Salisbury, Rhodesia. When he arrived there he found 'many harassed men and women opening packing-cases, pulling out an amazing variety of objects and arranging them on trestle tables'. In the course of the speech he had to make at the opening of the exhibition, he said:

> I pointed to the drums and bark cloths[1] from Uganda, the huge *carosses*[2] from Bechuanaland, the pottery from Basutoland, in short the wealth of traditional forms and designs from all over Africa. And then – *then* – I

---

[1] Made by beating the bark of certain trees to produce a kind of felt. Bark cloths are wonderful things, their texture almost exactly half-way between the finest chamois leather and ordinary sacking.

[2] Fur blankets sewn together with the split tendons of antelopes.

compared all this with the work brought in from schools and institutions. . . . The traditional work was good, because it still fulfilled its purpose; the new work fulfilled no purpose at all. . . . I pointed to these masses of *bric à brac*, doilies, embroidered cushions, all copied from tenth-rate European designs, and I felt bitterly ashamed of all this trash for which we, the white people in Africa, were responsible and which we, in the name of education, had inflicted on the people of Africa . . .

The exhibits which attracted his severest comments were those from West Africa. But it so happened that the delegate from the Gold Coast was the Deputy Director of Education there, and at the end of the speech he came up to Meyerowitz and said, 'Since we are so bad, I wish you would come over to us and help us.'

Shortly afterwards Meyerowitz was formally offered the job of running the art department at Achimota College, the most respected educational establishment in West Africa. During his eleven years in South Africa Meyerowitz had done well, and made a fine reputation for himself. But now he was presented with the opportunity to work in that part of Africa that had from the beginning attracted both him and Eva most. They decided to leave South Africa for Achimota.

But first they had to go to London, so that Vladimir could be properly inducted into his new job. They spent altogether eight or nine months in England, and it was during this time that he went to that 'New Education Fellowship' conference in Cheltenham, where I had first met him.

There was an element of greatness in H. V. Meyerowitz; and as with others who have been touched by that mysterious power, it produced contradictions in his character which are only surprising if one forgets that greatness often prefers to settle on a person in whom something of the original child has survived intact into adult life; and that this child is always liable to be in conflict with what the adult world or his own ambitions impose on him. Though he was by nature incapable of unkindness, yet there were moments when he could show arrogance. He was more sophisticated than I was, and far wiser in the ways of the world (his early youth could not be described as sheltered); yet he would denounce cynicism with a sudden ethical intensity which took me by surprise. 'Cynics are sinners, you know – that's not a joke, Michael: it is *true*.' He was ruled by the heart rather than the head, to a much greater extent that I was: it was startling to see how easily he could be hurt, considering how clever he could be in manipulating other people.

Early in May 1942 I received a letter from Meyerowitz: 'The mills of the Colonial Office, which grind very slowly, have at last ground out Nance's appointment, and he will be going out to Achimota as soon as possible.' He got there six or eight weeks before me. Meyerowitz also told me that the tileworks at Alajo, now in full production, was being managed by George Procter, an experienced tilemaker from the Stoke-on-Trent area. He was due to come to England soon on leave.

Meanwhile I had to go to Stoke-on-Trent, where I was taken round several big factories, and then to the head office of the Federation of Pottery Manufacturers to get full details about the army specifications for tableware, in order to see just what it was we had undertaken to make for the army at Achimota. Meyerowitz had landed a firm order from General Headquarters at Achimota for about 180,000 pieces of tableware for the troops, as soon as the new pottery at Alajo was in operation. It seemed a tall order to me, but Meyerowitz said the army was desperate for them: the soldiers were having to eat and drink out of tins.

Now something else had turned up. Since the fall of Singapore and the loss of Malaya, Britain was very short of rubber. The United Africa Company's rubber plantation at Sapele in Nigeria was trying to increase its output, but they needed latex-cups – little bowls about the size of a tea bowl, which are attached to the trees when they are being tapped, to catch the milky latex which oozes out. They needed 200,000 of these a year. Could we make them at Alajo? Meyerowitz immediately seized upon this as yet another powerful lever with which to move the authorities to give the green light for the Institute. He emphasized to me that there would be plenty of money and plenty of labour; that there were already nine throwers there, some of them very good, and that I could train others if they were needed (as I thought they surely would be). I asked what clays and glazes were available for all these potters. (I really did not have much technical knowledge about stoneware at that time.) But he assured me that I would not need to worry: Harry had done all the groundwork of local research, and worked out good bodies and glazes. This was quite true. But there was also the problem of producing these on the scale of hundreds of tons a year. I did not consider myself to be some kind of superman or ceramic wizard. I was simply carried away by Meyerowitz's persuasion, which always made anything sound easy, and my own enthusiasm for the scheme.

It was nearly the end of July 1942 when my sailing orders came at last. Mariel travelled with me to London and from there to Glasgow. We went by the night train, blacked out as usual, and very full. The train had to crawl through the industrial area of Merseyside where there had been an air-raid; but we reached Glasgow in the early morning and had breakfast together at the Station Hotel. There we received news that all civilian passages had been cancelled. Nobody knew why. We were at first advised to go home again by the next train, and many of the passengers did that. But Mariel and I were desperate, and most of our last hours together were spent feverishly trying to put a telephone call through to the Colonial Office. They were sympathetic, but, as can be imagined, powerless to do anything to help.

One of the reasons we were both so upset about the cancellation was simply money. During the past eight months I had been doing a lot of unpaid work for the Colonial Office (though they did refund travelling expenses). Mariel had given up her teaching job and gone back to Wenford, in the expectation of receiving what was called a 'family allotment' (one half of my salary of £600 a year) each month from the Crown Agents. But neither of us would be entitled to a single penny of that salary until I embarked on the boat.

But my eagerness to go was not entirely because of the money, nor even because of the Achimota pottery scheme itself. It felt more like what people call 'destiny' – the shadow of future events and experiences, calling me on. Something was saying to me, 'This is what you must do, this is your path, wherever it may take you.'

Eventually somebody who seemed to have some inside knowledge appeared, and advised us to hang around for the rest of the day on the chance of getting on to the boat. So we took the train out to Greenock and waited at the dock. There at the last minute the remaining civilian passengers were told that they were to be allowed on the ship after all. Mariel and I stayed together until the moment came when I had to go through the barrier and join the stream of passengers.

At last I was on the lighter taking me out to the boat, which was anchored in mid-channel. One of the sailors said, 'Looks like a Dutchman to me.' She was called the *Amstelkerk*, of the Holland–West Afrika Lijn.

At the age of forty-one, full of ignorance, misconceptions, illusions about the world and about myself, infatuated by something without even knowing what it was, I was about to embark on a new life.

Our convoy consisted of forty boats and an escort of four small naval vessels. There was very little to do on the *Amstelkerk* except sit around, talk with the other passengers, and worry about the likelihood of being torpedoed – 1942 was a bad year for shipping. After eighteen days sailing we entered Freetown Harbour, at night. The lights of the town were all blazing as if there were no war on. We leant over the rails and gazed at it all. A warm breeze was blowing. The air was like a bath of milk, so exactly the temperature of your body that you could hardly feel it. For some reason we lay in Freetown Harbour for ten days. I felt as if I had already reached my destination, though we still had about nine hundred miles of (probably) submarine-infested waters before we reached Takoradi, where I was to disembark. We left Freetown at last in the early morning of 29 August. And on 4 September we finally disembarked at Takoradi.

After passing through Customs I joined up with one or two passengers who, like me, were bound for Achimota, and they took me along to 'Adra's Government Transport Bus'. When all the baggage was on, the bus started, driven very fast, with much rattling and bumping and a furious, almost continuous, trumpeting of the horn. We passed trees with long black pods hanging from their branches, like giant beanpods; and tall fan-palms, their pale grey smooth trunks growing fat towards the top, like the stem of a leek when it flowers, or those truncheons which Victorian policemen carry in old pictures from *Punch*.

Farther on, the road ran parallel with the beach. Big dugout canoes were drawn up on the sand, and nets were hanging to dry. Two teams of fishermen, twenty or thirty together, were hauling in the ropes of a seine-net. Then the road turned inland again. In the roadside villages the men and women were wearing brightly coloured cotton, and carrying loads on their heads. Occasionally we saw cultivated patches in which maize was growing, looking rather dried-up; but nowhere any hedges or large fields. The country seemed to be solid Bush, a tangle of creepers and purple-flowering bindweed. In front of the houses in the villages there were shrubs entirely covered with a mass of purple or magenta flowers, the colour so intense that you had to look away because it made your eyes jump.

We passed Elmina Castle, and reached Cape Coast where we stopped to eat lunch, and I bought four oranges for a penny and was rebuked by the other Europeans for paying too much for them. After that the road turned inland again, through country which seemed to be full of activity and thickly populated. As the road threaded its way through all these evergreen shrubs and trees, I kept on having a curious illusion that I was on a visit to some great estate in the heart of England. Surely the next turn of this 'drive' we are following will bring us in sight of the 'great house' itself? But the great house is never there, only more miles of evergreen vegetation. As we reached the fringes of the rain forest, the vegetation began to change. There were immensely tall oil-palms with a small tuft of leaves at the very top. Gradually we began to see tall forest trees, rare at first, with smooth white or pale grey trunks which rose to a height of 100 feet (30 metres) or more before they began to branch. Some had great buttresses at their base, like vegetable sinews. We began to see cacao-trees, which looked to my eyes like small Spanish chestnut trees with coffee-coloured dead leaves covering the ground at their feet; and all the way, innumerable bananas, their leaves like enormous Venetian blinds, the bunches of fruit pointing upwards instead of hanging down, and their very surprising and indecent-looking fruit buds, hanging like the penis of a gigantic horse. Near Nsawam a great conical hill rose 1,000 feet (300 metres) or more out of the surrounding country, covered with tall, white-stemmed trees all the way to its summit, making it look like an enormous dome-shaped cake covered with candles.

After Nsawam the road turned south again; we left the forest and a sort of coastal scrub began. Eventually we saw the tall white clock-tower of Achimota College. Another great estate; but this time there was a 'great house' at the centre of it. We got there around five o'clock. It had been a long, unforgettable drive.

I had not known I was capable of such exhilaration; I felt like an enormous mainspring which had been wound up for the past five weeks and was now suddenly released. (It would be truer, I suppose, to say that something had been winding it up for the past thirty or forty years.) I wished I could have been born and have grown up from childhood in this country. In a sudden illumination I realized that Europe's war didn't matter, here, nearly so much as I had thought. I felt convinced that the only thing which really did matter was the art, whatever forms it might take, of the people who lived here.

16

ACHIMOTA

I did not relish the role of a colonial exploiter; but then I did not believe that I was one. The work that I had come to West Africa to do was not exploitation: it was beneficial. So I thought, in 1942. It is perfectly clear to me now that a white man working in a black colony cannot possibly win. In the eyes of any intelligent African he is either a shameless exploiter or a paternalist 'do-gooder', the cold truth being that he has no business to be there at all unless he has been invited to come by the free people of an independent country. But we are talking about history, about a certain period in the past when 'colonies' (that euphemism, that good word debased) were a fact. I am recording things that happened at that time, not what ought to have happened.

The very word 'do-gooder' is a symptom of the disillusionment and cynicism to which we in the present period cannot help being subject. Of course it is true, as Aldous Huxley said, that 'doing good, on any but the tiniest scale, requires more intelligence than most people possess.' But what people forget when they dismiss 'do-gooding' is that though it may often be mistaken, or even harmful, it is still very much 'better than the alternative', in Clement Attlee's useful phrase.[1] As for the inevitable reproach of 'paternalism', of this too it must be said that in the context of the colonial period it was better than the alternative. It was the natural, generous reaction of any good man when he first came face to face with what he saw as the deprivation of the people around him, and when he compared their material standard of living with that of himself, his white friends and the African élite. The trouble about paternalism is that it easily degenerates into possessiveness (in your relations with individuals) or into authoritarianism in your public attitudes. I fell into all these traps during my earlier years in Africa, before painfully acquiring enough good sense to avoid them.

Something else I only realized later was that, whatever kind of temperament a white man brought with him, the mere fact of being transplanted out of the

[1] On Attlee's eightieth birthday, a journalist asked him 'How does it feel to be eighty?' Attlee's reply was 'Better than the alternative'.

cold northern environment into these steamy tropics had an electrifying effect on him at first. What usually happened was that all his previous characteristics tended to be exaggerated. The conscientious man became more conscientious, the cautious more cautious, the earnest more earnest, the reckless more reckless, and so on. Or occasionally, the sudden transplantation into a hot climate would bring out some tendency which had been quiescent before, and in these cases an opposite result was seen: the apparently cautious became reckless, the apparently frivolous became surprisingly earnest. It was imposs-ible to be forewarned of any of this.

It was not only a climatic transformation: the job itself, the whole milieu, had a similar effect. The tight, narrow, expatriate society with its conventions, taboos, and ritual jokes; and above all, the challenges and responsibilities laid upon the neophyte, which, if he had any imagination, could either reduce him to a state of stammering indecision or else exalt him with hubris and arrogance.

These were some of the conditions which cause a well-recognized 'disease' in newcomers, which was known among the old hands as 'First Tour Fever': the symptoms were a kind of mania, a feverish energy, an absurd keenness, a ridiculous attachment to proposed tasks, or a childish moodiness. There was also a rather endearing after-effect of the First Tour disease, which caused a European to the end of his West African service (which in the earlier decades all too often coincided with the end of his life) to have an ineradicable belief in the superior merits and virtues of the African people with whom he had been in contact at the beginning of his career, whether these were Ga motor-drivers, Ibo traders, Hausa farmers or Togolese craftsmen.

For myself, I found that the work I did and the life I lived were much fuller, more challenging, and more exciting, than they had been at home. At the same time they were harsher, more serious, more exacting, more real; and I began to look back at my former life as if it had been spent in a kind of dream world, beautiful perhaps, but not quite real, and from then on, never really relevant. Even though I was already forty-one when I first arrived, I could never afterwards take that previous life quite seriously. It seemed to have been filled with rather trivial and doctrinaire debates about things like 'handcraft versus machine production', about 'art in industry', or stupid, snobbish questions like 'Are you an artist or a craftsman?' All those rather narrow, purist attitudes I saw as luxuries which I could not afford and did not need, now that I had entered into this glorious new dispensation. My friends and acquaintances must have noticed that the First Tour Fever had hit me with special virulence; but from my own internal point of view my first four months in Ghana were pure bliss. Fortunately the letters I wrote to Mariel at this time have been preserved: and though I would now repudiate many of the opinions I expressed, both then and much later on, it is perhaps better to quote from them because they give a more immediate and vivid idea than I would now be able to convey, of my excitement at that time.

> *Achimota College, 5 September* (the day after arriving) I am sharing a house with Thurstan Shaw, who at the moment is away digging a site; his wife and baby are 'on leave' in South Africa. Harry Davis and Dicon are sharing a house (No. 5) with John Scholes, a young science teacher on the College staff. Their house is very bare-looking, except for some *ravishing* Nigerian textiles. It will take a few days or a few weeks to get over the stage of gasping and gaping at everything. . . .

> *14 September* Most evenings I spend down at No. 5 with Harry and Dicon and John Scholes, discussing pottery and tileworks 'policy' and the technicalities of blungers, pugmills and so on; also being initiated by Harry into the mysteries of felspar (which he recognizes by its 'characteristic pearly lustre'), pegmatite, aplite, dolerite, diorite, etc., etc. – all very difficult and confusing. Harry knows *a lot* about all these things – he has had to learn it, in order to be able to start the pottery here at all.

That was an altogether new dimension that was being given to pottery; and once again I had a feeling of the unreality of all my 'pre-African' life. Even in simple technical matters – clays, the raw materials for glazes and how to grind them – I saw that in England we had been coddled and spoon-fed, insulated from the realities of what was involved; and I thought: 'All this cushioning can't have been good for the quality of our pots!'

> In the mornings I get up at 6 or 6.30, shave, and eat a few bananas or an orange or two, and walk down to the 'Water-cooler Unit', where they start work at 7. This was Harry's original pottery at Achimota, and I am working there, because it gives me a chance to 'feel my way' into this great work. (The tileworks at Alajo is a great *factory* – about 100 men – where I get rather lost, and begin to despair of ever being able to distinguish one African face from another.) This 'Cooler Unit' at Achimota is at the far end of what they call the 'Maintenance Yard'. It consists of a few open sheds and half-open dryers; two or three rectangular downdraught kilns and one small round kiln for glazed ware. . . . This 'Cooler Unit' is the training ground for the workers in the future 'Glazed Ware Unit' down at Alajo. That (so far) is only a shell, or rather, about a quarter of a shell. . . .
> After breakfast I go down to Alajo tileworks. Lucky if I catch Harry

or Dicon before they leave in the tileworks lorry. Otherwise I borrow Harry's or Dicon's bike and ride along the rough and sandy dirt roads between the rectangular plantations of the Achimota College Forest Reserve – coppiced *neem* and *cassia* trees which look something like young ash trees. It's about $2\frac{1}{2}$ miles to Alajo if you go this way, $3\frac{1}{2}$ if you follow the main road. The tileworks: mostly long open sheds roofed with red tiles – beautiful. . . .

The 'Glaze Unit' is to be next to the tileworks. . . . The main plan has already been laid out by Harry, but only one of the (enormous) buildings has a roof, so far. The roofing is held up for lack of tiles. The army takes all the good ones, and we use the 'seconds'. There are four or five good carpenters, each with three or four young apprentices. The carpenters' shop is in the shade of a big spreading mango tree, and the timber is stored in the branches overhead. Then there's a large gang of builders and bricklayers, each with their apprentices and labourers. The Head Man is J.H. Dadey, a Dahomeyan who Harry says is the best man in the whole place. He wears an old but very high-class sun helmet, a loose blue boiler suit, with bicycle clips and white sandshoes. He has a three-foot ruler sticking out of his pocket and an English tobacco pipe pushed into his belt, like a dagger.

At 12 noon a whistle blows and everyone 'goes for chop' – to a great gathering of vendors and their babies under the mango trees. We three whites jump into the lorry and Harry or Dicon drives. We bump along the dirt tracks to Achimota Dining Hall; late as usual. Dinner: one huge lidded enamel pot full of stew, meat or dried local fish, very good (but too many fish bones for you!). . . . Then more coffee at No. 5, and [Harry and Dicon] return to Alajo and I to the Cooler Unit. . . .

The apprentices are very good at making the water-coolers, but when they start on teapots, or tea cups, or pitchers, or anything else, they make awful things. So I am doing quite a bit of throwing.

At 4 p.m. they close for the day, and we sometimes have tea at No. 5 and then go down to Alajo again to look after the evening shift making Marseilles tiles, or the firing of a tile kiln or a brick clamp. At sunset, we bump along up to Achimota again. . . .

Yesterday (Sunday) we made an excursion fifty miles north-east, to Kpong on the River Volta, to get rock (nepheline syenite) for making glaze, and to investigate a promising tile clay. . . .

The expedition to Kpong was memorable. On our way from Achimota we followed the foot of the Akwapim Ridge, which runs eastward all the way to the Volta gorge: high, thickly wooded hills with quite large towns perched on top. On our right were the bare, serrated Shai Hills, not high but wildly rocky, rising dramatically out of the gently undulating coastal plain on which we were travelling. As we went along the road we continually passed women carrying beautiful black pots, mostly very big, with a capacity of 8 gallons (36 litres) – the standard size for carrying water. This was the first time I had really looked at African pots and taken them in. They were globe-shaped, black; incredibly light and well-potted, like miraculous balloons made from clay.

18 October 1942 Mr and Mrs Southern invited me to dinner, to meet two African members of the Achimota College staff. As he rightly says, one can talk to them on completely equal terms intellectually. Intellectually, yes; but in another sense you can't, because of all those underlying differences in history, traditions and above all language, which as well as being a vehicle for intellectual communication, contains in itself all the traditions. Of course you can communicate on the intellectual level, rationality being the first and most obvious thing that 'unites the human race'. Intellectual people assume that that is the only thing that matters; given an intellectual understanding, all the other faculties of humanity will be automatically taken care of. But I feel somehow strained and unnatural, even a bit insincere inside when I am with them. And I suddenly realize, *this* is what I find tiresome about Achimota College and most of the white staff there. It's something like the kind of *fausse bonhomie* you get in those uplifting 'Boys' Clubs', the strain of pretending that you completely understand one another when you don't, really ... I find it subtly condescending ... It's insincere, because you're pretending that you have a whole lot more in common than is actually the case.

Good manners dictates that you must behave constantly *as if* you did have all that background in common – the alternative would be (metaphorical) mud-slinging. It may be a strain; but once more, 'better than the alternative'. But I still can't help observing that the good manners produces relationships which are forced, and slightly false. At the Southerns' they expressed their disappointment at finding that in that weighty 'book' compiled by the Principal and Meyerowitz, 'Proposals for a West African Institute of Arts, Industries and Social Sciences', there is *nowhere* any provision for any kind of African control of it and its policies. I hadn't thought of that.[2]

---

[2] *Touché!* The whole concept of the Institute was fundamentally paternalistic.

My outburst about the *fausse bonhomie* at Achimota is a revealing indication of why it was that I, in common with many other whites in the West African colonies who had urgent, absorbing practical work to do, felt so much more at ease with 'uneducated' Africans. By African eyes, this undoubted fact is always seen as proof of the pervading paternalism of the whites, who prefer the 'uneducated' Africans because they are able to patronize them and feel superior to them. But that, in my own case anyway, is far from being the whole story. Before I left Ghana I had learnt that the intellectual is the significant and important African. Ten years later, in Nigeria, when I heard the painter Maurice Fièvet telling the District Officer in Abuja, 'Of course I'm not interested in the collar-and-tie African', I realized how profoundly I disagreed with him.

In the euphoria of those first weeks in West Africa I was even pleased to find that the new pottery at Alajo was much less advanced than I had supposed it would be. I wrote to Mariel, 'It's even better than I expected ... No kilns begun, the buildings only half up, no china clay obtained yet. It will be a bigger job to get it started and, much more than I expected, a case of making a pottery according to my ideas, rather than of simply running one made according to ideas already laid down.'

However, Harry, with his much longer experience of the work, was convinced that the rapid expansion of production at Alajo was a mistake. He was alternately happy to be leaving, and worried to think he was saddling me with a hopeless task. After many delays, he finally got away on 10 November.

The year 1943 dawned inauspiciously. The Bursar's Office at Achimota announced that the tileworks was making losses at an annual rate of about £2,000. In the previous May, special funds had been allocated so that its output could be doubled, and in order to achieve this with the existing equipment, large numbers of additional employees had been taken on. This had increased the running costs but, perhaps predictably, had failed to double the production. Moreover, the increased demand had come from the army; and now it was suddenly doubtful whether the army would want any bricks or tiles after all. Everyone was in a panic about money. George Procter, the tileworks manager, had been on leave in England when I arrived, but had now returned. He understood far more than I did about book-keeping and business methods, and he became extremely depressed. To me, the whole situation was rather a mystery, since this doubling of the tileworks' production capacity had been part of the great Achimota success story which I had listened to in London. I began to understand the difference between grand planning at the top and the bumpy, dusty rides ordained for the poor wretches who have to carry out the grand plans in the field.

As part of our dusty duties, Procter and I had to begin the painful task of cutting down the numbers of employees. Cutting down the numbers, a phrase easy to pronounce in the counting-house, felt at the tileworks more like casting off the members of a family. Every relationship here was a personal one. These men, from a mixture of poverty and adventurousness, had left their villages in Togo or in the Northern Territories and come to join the urban proletariat in Accra, hoping for employment and new experiences. They had found both of these at Alajo, where they had been working not only for their miserably low wages, nor even for the novelty and interest of the work itself, but above all to please a person. Then that person was forced to give them the sack because the money for paying them had been cut off. It was hard when confronted with their enchanting but infuriating capacity for sulking, to carry out the decree from higher up, or to convince them that there was nothing personal in this. The capitalist idea that a man's labour is just a commodity which he is selling by contract in a market was totally unknown to them – as indeed it was in Western Europe until recent times.

I was at this time working on a pamphlet which Meyerowitz had asked me to write about the tileworks, as part of an effort to promote our image. For nearly six weeks I worked hard on that pamphlet, and learned a great deal about brick- and tilemaking that I hadn't known before. At the same time we had to compile a financial report on the tileworks and a sort of cash-flow forecast including new estimates for the pottery, as well as preparing detailed plans and drawings for the kilns, the clay-washing arrangements and clay-storage cellars for the pottery. All these and a dozen other things needed to be done, and they all seemed to be equally urgent. Every night, after a hard day's work, I sat up late, writing or making drawings, till two or three in the morning. Harry Davis's excellent advice when I first arrived, that 'in this climate' it was more than ever important to go to bed early, was not indeed forgotten, but had to be thrown overboard from sheer necessity. This perpetual overwork aggravated my condition of exasperated emotional sensitivity. The gravity of my situation was becoming clear. How on earth, within the necessary time limits, was I going to build and organize a pottery which would be adequate to carry out the production tasks which had been set and which I had so enthusiastically taken on?

In addition to our commitment to making the 180,000 pieces of tableware for the army, and an annual production of 200,000 latex-cups, we had accepted an order for 1,000 salt-glazed drainpipes for the Accra local authority, and a request from the Cacao Research Station at Tafo for several hundred special flower pots or 'tree pots', taller and more slender than standard flower pots, for their seedling cacao trees. The making of these pots, and of the drainpipes, was already in full swing, while the pottery itself was less than half built. Now a man from the Posts and Telegraphs Department came to say that they were in desperate need of electric insulators, and imploring us to make them. Again I agreed.

At the beginning of January we started building the first kiln. I had made the drawings for it towards the end of 1942. It was to be a round, downdraught kiln with eight fireboxes and an internal diameter of 12 feet (3.5 metres). At every stage in designing it I had had to make bold decisions on an inadequate basis of experience, a series of frightening leaps in the dark. One of the first of these decisions had to be about the fireboxes; and in the event it turned out to be an inspired one. I had taken part in many firings of the 45 cubic foot (1.27 cubic metre) kiln in the College at Achimota. Its three fire-mouths had firebars which had been made by cutting up old rails, and after a few firings these bars became so twisted and slagged that they had to be replaced by new ones. During firings a piece of corrugated iron was hung in front of each fire-mouth to prevent excess air from going in. When it was time to stoke, this sheet had to be removed and the stoker had to work in the full blast of the heat. Then the hot iron sheet had to be replaced. The prospect of having eight such fire-mouths was hardly to be borne. A drawing in Bourry's *Treatise on Ceramic Industries* came to mind. It showed a firebox in which the wood, instead of being supported by firebars, was resting on hobs at each side. Air entered at the top and was drawn down through the wood. When the bottom sticks burned away, their embers fell into the ashpit, and the next layer of sticks caught fire. The flames were drawn downwards into the throat arch. Bourry, with his habitual economy in the use of words, only remarks that this type of firebox is 'suitable for temperatures above 1100°C'. I decided that this was what was needed: no iron firebars and yet no problem from accumulations of unburnt embers; above all, no roasting of the stokers' legs and bodies. Questions were raised. Had I ever actually used such fireboxes? No. Would it be possible to obtain reduction with them? I didn't know, but I felt it was worth trying.

At about the time the kiln-building began, the machines for the pottery arrived from Stoke-on-Trent, fifteen extremely heavy crates, including three barrels which contained between them a ton of 1 inch (2.5 cm) porcelain balls for the ball mill. Next day, the ball mill itself arrived, on a three-ton truck which sailed like a ship across the undulating plain of dried-up grasses and came to rest alongside the mill house. The porcelain-lined iron cylinder with its pulley and transoms weighed nearly two and a half tons even without its ton of porcelain balls. We called all hands, the tileworks men, the potters, all the builders, and they brought up all the available timber baulks. It took us more than one and a half hours to unload it, with much shouting and running hither and thither and much fear on my part that one or more of the black bodies that were climbing all over and under the monster would be crushed. At last, with no damage to itself or to any of the workers, it lay safely on the earthen floor of the mill house to await installation, a cast-iron cylinder about 6 × 5 feet (1.8 × 1.5 metres), looking like part of a very large steamroller.

At this stage the mill house was the only one of the major pottery buildings that had a roof. Five other big buildings were still roofless. These were the huge kiln shed; two large open sheds, one to house the blunger, clay-washing equipment and pugmill, the other for the hand-powered wheels used by the water-cooler makers; and two closed buildings, one to be the main making shop and dryer, the other the biscuit warehouse and dipping shop. There was also to be a stock store and packing shed, which had not yet been begun.

By early February the wall of the kiln was up to springer level, and we were ready to build the dome. There was great curiosity among the bricklayers and I was asked the inevitable question, 'Don't we have a form to build it on?' But by the time it was half built, they were all enthusiastic dome-builders. No mistakes were made and each successive circle of bricks kept its correct level. When the dome was two-thirds built, Mr Dadey told Dicon that it looked to him 'just like an egg, and the heads and shoulders of the builders like chickens coming out of it'.

As soon as we had finished the first kiln we started on the second one; but after reaching ground level we decided to leave it there until we saw how the first kiln worked.[3]

Towards the end of February there was a brief time of calm. I wrote home:

> Suddenly the crises seem to be over: no Plans, no Estimates, no Reports, no Proposals, evenings are free, and I can go to bed early; no doubt it won't last long. . . . I am busy with experiments for raw-glazing and with glaze-firings in the little kiln at the College. What I really want to see is the first firing of the big kiln, but that won't be for another month or two yet.
>
> We've had some rain at last, and everywhere at Alajo there are suddenly lots of little beetles with bright vermilion backs, like *velvet*. Also a few birds: very tame buzzards, and the white egrets, slender and so beautiful they make you sit up every time you see them. The egrets follow the cows, which are black-and-white and extremely thin. . . .

---

[3] This second kiln was later completed. The two kilns shared one chimney, and were fired alternately.

Lately I dreamt that Meyerowitz said to me, 'What? Haven't you got out your Production Estimates for 1975 *yet*?' Lord, I thought, that means I must be about 73 or 74 years old! I'd better be getting home to Wenford soon, or it will be too late to see Mariel and the boys. . . .

The Glaze Unit buildings are nearly finished now; only the roof of the enormous kiln shed remains to be done, but that will take a few weeks yet. . . . I have at last succeeded in getting a working-shirt like the blue-dyed ones which are worn by all the 'N.T.' [Northern Territory] men here. You can't buy them in Accra in the ordinary shops. . . . It took me quite a time to find out where and how to get one of these nice blue things. I had to buy a five-yard [4.5 metre] piece of 'grey baft' (un-bleached calico), and after much hunting and questioning I was guided at last to the place where I could get it dyed – in an incredibly picturesque backyard somewhere on the outskirts of Accra. It was full of indigo dye-vats and lovely women with wrinkled *blue* hands, who don't know a single word of English. They charged me half-a-crown [12½p] for my five yards and have dyed it a beautiful dark blue. (For the real 'black' blue the charge is double, but I don't think that is really suitable for shirts.) They do all sorts of nice fancy things with their dyeing. They sew the stuff up with bast into patterns, and tie it into little twists and so on; and it comes out with lovely free resist-patterns – stars, flowers, strings, stripes – in white on a blue ground. I'm going to bring some home for you.

Am I going to spend the rest of my life here? I don't really know yet; but I'm inclined to think I must stay for more than the two years of my present contract – if they'll have me, and provided I get £800 a year (£600 is absolute penury I find).

It was true, as I had said in my letter, that the major buildings at the pottery (except the kiln shed) had now got their roofs on; but we were still a long way from being able to start full-scale production. Apart from the buildings, my biggest problem at Alajo was the clay. The Alajo clay was very bad. Even when fired at stoneware temperature the clay was not vitrified, but still quite porous. And it threw off all the glazes. Harry Davis had developed a stoneware body which was a mixture of sieved Alajo clay and semi-decomposed pegmatite from the Achimota quarry, but this was not nice to throw with. I was determined to get a satisfactory clay, or mixture of clays. Of all those we tested, a white plastic clay from Koforidua was the most promising: it made a grey vitrified stoneware which took the glazes very well. So I made arrangements to go to Koforidua to obtain more.

I decided to take Kofi Athey with me. Clement Kofi Athey had been taken on at the pottery towards the end of 1942. At first he worked as a labourer, but soon it was clear that he had more than average ability and interest. By the end of January he knew how to knead clay in the Japanese way, and by early March I was teaching him how to throw saggars.

We travelled to Koforidua by train, in the second class. The district engineer had arranged for us to have the help of two labourers, with shovels and headpans. We began removing the overburden of white sand – the good clay was 4 feet (1.2 metres) below the surface. When I read my records of that week's proceedings, the only comment that comes to mind is 'Pathetic!' Here we were, for only four and a half days, armed only with picks, shovels, headpans and earth baskets, with a labour force of four men (though by Saturday morning it had grown to ten), trying to obtain an adequate supply of clay for the monster which was Alajo Pottery, and the vast scale of production which I had so rashly agreed to. By the Saturday morning we had filled one railway truck (10 or 12 tons of clay), and we went back to Achimota.

Kofi and I returned to Koforidua, for more clay, in May. This time we stayed for nine days altogether, and sent back two truckloads of clay, 34 tons. We also spent a whole day looking, rather desperately, for some source of similar clay somewhere in the country round Koforidua. We came upon women making lovely small bowls, but the clay they were using was a brown gravelly material from near the surface. We asked a woman who was standing at the door of her house for water, and while drinking it I noticed a black Ashanti water pot lying abandoned in the ditch because it had lost one of its two handles. We exchanged it for a small Achimota water-cooler and the sum of 2s. (10p). At that time the villages and small towns of Ghana were still full of the evidences of a creative popular culture untouched by its long acquaintance with the forces of colonialism; works of art like this water pot were discarded lightheartedly by people who knew they could easily make or obtain new ones to take their place. They were not, and did not need to be, interested in preservation, because new creation was still a feature of everyday life. The prodigality of new creation made any idea of preservation irrelevant. Something is worn out or broken: good! that means we can make a new one! – the true spirit of cultural continuity.

Back at Alajo, the new kiln was at last ready to be fired. The bungs of saggars were set with water-coolers, tree pots, moulds and hundreds of pan-rings. We lit the fires, and smoke began to come from the chimney. All went well: the downdraught fireboxes worked exactly as Bourry had indicated. The kiln took nine days to reach 1000°C and eleven days to cool. When we unpacked we found that there were very few breakages, and above all, that the temperature distribution in the kiln was remarkably uniform (as I had planned, and predicted, and hoped).

One of the most extraordinary features about firings at Achimota and Alajo was the immensely long time-schedule which Harry Davis had early discovered was necessary, if the Alajo clay was to be fired successfully. We sometimes made attempts to shorten these schedules, but always without success.

While the kiln was cooling, I taught some of the apprentices how to make the small latex-cups on the wheels. I did not think of the making of the latex-cups as a purely quantitative 'industrial' programme, but rather as a unique opportunity for the throwers to explore the depths of this simple, basic bowl shape. In fact I have never thought of the throwing of any simple shape except in terms of absolute form. The fact that thousands had to be made was not an obstacle to this; it simply provided even better opportunities to explore the shape in all its inexhaustible dimensions. I therefore took considerable trouble with each thrower, to encourage him, if he was capable and willing, to explore the true nature of the shape, and I took the opportunity, whenever I had the chance, to make dozens of them myself in the same spirit.

There were not many opportunities for me to do that, however, because the burden of management had become quite heavy. The finance people insisted that records be kept of everything. And I was now making preparations for moving all the work from the old pottery at the College to the new one at Alajo, which was nearly ready to begin full-scale production.

Transferring the work had to be a gradual operation. It involved fifteen people and a good deal of equipment, mostly potter's wheels and glaze materials. Of the fifteen men, five were officially described as 'labourers'; but having worked there for a long time, they had acquired a certain amount of specialist knowledge. Then there were the six apprentices who had been taken on in 1942, shortly before I arrived; and the three senior apprentices, who had come in 1940: David Ziga, and his two adjutants, Daniel Cobblah and Joseph Ahia. The fifteenth man was Reynolds Amponsa, whose home was Ashanti-Mampong. He had become interested in the pottery as a schoolboy at Achimota, and was the first student in West Africa to take pottery as a special subject in his School Certificate. The external examiner had awarded him Distinction on the strength of his practical work. Meyerowitz and Harry had proposed, as part of a general plan for his career, that on leaving Achimota school he should spend two years doing practical work at the new pottery. After that, they hoped he would go to Stoke-on-Trent for a full technical course, and that eventually he would return to the pottery as a qualified ceramist, and a key man in the future industry. He was a remarkable young man, who radiated warmth and charm. Meyerowitz used to say, 'He's like a *stove*. You can sit and warm yourself in front of him.'

Amponsa was the first of these potters to move down to Alajo, followed soon after by Daniel Cobblah, Joseph Ahia and the six younger apprentices. David Ziga remained at the College for the present, to carry out a sequence of test-firings on the latex-cups in the old glaze kiln.

Though at the time I did not recognize the fact, I can see now that the idea of moving from the shelter of Achimota College to Alajo was never popular with the apprentices, or at least not with the six younger ones. To me, the move away from the makeshift conditions at the College to the enormous and magnificent (even if unfinished) new pottery at Alajo seemed to be a clear gain for everyone. But the apprentices found the new conditions of work very arduous and ungentlemanly. They complained that they were being made to work like labourers – a thing to which they evidently had no intention of reconciling themselves. They were not here to labour for an ideal; as Achimota College apprentices, they were embarking on their careers. George Procter, who was far less excitable than I (and possibly less excited about the whole project) had had six tileworks apprentices for a year already, and had the same difficulty with them. Being a fair-minded man, he said, 'Maybe they really do have a legitimate grouse. I don't know, and *you* don't know, what those Achimota College people promised them – an education in physics and chemistry, geology, accounting, commerce or God-knows-what.'

Someone has observed that 'when men have to work under great pressure on something which they believe is important, they generally become over-excited.' It was certainly true of me at Alajo. I summoned up all my reserves of willpower; no task, surely, was ever beyond the power of human will to accomplish. I told myself that I was extremely lucky, in the middle of this world war, to be set such a task, especially as it so nearly coincided with all my dearest ideals in pottery. I thought I could overcome all my present obstacles and troubles by the same methods I had used in Winchcombe in the 1920s: by working harder and working longer. At Winchcombe, this treatment usually caused my difficulties to dissolve after a few months. So now I said to myself, this is another of those great tests for flesh and blood: I must work harder and with more concentration.

But the only effect this régime had on me was that I became more than ever a victim of toothache, sore throat, colds and continually returning tropical sores; more given to ranting and raving and less able to cultivate *patience*, the supreme African virtue. Flesh and blood were telling the tyrant Will that there were limits to his power and that where a great mountain of work had to be moved, this way of doing it was not likely to succeed.

17

THE
WEST AFRICAN
INSTITUTE

In May 1943 the British Government in London gave the green light for the creation of the West African Institute of Arts, Industries and Social Sciences. It was an immense personal triumph for Meyerowitz. Only the power of his magnetic eloquence (backed by the pressures of the war) could have persuaded the Colonial Office to support the project, and the Treasury to release the necessary funds.

The Arts and Industries included in the West African Institute were bricks, tiles, pottery and textiles, and there were plans to develop cabinet-making and leather-working. The Social Sciences were chiefly social anthropology and economics. The function of this 'academic' side of the Institute was to take care of the social and political side-effects consequent on developing traditional crafts into small local industries.

But there was a serious weakness at the heart of the scheme: the industries were regarded as potentially profit-making. The funds for the tileworks were authorized because the impression was given that tilemaking in West Africa would be a very profitable undertaking. Similarly, with the pottery it was always assumed in discussions with the Colonial Office that not only would it be possible to manufacture 200,000 latex-cups a year, but they would be purchased by the rubber plantations at an economic price. The crises that we faced in the tileworks and the pottery illustrated the great gap that existed between the success story that was heard in London and the facts as they were known on the spot. Already in April 1943 I was writing in a letter home, 'I am realizing that this work is about two-thirds "education", in the sense of training workmen in specialized skills, a sense of industrial responsibility and experience (which takes the longest of all) and that it will have to be more heavily subsidized than anyone imagined at first.'

When Meyerowitz returned to Achimota in the middle of August 1943, we found, like the children of Israel, that our tasks were increased, not made less. But I felt that at last the demands were coming from one who was on our side and knew what all our efforts were for. He told us that his function was to help us to get supplies and facilities, and to relieve us of the official pressures from which we had suffered. This meant, for instance, that I could now go ahead with completing the pottery without having to worry that our funds were coming to an end. However, there was an urgent new job to be done. In Stoke-on-Trent Meyerowitz had persuaded the Principal of the North Staffordshire Technical College, Dr Harry Webb, to act as the Overseas Consultant for the pottery and tileworks, and now it was necessary to gather up information for him: he would need drawings of all the kilns, details of our equipment and machines, descriptions of all our raw materials and where they came from, with samples for analysis, and specimens of all finished products from bricks to glazed latex-cups.

Meyerowitz also proposed that I should give the apprentices instruction in ceramic theory and the technical history of ceramics. I had anticipated this and had raided Achimota College library for books on geology, petrology, and the history of chemistry. But though I had made copious notes of all this reading I felt quite unequal to the prospect of teaching these subjects in any way that would be relevant to the apprentices' needs.

Meyerowitz's return at first acted on me as a tonic. He used to come down to the pottery whenever he could get away from the office in Achimota, to discuss plans, both short-term and long-term; and he often invited me to his house, where he and Eva gave me proper, civilized meals, which were a welcome relief (though I did not like to admit it to myself) from the spartan régime at Alajo. He introduced me to Professor William MacMillan, the author of *Africa Emergent* and an old friend from his South African days; also to other interesting people who happened to be in Accra at that time, notably Maxwell Fry, who was then in the army, and was enthusiastic about the beautiful buildings at Alajo.

However, my exhilaration became fitful, turning more easily to dejection. My enthusiasm began to degenerate into fanaticism, my sense of proportion became distorted by impatience. Life was a hopeless race against time, a reckless gamble with every kind of known and unknown technical hazard, all conducted on a scale much vaster than any I had ever experienced before. I attempted to obtain co-operation and a comparable measure of hard work from the six younger apprentices by applying a high-pressure injection of my own enthusiasm. But they were not convinced. Defeated in this, it would happen to me as often happens to paternalists in a situation like this where so much had to be done in so short a time, and for such a good cause: paternalism hardened into authoritarianism. All these troubles were complicated still further by an emotional turmoil in my own heart, a dilemma and a contradiction in myself which month after month refused to be resolved or to go away. I felt myself becoming bound to this place and these people, and particularly to one man, Kofi, in a way which was going to cut me off altogether from the wife and children I had left in Britain, make nonsense of my whole life for the past twenty years, and contradict all the most firmly held principles on which I had built that life.

I am sure that in other places tasks just as overwhelming were often imposed during the Second World War on people with better organizing abilities than mine, people who somehow managed to rise to that kind of challenge without half-killing themselves, and were able in later years to forget it, or to dismiss their struggle as a necessary incident of their experience of war. But in my case it was somehow different. Something in me had begun to undergo a permanent change. I believe, now, that this irreversible change that was taking place inside me was the first stage of being cured of unconscious racism. Racism is a stubborn disease. The treatment is painful and humiliating and goes on and on, so that you begin to think it is worse than the disease itself. But it is necessarily as long and painful as the disease is deep-seated. Of course, I thought I was quite free of racism when I first arrived in Ghana. But we all carry the germs of this disease unconsciously in our entrails.

In November Kofi and I went to Koforidua again. We stayed thirteen days, but only sent down 30 tons of clay; my maniacal energy of previous visits was beginning to flag after fourteen months in West Africa. The visit was memorable for the expedition which Kofi and I made on the second Sunday. We followed the Bisa road for a few miles. The morning was fine. Mist was still clinging to the flanks of the hills and their rocky wooded summits stood revealed in the morning sun, looking like the mountain tops in Chinese paintings. Near Aboabo village we found a promising clay, micaceous and plastic, not too far from a road. In the afternoon we came upon a house hidden in the forest, where there was a group of people engaged in making glass beads and buttons. Their workshop was a small shelter which was more like a tent than a shed: bamboo poles and a steeply pitched roof of palm leaves coming to within a foot or two (30–60 cm) of the ground – you had to bend low to get in. Inside, their little kiln was built of mud, 2 or 3 feet (60–90 cm) high and about as broad and long, with one fire-mouth, another entrance for the bead moulds, and a hole on top which was the chimney. It was rather like a *raku* kiln, and was kept all the time at a good red heat, perhaps about 750°C, by periodical restoking with dry firewood. There were five people: a young girl of about seventeen, three handsome old women, and a charming but ineffectual-looking young man who managed the fire with easy efficiency. The women were busy filling the bead and button moulds, while other moulds were glowing red inside the kiln, on a perforated iron plate.

The moulds were small blocks of red clay which had been dipped in a white slip. Their surface carried numerous round cavities, just deep enough to make a bead, or a button. In the centre of each of these little cavities was a small hole to take a short length of piassava fibre. The button moulds were shallower than the bead moulds and had three little piassava fibres instead of only one. When the mould was ready for filling, each cavity was provided with its short spike of piassava; then with a tiny metal spoon the girl would take powdered glass out of a container and deftly fill up the cavity, tamping the powder carefully round the fibre which projected in the centre. Usually the glass powder was plain green; but sometimes she would put different powders in layers, so that the bead came out with green, blue, red or white horizontal stripes. The plain green powder was made by grinding up broken beer bottles. The other colours had been made by grinding old medicine, scent or ointment jars or bottles; these colours were more precious, especially the opaque white, because such bottles were hard to come by.

When all the numerous cavities had been filled, the mould was ready to go into the kiln. With a flat iron spatula, rather like a baker's wooden peel, the kiln man would take one of the red-hot moulds out of the oven and then insert the new one. The piassava fibres had all burned away, leaving in their place a trace of grey ash; and now one of the old women, armed with a short length of galvanized wire, inserted this into the holes left by the piassava and clicked out the completed beads or buttons one after another, ready when cool to be strung up and taken to market. It was not easy to tell how long each mould remained in the fire, because it was a continuous production; every few minutes a new mould would be slid into the furnace and a fired one taken out.

Surprisingly, we found that here, only about four miles from Koforidua, we were no longer among the Ashanti people of New Juaben but in Krobo-speaking country. Kofi knew Ga, Twi, Fante and Hausa as well as his own Ewe, but none of these was understood by the people here. As for me, I had made some attempts to learn Ewe, and Hausa; but I did not make much progress, the fatal obstacle being that there was always just enough English spoken, even if it was only pidgin, to get along with, without the trouble of having to learn an African language. It was only much later, in Northern Nigeria, that I succeeded in teaching myself Hausa – from necessity, because no English was known. And it was only there, when the language barrier was turned the other way, and I in turn became the stupid one, that I fully appreciated what an obstacle a foreign language can be. I realized in retrospect, and with sorrow and regret, that at Alajo many of our difficulties had been due to the fact that whereas I was speaking to the men there in my own language, they, if they wanted to say something to me, were having to use a foreign one. A simple point: but I truly did not appreciate it until after I learnt Hausa.

One of the first things I did in 1944 was to fall sick with malaria. Lying in the Ridge Hospital in Accra, I had time to reflect on how committed I was to West Africa and the potters at Alajo, and to Kofi. The people I was working with in Africa seemed to me much more open-hearted, more generous and lovable, and therefore more capable of making good pots, than the cold, tightly closed-up inhabitants of Europe, obsessed as they were with abstract ideas which obstructed the flow of their natural affections.

Meanwhile Meyerowitz was finding it even harder to get the West African Institute working at Alajo than it had been to persuade the London people to launch it. All those of us who were on the scene were trying to do the work of three men, and he himself was no exception to this. Now the London Advisory Committee of the Institute was beginning to question the whole programme on the grounds that it was too ambitious, and the acrimonious correspondence that was exchanged did much to exacerbate his position.

I continued to run the pottery in a quick-tempered and high-handed way. It was a bad way to run it, but I found it impossible to control the excitability that was the outcome of my fanatical belief in the urgency and importance of the work. The apprentices, on the other hand, believed in neither its importance nor its urgency.

I had for a long time been advocating that the status of apprenticeship, with the quasi-parental role it called for on the part of the College, should be abolished altogether, and that the apprentices should be employed simply as skilled workers on an equality with others of similar skill at the pottery or the tileworks. I hoped that in this way, instead of clinging to their status as part of Achimota College, they would perhaps acquire the ordinary virtues of skilled craftsmen, a natural self-confidence and a recognition of the value of hard work. But this revolutionary proposal found no favour with Meyerowitz and still less with the others at Achimota – they had all invested too much moral capital in the idea of apprenticeship. However, in 1944 it was proposed that the Institute should take over the apprentices' indentures from the College, and that they should move down to Alajo as soon as living arrangements could be made for them there. In the eyes of the younger apprentices this plan was anathema. They resisted any proposal to separate them from Achimota and hand them over to Alajo.

At a meeting called to discuss the matter, the apprentices openly declared that if they were moved away from Achimota it would constitute a breach of the terms of their indentures. They told Meyerowitz they had consulted their lawyer, Dr Danquah, the eminent politician, and threatened legal action against the Institute to protect their existing status. This was embarrassing for Meyerowitz, since he had always considered Dr Danquah a friend. It was also infuriating, because it was an attack aimed at the very heart of the organization he was trying to construct. At last he became extremely angry, and shouted, 'All right! Bring your case. Go back to your Bush lawyers, clear out, and stay out.'

It was an extremely uncomfortable scene, especially for me. I felt I was to blame. The apprentices may have opposed the move chiefly because they felt separation from Achimota would mean a lowering of their status. But they would not have been so hostile if they had not resented the way I was running the pottery at Alajo. Why had I not had enough political sense to realize how much power these apprentices had, to harm the Institute and to hurt Meyerowitz, whom I had been in the habit of looking up to as always wise and right? It did not matter so much that I, deep in the mud and sweat of the job itself, should shout and swear at people as an admittedly stupid way to get work done; but this outburst from him felt like (and indeed was) the beginning of a disaster.

In the end, the apprentices went home to talk over their future with parents, guardians and lawyers. I breathed a sigh of relief and hoped they would not come back (some of them didn't). For the time being life at the pottery went back to normal. There was one major advance. The Gold Coast Geological Survey Department, at Meyerowitz's request, had been sending us samples of clays from all over the country for testing at Alajo. They were mostly brick or tile clays, but some were white and plastic – as plastic as any red earthenware clay I had ever met in England – and were refractory. Testing them gave me much-needed opportunities for getting back on to the wheel.

Meyerowitz took me again to the Cacao Research Institute at Tafo and I brought back another order for tree pots – they wanted 3,000 of them this time. I welcomed this because it diverted attention from my failure to deliver other goods. (In all my time at Alajo I never succeeded in producing any of the tableware for the army; and we only managed to make a few thousand of the latex-cups.) I made and fired some clay rollers, so that these tree pots could have some decoration. I also gave some of them to the tilemakers who were testing a special sample of tile clay. The result of this was dramatic: their cheerfulness and speed of production increased miraculously. I thereupon made other clay rollers, with different patterns, and took them along to where the regular tilemaking was in progress, with the same result: a renewed and continuing happiness.

It was probably at this time that I made some biscuit-fired seals for the Alajo pots. The acronym for the West African Institute of Arts, Industries and Social Sciences (W.A.I.A.I.S.S.) presented a nice problem which I solved by using only one A and one I, and putting the two Ss between the arms of the figure and his head. W. Michael Gina, the tileworks head burner, was fascinated by this seal and asked me what it meant, so I interpreted it to him at great length, in voluble French: 'It is a picture of the good workman. He is wearing his loincloth about his middle and raising his arms ready to begin work; and these are the thoughts which dart in and out of his head like streaks of lightning.'

About the beginning of August 1944 I was told I would be returning to England for a long leave at the end of September. I wrote to Mariel, 'I have about seven weeks left in which to finish up hundreds of jobs, and I find that my efficiency is desperately low. . . . I am in a state I never thought possible for me: of just keeping my head above water with only one object in life, to get through the next few weeks and into that aeroplane . . .'

Soon after I had written this letter the second disaster of this disastrous year occurred. We were now ready for the third glaze-firing of the big kiln, and we loaded it with pots of various kinds – hundreds of plates, cups, beakers, beer mugs and pitchers, and one experimental bung of moulded dishes set out on pan-rings. All went well until the fifth and last day of the firing. At 7 a.m. on that day Seger Cones 5, 6 and 7 were all bent or bending, but Cone 8 was still standing. The glaze of the test-rings was melted, but not quite mature. We began the soaking fire. When I looked in again at 4 p.m. there were no cones to be seen at all, and no rings. The saggar top on which they stood had melted, and as far as could be seen the whole bung below them had collapsed. It was of course an absurd, and to me now incredible, mistake to have allowed nine hours for a temperature rise of only 20°C. It is fatally easy to overfire kilns of this type. But the blunder may not have been due only to my want of experience with these kilns. I think the general condition of exhaustion I had reached must have been a contributing cause.

Of the day or days of unloading I cannot remember much, because having seen the inside of the kiln – all the bungs had melted into a formless mass of black slag – I had to go away and lie down in a state of psychosomatic collapse. I remember lying in a shed nearby, listening hour after hour to the hammer blows which were breaking up the masses of slag, and (it seemed to me) all the hopes and labours of the past year. The only pots that survived were, surprisingly, most of the oval dishes in their bung of pan-rings.

During these weeks the 'Webb Report' – as we called it – had arrived from Stoke-on-Trent. I carefully studied all the analyses of the raw materials we had sent. In reading the report itself I found, as I had expected, that some of the comments were unavoidably off the mark, but I read on with great respect until I came to the part where Dr Webb recommended that the pottery should obtain plaster moulds for casting, so that we could manufacture a line of 'ornamental birds'. He then went on to say that while it was evident that a meritorious beginning had been made, it would be a mistake to continue with the system of low-fired biscuit and high-fired glaze, and recommended we should adopt the Staffordshire system of high-fired bisque and low-fired glost. At that point I thought to myself, 'If the Institute accepts this, I shall be obliged to leave!' But there was more to come. I read on, and found that whereas some good groundwork had evidently been done, it was noted that the ceramist in charge was of the kind which is usually described as a 'studio' potter, and that such potters, though often gifted artistically, were lacking in sufficient technical and scientific knowledge to conduct a manufacturing enterprise. Dr Webb ended his report by saying that he knew of a very suitable man, with excellent technical and managerial qualifications, who would be likely to be interested in this post.

Meyerowitz was away in Nigeria when the Webb Report arrived. When he returned, he was pleased with the report in general but like me was upset by the references to 'ornamental birds' and by the proposal that Dr Webb's nominee should be appointed in place of me. He described my role as he saw it. 'I don't want you, or George Procter, to think of yourselves as works managers. You are here to be the inspirers, the setters of standards, to see that what is made is worth making – without which no management is worth having.' He did, however, suggest that when I got back to England I should go to see Dr Webb, and obtain from him all the technical advice I possibly could, about our raw materials, our firing difficulties, everything. 'Above all, try to establish friendly, human contact with him; of course I don't know how you English people do these things, but I suggest you should go to see your friend Josiah Wedgwood and get him to invite you to lunch at Barlaston and to invite Dr Webb at the same time, so that you can meet socially on neutral ground . . .'

Just before I went home Meyerowitz was taken into the Accra hospital. I went to visit him there: he was in a state of dejection such as I had never seen in him before. All his confidence seemed to have left him, even his belief in his own guiding idea. He told me there was going to be no place for artists of our kind in the industrial world of the future. I tried to raise his spirits by an impromptu repetition of his own doctrine, that the function and place for artists in the future world was inside the industries which we had so often been accustomed to think of as enemies, working as designers (that is to say, humanizers) of industrial productions. But, not surprisingly, this had no effect. It was the last time I ever saw him. About the same time that I left for England, he and Eva went to South Africa and Lesotho; and then, in April 1945, to England.

I had, and still have, a very bad conscience about Alajo. Granted that the burden of work was too much for any man to carry, yet there was no need to be so impatient, provocative, and intolerant of the less efficient or industrious workers. What had really been the matter with me? Strain. Yes, but what caused the strain? The determination not to fail. But I had got the values wrong. Success would not have been much use without goodwill; it would have been better to keep that, even if it led to failure. As it was, I found I had failed and had also lost goodwill. On a small scale, I had been doing something which is distressingly common in the history of Western Man. Captured by a grand idea, and failing to notice that my individual powers were limited, I had attempted to make myself equal to a superhuman task by blowing myself up to heroic size, a dangerous exercise which usually ends like the fable of the frog in Aesop.

I enjoyed the flight home. It was my first experience of flying. Kofi and his friend Yawo Kuma came to the airport with me to see me go, on the last day of September. Most of the passengers in the D.C. Dakota were army officers. The pilot spent what seemed like a very long time revving up the engines on the ground, until the whole fuselage where we sat was filled with an over-whelming smell of fuel. Suddenly we were seeing Accra below us, and the Alajo plain, and the red roofs of the pottery and tileworks. Then, as we approached the red-earth landing strip at Takoradi the palm trees came up towards us looking like cabbages in a kitchen garden. Our second stop was at a bush landing strip somewhere near Freetown, for refuelling, and we reached the Gambia in the evening. Here we all got out and were driven in the dusk through a West African scene such as I had not seen before: the air was dry and hazy, and the villages we passed through had round thatched houses, with venerable-looking old men sitting in front of them. We slept in wooden army huts somewhere just outside Bathurst. Next morning we were away at 4 a.m.

and landed for refuelling at Port Étienne on the Sahara coast. Here we had to wait about three hours or more while something – we were not told what – was repaired. There was nothing to be seen except the sandy beach on which we had landed, and an abandoned-looking French fort, and nothing to do but walk along the unending beach in a strong, dry, bracing north-east wind. We had definitely left West Africa behind. At last, very late, the repair was completed and we flew on along the coast, in the dark now, at 15,000 feet (4,500 metres).

After refuelling again in Rabat we went on through the night until we saw the bright lights of neutral Lisbon. Here we landed about midnight, and slept in a hotel the external walls of which were entirely covered with polychrome glazed tiles. In the elevator going up to our rooms, we remarked to the attendant, a stocky, wizened old man who looked as if he had the experiences of all past ages deeply scored into his soul, that Hitler was pretty well finished now. He gave us a look of pity at our childish confidence, and said something like 'Don't be too sure.' Next morning at about 5 a.m. we left again (we were told this was the first daylight flight since 1940), across the Bay of Biscay and past the coast of Brittany. When we reached Cornwall the pilot began to enjoy himself, flying low over Porth Curnow and up the whole length of Cornwall; right over Wenford – I could see the clothes line between the two granite posts in the garden – then nearly grazing the top of Brown Willy. We finally landed at Bristol in the evening of 2 October.

18

HOME LEAVE

At home, Mariel was struggling to keep the Wenford Inn (as we still called it) alive and habitable. It still had no piped water, and luxuries like electric light were nearly twenty years away in the distant future. She was supplementing the miserable half of my small salary, which was sent regularly to her through the Crown Agents in London, by teaching art three days a week in schools at Launceston and Bude. This involved long journeys in all weathers, mostly bad at that time of year. She had acquired a secondhand motor-bike, and having encased herself in various rain- and windproof coverings she rode this dangerous and unreliable vehicle to and from the distant schools. One of the few good things I was able to do during my time at home was to persuade her to find, through a friend in St Tudy, an ancient but reliable Baby Austin, so that the journeys should involve less difficulty and hardship.

Ennis, our youngest boy, now six, was walking every day to the village school in St Tudy, but the two older ones, ten and eight, were away at St Blazey, a little town about sixteen miles from Wenford near the south coast. Mariel had discovered that the Canterbury Cathedral Choir School had been moved away from Canterbury because of the air-raids, and it was now functioning as well as it could in its temporary home at St Blazey. She took her two boys there for an audition, and they were both accepted: the younger one, Cornelius, having especially impressed the music master not only by his voice but even more by his 'natural musical intelligence', as the music master called it – for instance, his ability to sing the middle note of a chord.

I had come home thinking hard about how I was to resist Dr Webb's recommendation that we should be making earthenware in the English industrial tradition, rather than stoneware on the Oriental system. I knew Meyerowitz was entirely on my side about this, but he was not here, and he was not a potter. My trouble was that I still had no concrete proofs of successful production along these lines, no body of solid achievement to back up my argument, which itself was not really an argument at all but merely an organic conviction of the heart, that pots ought to be, and deserved to be, were *entitled* to be, made by the Oriental system, especially pots made in West

Africa, for West Africans. Dr Webb's insinuation that I probably did not know much about science or the theory of ceramics had stung me because I know it was true; and so, instead of making efforts to revive the pottery at Wenford, I now spent most of my time working out the molecular formulae of all the Alajo glazes and bodies, using the analyses we had received, in order that when I went to Stoke-on-Trent to see Dr Webb I could meet him on common ground, and perhaps even begin to convince him that I was not quite what he called a 'studio' potter.

I went to Stoke-on-Trent and stayed (by courtesy of the Crown Agents, who were paying my expenses) in the artificial tropics of the centrally heated main hotel. The sessions with Dr Webb were useful. At first his manner was rather like that of a headmaster interviewing a troublesome or unruly school-boy. But I had so many purely technical questions to ask him, and listened so reverentially to his oracular replies, and made so many studious notes of them in my notebook, that he gradually relented and became more friendly. I learnt a lot from him; and when he saw that some parts of his explanations were leaving me in a state of incomprehension, he produced three or four technical papers written by himself and gave them to me. I took them back with me to the hotel, read them carefully, didn't understand them, read them again, making a note of all those terms he was using (for example, thermal expansion, acceleration due to gravity) about which I was ignorant; and so, step by step, I worked on them until some light began to dawn in those rooms situated somewhere inside my skull, which had up to then not needed to be lit. As a last resort, where all other attempts at understanding failed, I would copy out the entire passage into my notebook, underlining the terms which I found uncrackable. In this way, I would remember them and whenever I read a technical book or paper I would keep watch for these terms, hoping that if they reappeared I would find a definition or at least something in the context that would throw additional light on them. It was hard work, but curiously exhilarating, like being given a food of which your body, without the knowledge of your conscious mind, had long been in need. I treated Dr Webb's technical papers as treasures, often rereading them; and eventually had them bound into a slim volume.

While I was in Stoke I joined the British Ceramic Society, and was agreeably surprised to find that my subscription was retrospective; they sent me all twelve issues of the 1943 volume as well as the current ones for 1944. I continued to subscribe and received them regularly from that time until about 1967; by then they had become so specialized and scientific that I found them too difficult to understand, and had to let my membership lapse. But in the 1940s and 1950s and early 1960s, I used to devour them almost from cover to cover, digesting from them a great mass of useful notes. Most of the papers then published were written by authors who were actually working in one or other of the ceramic industries, or by researchers who still retained the practical outlook of clay-workers or potters. The language they used struck me as perhaps the best English then being written by anyone: plain but lucid and above all conscientiously unambiguous. Without their help I would never have been able to write *Pioneer Pottery*.

In January 1945 I went back to Stoke again. This time I stopped on the way to visit Beano at Coleshill, and to find out whether she still possessed her notes on Matsubayashi's old pottery lectures of 1924. She produced them, and I copied them out. She was still living in the mill at the bottom of the park, pining for the war to come to an end so that she could start potting again. Her mother had died, her sister had moved to another part of Wiltshire, and Coleshill itself was about to be sold to someone who intended to hand over that perfect example of the Palladian style of the 1650s to the National Trust. We walked all round the house. It was a dark, windy January afternoon; the patriarchal elms and beech trees were waving their bare branches in the wind, and rooks were sailing around the massive chimney stacks of the house in irregular, unpredictable lifts and swoops, like black flakes of soot carried hither and thither by the gale. The great house stood in deserted majesty, its life destined within a short time to be disastrously brought to an end by an accidental fire.

The second round of sessions with Dr Webb went well, and a few days later we met again, exactly as Meyerowitz had planned, round the Directors' lunch table at Wedgwoods.

From Stoke I went on to Derbyshire, to visit the big stoneware factory at Denby. Here everything was much more relevant to what we were doing (or trying to do) at Alajo, than any of the potteries in Stoke-on-Trent. At that time, their system of clay preparation was quite simple. The fat vitrifiable clay from a nearby deposit was shovelled into the blunger with about 10 per cent of a sandy (or rather silty) material, a kind of fireclay. After passing through a vibrating sieve the slip was pumped into a filter-press, and the filter-cakes were put once or twice through a large horizontal pugmill. At that date most of the ware – bowls, casseroles, bottles and even pin-type electric insulators – was being thrown by hand and subsequently turned or trimmed on an ordinary wheel-head. It was here that I first saw screw-threads being tapped out by hand; but the stoppers had to be slip-cast.

In London, my brother Philip gave me the sad news that our beloved Alice Clara Mason was very ill. We went together to visit her. She was living then in my sister's house at Leatherhead; but less than a week later she had to be taken to the hospital in Epsom. When we visited her at the hospital she was very weak and looked pathetically tiny in the narrow bed; every now and then in bad pain. Two days later, she died; but I was not present at her bedside because I had arranged to go to Winchcombe – a visit that could very easily have been postponed. At Winchcombe, Ray gave me a bed in his house in North Street. On the night she died, 29 January 1945, there was snow and a very hard frost. All night I kept waking up from dreams about her and lay accusing myself for not staying beside her. On the day of the funeral the ground was covered with snow and hard with frost; but a grave had been dug in the soft, pure-white chalk. Her brother was there, and my sister, and all my brothers except the oldest, who was in the army in India.

I went home to Wenford, to wait for sailing orders. At last we heard I was to sail from Liverpool on 17 March. Mariel came with me, and we took along our youngest son. The ship was the very same *Amstelkerk* in which I had sailed in 1942. We three walked along the quay until I was told to embark, Mariel haunted by premonitions of unknowable future disasters which I tried in vain to dispel.

19

SHATTERED
DREAMS

When I reached Alajo at the beginning of April 1945, I was met by what seemed like the end of all our hopes. The Institute Council had convened during Meyerowitz's absence and had decreed that the tileworks should be closed down. The pottery was, for the present, to be allowed to continue, but only on a provisional basis and in a crippled condition, until a final decision could be made about the future of the potters concerned. There were to be no more firings of the big kilns. George Procter and Dicon were in a state of deep depression. Dicon was waiting for a boat to take him home, and Procter was stoically standing by, waiting for orders. The West African Institute was evidently in ruins, and I could not escape the feeling that the responsibility for all these misfortunes was mine. I felt irremediably disgraced. All the faults and failures of the past years, the most overwhelming of which had been the disastrous glaze-firing in August 1944, when we had melted the entire setting, were attributable to me. My main obsession, ever since that firing, had been to wipe away its memory with a spectacular sequence of glaze-firings in order to justify the continued existence of the pottery. But now it was too late. There was to be no second chance.

However, there were some small chinks of consolation in all this gloom. I had plenty of time now for throwing, making teapots, pitchers, storage jars, bowls, casseroles and pots for flowers, even though there seemed to be no immediate prospect of glazing them. And I was able to give individual tuition to the potters, whose throwing had been so narrowly confined to one or two production lines during the past two or three years. To circumvent the veto on firing the big kilns I designed and built a test kiln – round, downdraught, top-loading, with a capacity of about 6 cubic feet (0.17 cubic metres) and a removable dome made in two or three pieces – so that we could try out materials and fire a few small pots from time to time. I also started the long-promised evening classes in ceramic theory, dividing the course into three stages: Refractories, Bodies and Glazes; in that order, seeing that our most urgent need was for a good refractory material, and next to that, for a reliable body which did not shatter.

The war was evidently coming to an end; and for the pottery it was clear that the time of crisis and emergency was past, together with all the pressures of that huge production programme. A clear idea began to take shape in my mind about the true function of Alajo Pottery – that it should act from now as a model workshop for the training and activity of Ghanaian potters. This after all was the real core of Meyerowitz's idea, to provide a modern channel for the special talent of West African people.

Then out of nowhere, as it seemed, the sculptor Leon Underwood appeared in Accra – my old friend and supporter from 1931, the distant days when I had first joined the National Society. He was doing a six-month survey for the British Council on West African Art. It was like old times. Here was another European who, I felt, was 'the same animal' as myself – that is, an artist, with whom I shared a similar scale of values and to whom I could at last talk as to a friend who was prepared to listen.

On Underwood's travels in Nigeria he had met and talked to the three or four Europeans there who cared about and valued the art of West Africa – Kenneth Murray, E.H. Duckworth and one or two others. He had found that Meyerowitz during his brief trips through Nigeria had somehow managed to antagonize all of them. I suppose this was partly Meyerowitz's own fault – he would have found their ideas much too narrow and purist.

I had been writing to Meyerowitz ever since I had returned to Achimota, with news of what was going on at my end, and had had two or three rather depressed letters from him. In May he wrote, 'Meanwhile the war seems to be rapidly coming to an end, and this will mean perhaps some wider opportunities for our ideas – or more likely, further attacks on them.' It was the last letter I ever had from him.

I decided that however badly things were going for him, my function here was to maintain as far as possible a holding operation. Even if Meyerowitz was being cut off and all his schemes shelved or curtailed I told myself that the obvious thing to do, for him as well as for me, was to continue our work, even if on a less ambitious scale, and even if his ideas were misunderstood. In the end people would come round to supporting him; I kept telling myself that he would come back and eventually things would right themselves.

Then, suddenly, the news came that Meyerowitz was dead. Two days later we heard that it was suicide.

Meyerowitz's suicide took me completely by surprise, I having never in all the ups and downs of life even remotely contemplated such a thing, being far more preoccupied by problems of how to survive. My first reaction was a feeling of bitter resentment against all the mediocrities of the West African Institute, its ridiculous Council and London Advisory Committee, who, as I imagined, had collectively persecuted him until in the end he made this futile gesture.

There was a private tragedy which may also have contributed to Meyerowitz's suicide. When he reached London in April 1945 he made inquiries at the Soviet Embassy for news of his mother. He learned that during the long and terrible siege of Leningrad, which lasted from the beginning of September 1941 to the end of January 1944, she, like many other civilians, estimated at one million people, had perished from starvation and cold. This news, now reaching him for the first time, may perhaps have extinguished in him any remaining desire to save the West African Institute from the jackals.

At the inquest, evidence was given that Meyerowitz had shown symptoms of manic-depressive cyclothymia. Religious rituals are a kind of first step towards consolation; but official rituals often have a trivializing effect, and an inquest can be a kind of insult to the spirit of the victim.

So, the man had conceived a great idea, failed to carry it out, was not willing to live with this failure, and killed himself. It is not good enough merely to say, by way of explanation, that he suffered from a disease. In contemplating the Promethean achievements of Western Man, I am continually amazed at the power of the human intellect when it is applied in those fields which are appropriate to it – the exact sciences and their practical applications; and at its impotence and imbecility when those who work in the fields of the empirical sciences try to apply the same methods to the operations of the soul, imagining that the small portions of evidence available to them constitute the whole explanation. As Hilaire Belloc said, 'Modern men, knowing a dozen out of a million causes, reason downwards from the rules they have, instead of trusting to their perceptions as their fathers did.'

After the death of Meyerowitz, it was obvious to everyone except me that the Institute, and with it Alajo Pottery, were doomed. But I still clung with blind and fanatical determination to the idea that the pottery, in its post-war form, must somehow continue to operate. I could not forget all the promises which I, and Meyerowitz, had made to the potters who worked with me there. And I also felt a duty to fight on in order to defend and promote what to myself I called Meyerowitz's idea. I thought I only had to prove its rightness by means of my own sincerity in adhering faithfully to it; and in the end the great world of official policy-makers would recognize that from any long-term point of view it was the only right programme for the true interests of West Africans and of the human race as a whole. I see now, in old age, that I was pathetically naïve to believe such a thing. A great, good and fundamentally right programme has no particular chance of being adopted as a policy simply because of its long-term rightness. Generally, what the policy-makers are looking for is short-term expediency. I see now that the first question the policy-makers would have asked themselves was 'If we close down this Institute, will there be a popular outcry in its favour?' The answer was obviously no, seeing that instead of producing the results which had been promised in 1942 – profitable industries, vast deliveries of high-quality goods, a contented body of workers forgetting their political grievances in the joy of their creative work – all it had to show was heavy financial loss everywhere, no goods to speak of, and (worst of all) a wave of native non-co-operation. A decisive blow against the Institute had been delivered at the time of the rebellion of the apprentices in 1944, a popular revolt (or, rather, what in that context was worse – a surge of rejection by a small group of people who saw themselves as an élite) repudiating our idealism, at any rate in the form which it had taken in practice.

None the less, I was determined at all costs to continue to defend Meyer-owitz's idea in so far as that was possible for one man with no private wealth, no influence, and no great fund of local goodwill, whether among whites or blacks; but in trying to define just what that great idea was, I am beset with doubts whether my interpretation corresponds with his.

> It is one thing to know that a friend is dead and another thing to accept, within oneself, that answering silence. . . . One no longer knows if one ever really knew the person, but what's worse, that no longer makes any difference; one is stuck with whatever it is one thought one knew, with whatever filtered through the complex screen of one's own limitations.[1]

In giving my version of the idea I can never be sure how much of what I write is his doctrine rather than my variations on it, or even how clearly he formulated it in all its implications.

In its widest terms, it was that the contacts and even clashes between different human tribes and cultures are not merely the necessary conditions for the progress of the human race, but also a highly desirable instrument for that progress. The word 'progress' is at the present moment unfashionable because most recent progress looks more like the biblical progression of the pigs down the Gadarene steep place. But that simplistic interpretation of the word is merely the product of our nineteenth- and early-twentieth-century intoxi-cation, from which we are now painfully trying to recover. Progress is both necessary and supremely desirable to man, because all real progress is a progress of the soul. The alternative to progress is not stagnation but retro-gression or degeneration. And in modern times, or at least since the nineteenth

---

[1] James Baldwin, *No Name on the Street*, Michael Joseph, London, 1972

14

15

An oval earthenware pie dish with a bird design in trailed brown and green slip on cream slip, under a yellow glaze. Width 12 in (30 cm). Made at Winchcombe, c. 1938. *City of Bristol Museum and Art Gallery.*

An oval earthenware pie dish with a heron design in dark slip on white slip, under a dark galena glaze. Width 14½ in (37 cm). Made at Winchcombe, c. 1928. *University College of Wales, Aberystwyth.*

An earthenware dish with a design of two fishes in trailed white slip on black slip, under a thick galena glaze. Width 13 in (34 cm). Made at Winchcombe, c. 1933. *University College of Wales, Aberystwyth.*

17 H.V. Meyerowitz, 1941.

18 The Alajo Pottery, *c.* 1944. The large buildings are, from left to right, the glaze mill, the clay-washing shed, with the throwing shop behind it, the dipping shop, and (almost hidden by the mango tree), the kiln shed. In front are the sun pans, with the toy truck for transporting clay.

19 Cardew at a native clay-wedging table, with onlookers from Vumë – and elsewhere, 1947.

20 The Volta Pottery, Vumë, 1947. The building to the left of the kiln is the corn mill. The pottery shed is behind the kiln. Cords of firewood are stacked in front.

21 Kofi Athey and Cardew, Vumë, 1947.

ABOVE LEFT A stoneware teapot, with lily motif.
Height 6 in (15 cm). Made at Vumë, *c.* 1947.
The British Council.

BELOW LEFT A stoneware jar, with lily motif.
Height 9½ in (24 cm). Made at Vumë, *c.* 1947.
The British Council.

24 A stoneware lidded bowl with brush
decoration in brown iron-oxide over a green
glaze. Height 5 in (13 cm), width 8 in (20 cm).
Made at Vumë, *c.* 1947. *Collection of Simon Fox.*
Photograph by Stephen Brayne.

25

26

25 Cardew stoneware made at Vumë. British
   Council Exhibition, Accra, December 1947.

26 Cardew playing his recorder to an audience of
   aborigine children in Milingimbi, Australia,
   1968.

27 Cardew giving a pottery demonstration, Venice, California, 1967. *Photograph by Sam Calder.*

28 Cardew at Wenford Bridge, 1981. *Photograph by John Coles.*

century, the alternative to the clash of cultures is not merely stagnation but, as Meyerowitz said to me on more than one occasion, 'reservationism'. That culture which is more powerful in terms of technology segregates and imprisons the less powerful in reservations – zoos, in fact – which can be visited by the heirs of the self-styled superior culture for purposes of recreation, sightseeing, photography or even to carry out seemingly respectful academic studies; never to know the inhabitants as people just like ourselves, by which I mean, never to love them.

Whether or not Meyerowitz would have formulated these ideas in exactly these terms, it is certain that I would never have become so conscious of them if I had not come under his influence. I will even dare to assert that had it not been for his death, it is unlikely that I would ever have undertaken the reorientation and the fundamental reassessment of my scale of values which enabled me eventually, in my relationships with West Africans, to become at least partly capable of that disinterested love which is called friendship. 'Love is when you desire for another that happiness which previously you wanted for yourself' (Pierre Louÿs).

As for the practical application of his idea to the Institute's industries, Meyerowitz certainly saw the industries as instruments for effecting 'the marriage of the old aesthetic skill and power to modern techniques', to use the phrase of the original (1942) blueprint for the Institute; and he was confident that in the process of transferring, adapting and developing old techniques to new, nothing of value would ever be lost of the essential genius and style of the people involved in the transition, provided the transition was being conducted in the right way. By 'the right way' he certainly meant, as I did, the way of craftsmanship. This is a point on which he often insisted in private and also in his public pronouncements.

What he in common with all other whites at that period failed to perceive was the inevitability of conflict between the people of the two cultures. Whatever he undertakes to do, however disinterested and however philosophically correct it may be, in the eyes of a politically awakened black man a white man in a black country is bound to be wrong. If he proposes to bring progress he will be trampling on sacred traditions, manners and customs. If he announces his respect for sacred traditions, and insists that native custom must be studied and conformed with, he is 'holding our people back' from their natural progress by trying to impose a tribal stereotype. If he tries to promote craftsmanship rather than machine production, he is one of those paternalists who consider that 'arts and crafts' are all a black man is fit for and that his industries should be limited to hand manufactures lest they should compete with the modern industries of white men.

It might be thought that the answer to all this is that none of these jobs ought to be undertaken by a white man; it is the job of the black man, in his own country. But even if a black man did the job, he would still be doing it because of the white man and his intrusive civilization. There is a real conflict here. The contradiction and clash of two cultures, the element of imposition, even of hostility, is essential and inevitable and cannot be removed, though it can be modified by the forces of love and laughter, which overcome all barriers; or else by successful production, which goes a long way to eliminate opposition and to sweeten criticism. I could not forget that not only my rows with the apprentices, but also my many technical failures, had become nails in the Institute's coffin.

In July the Institute Council met again for their final deliberations about our fate; and though their decision may have seemed to everyone else a foregone conclusion, nevertheless when it was at last delivered it was more than I could bear. The news was brought to me while I was in bed with another bout of malaria. For two whole days and nights I lay in a state of incredulous indignation and blank despair. Two days later I went down to Alajo to tell my friends. It was a Sunday; there were not many people there; Kofi and his friend Yawo Kuma were busy planting cassava on their 'farm' – that was what they called it, but it was only a tiny patch of cultivated ground which they had dug in the open grassland a little way to the north of the pottery. I tried to tell them the news, but when I began to speak, a sudden realization came of the enormity of what had happened. I was overwhelmed by a convulsion of helpless grief and collapsed on the ground, speechless in my despair, and watering the dry grasses with my agonizing tears.

There is nothing to be done, when you are suddenly the victim of an obliterating emotion. You are excommunicated, cut off, alone in the struggle with your demons or angels. Physically, it is like some sort of possession or seizure, like a fit of sneezing or vomiting, or a long spasm of uncontrollable coughing. While it lasts, there is no hope of resisting it, no chance of any rational control or of any human contact. Nobody can help you. Kofi laid his hand on me to comfort me, but I was cut off, and beyond any help; the mere thought of being comforted gave added force to the storm. In this kind of crisis there is enough rationality still present somewhere inside you for you to be able to tell yourself you are acting in a dumb, stupid, inarticulate, and subhuman way; and yet subhuman is what in those moments you certainly are not. You are more human than perhaps you ever were before. Your affliction is an ancient and universal one, the proof and witness of your humanity. 'A tear is an intellectual thing', Blake said in 'Jerusalem' – how did he find it out, or how did he dare to say it? While you are in the grip it seems the antithesis of anything that could possibly be described as an intellectual thing; but in tranquillity it is found to be as close to the heart of man's nature as the sovereignty of the mind itself. Just as the intellect 'never rests until it has gained a hearing', so the message of those tears is never forgotten. Even after many years some chance of circumstance can still reopen that old wound, with all its pain unabated by the passage of time – the memory of Alajo Pottery, of those who worked there, the songs they used to sing at work, the desperate urgency of our labours together, and the unspeakable grief in which they ended.

From that day I knew, beyond any question of free will, that I was bound to West Africa by ties that I could never undo; that I could never leave it now, or at any time, as long as I could still enjoy the ability to work there.

I could also see the apparently irreconcilable conflict which was implied in this, for all my former ties of affection and duty to Mariel, our three boys, and the pottery at Wenford (or, rather, those poor beginnings of the pottery there, which I now felt compelled to abandon). I could see, indistinctly as yet, what the penalties would be. It would be unjust and unkind to Mariel and the boys, inflicting hardships and unhappiness; it would mark me with the brand of an obsessed, monomaniacal and selfish idiot who was proposing to abandon all the duties of a husband and a father in order to stay in West Africa, working for a hopeless cause there. I caught glimpses of what it would involve to pit my negligible one-man strength against what everyone agreed to call right, and of how much better it would be for all concerned if I could somehow avoid the course to which I was now committed. But I was not governed by any conscious, rational decision. It was simply a bleak realization that this was what had to be done.

We still had the use of the lovely pottery at Alajo for a few precious weeks, and I didn't intend to waste them. Leon Underwood and I planned together that he should organize an exhibition in London, of West African carvings, stools, textiles and pots, including glazed pots from a last firing at Alajo. We spent our last few weeks making great numbers of pots to fill one of the big kilns for this firing. Under the shadow of the end, we made lovely pots, water-coolers, casseroles, small and medium bowls with lids, with scratched decoration.

But the clay bodies we were using all contained a fairly high proportion of the fatal Alajo clay. They had been tried out in the little test kiln, but I had not yet learnt to appreciate and allow for the difference between the behaviour of a clay body in a small test kiln and that of the same body when fired in a large production kiln. The time–temperature schedule is much longer in the big kiln and a marginal body (as these evidently all were) is therefore much more likely to develop an excessive amount of cristobalite, both in the firing and during the cooling.

In early October we fired the big kiln for the last time. All the new pots came out shattered. It was another appalling, but enlightening, ordeal.

20

VUMË

A few weeks before the Alajo Pottery was due to close, I met by chance a Swiss entrepreneur named Friedrich. He was part-owner of a small limeworks at a place called Vumë Dugamé ('The Great Town of the Kapok Trees') on the River Volta, about seventy miles from Accra. He was now planning to move to Liberia, and wanted to hand over his various enterprises before he left. When he heard that I intended to stay on in West Africa, he suggested that Vumë might be a good place to start a small pottery. He offered to take Kofi and me for a visit, so that I could see the place and its possibilities.

We left on a Saturday afternoon, driving along the straight, dusty Ada road as far as the fork which branches off to Tefle. Vumë was a long, straggling roadside village, immediately remarkable because all over the space between the houses and the road there were pots everywhere: wonderful globular water pots, small, medium-sized and enormous. At the far end of the village we came to the lime operations. We turned off towards the river bank. There, before our eyes, was the vast expanse of the river, nearly three-quarters of a mile broad, and flowing swiftiy towards its mouth at Ada, about sixteen miles downstream. Friedrich explained that the flood season was now approaching and that the water would go on rising through September and then sink back to its ordinary level, at which it would become slightly tidal. Next morning, after swimming in the river, Kofi and I visited some of the pot-makers in the village; I obtained a large sample of their clay and bought one of the biggest pots. We left for Accra early in the afternoon; Kofi and I stuffed the big pot with our blankets so as to give it some ballast, and nursed it on our knees all the way back. (This pot now belongs to the British Museum.)

When we got back to Alajo I immediately began making tests on the Vumë clay. I wrote home, 'The clay *looks* and *feels* lovely. . . . The village is entirely given over to making the most impressive pots I've seen here. They are huge, and decorated with fat red ochre; – capacity 20, 30, and up to 40 gallons [90, 135, 180 litres]. We watched an old lady making one of them: fine! – real professionalism in every movement.'

Everything depended on those clay tests; but if they were successful, the other advantages of Vumë were obvious. The lime operations had already provided a clear site for the pottery; labour was even cheaper than in Accra; and there were two or three skilled men who could help with putting up simple buildings. There was a beautiful round-house which I could occupy rent-free. I had already arranged to buy various materials and pieces of equipment from the pottery at Alajo: six thousand bricks to build a kiln, three tons of raw bauxite, two potter's wheels, timber for the stillages, ware boards, sieves, glaze tubs and nearly three-quarters of a ton of water-ground glaze materials, enough to last until we could grind our own. All these could be brought in Friedrich's ancient lorry, which with its four-wheel trailer came down to Vumë from time to time to collect the loads of lime.

The prospects for firewood for the kiln were good. All along the river bank upstream from Vumë ᴜere was a belt of scrubby riparian woodland, and the people of the small hamlets there were already accustomed to cutting cords for Friedrich's lime-kilns and stacking them by the waterside. When enough wood was stacked, his men went up to collect it in the large flat-bottomed canoe which he kept at the landing stage just below the bungalow. The great river which gave such majesty to the scene was an important practical asset as well, transportation by water being much cheaper than by road. And there was that magnificent pottery industry in the village.

But it all depended on the clay tests. They were too late to get into the firing of the big kiln, but we had a last firing of the little kiln: the two or three pitchers and flower jars which I made for it all came out well, except for one small mug, in which the glaze flaked slightly on the handle – a small but unmistakable sign of future troubles, to which I should have paid more attention. I told Friedrich I would take over the limeworks for a pottery.

The last days at Alajo were spent packing up all our things and materials: the first load of them was sent away on Friedrich's lorry on 4 October. A few days later I wrote to Mariel:

> I've been waiting to tell you about Vumë until I was sure I was going there – as I now am. ... The Institute has decided to pay me twelve months salary from September 4th – eleven months instead of only six. With 'allowances' and gratuity it will come to about £900; and they offer me a passage home, provided I go within the next two months.
>
> Now I know you will think it is mad of me, not to accept the offer of a sea passage and come home to start again at Wenford with all this money. But it is no good, I can't help it. I absolutely believe in this West African pottery idea. Those Institute people are not serious about it, but that only makes it all the more necessary to prove that I am, and they will have to respect that, in the long run.

After that, it seems terrible to say that I've asked them to stop the 'allotment' to you after the one which you've just had. But I must keep this money as capital for starting the new pottery, and then as soon as I begin to earn something I'll send you as much as I can, and consignments of the best pots when we make them. . . . If I came home now I should be miserable, and would be sure to make you and the boys miserable as well.

It is painful and embarrassing now to read again the letters I wrote to Mariel at that time, chiefly because of the feeble attempts I made to justify what I was doing. My decision to stay on was much harder on her than it was for me, but in my mind there was no room for any doubt or hesitation. I was obsessed by one idea, and obsession made me absolutely selfish and totally impervious to any argument about what was just, or right, or proper. My attempts to defend myself by invoking high-minded motives were not exactly false but they sound a bit false to me now. I hate those interpretations of motives which want them all to be high-minded just as much as I despise those which want them all to be low-minded. Everything we do springs as much from our faults and failings as from our strength and courage, like fruits and flowers nourished by compost and dirt as much as by the sun and the rain.

My obsession was that I must prove to 'them' (the Institute people) that they were wrong to close down Alajo, and that a small pottery in a village would be successful in every way, provided it was allowed to develop naturally. I had nearly £900 in capital, considerably more than I had ever possessed before. At Winchcombe, and at Wenford, I had been able to move mountains, using almost no money at all. (Nevertheless, I was gravely underestimating the capital needed for starting a pottery 'in the Bush' – as I was soon to find out.) I was also furiously indignant at seeing all those promises broken – promises made by the West African Institute, by Meyerowitz himself, and by me. I had believed in them when I made them and I still fiercely believed in them: especially those I had made to Kofi Athey. I was determined to enable him to become a potter, and to set him up in a pottery of his own.

I saw clearly that these aims were incompatible with any idea of returning like a dutiful husband and father, or of picking up again the tame, constricted life of a small potter in England. If I had returned then, it would have been as a plain failure with a hard luck story; or (more likely) as a raging irreconcilable, nursing a grudge against everything and everybody, especially those who were dearest to me. Or I would have wasted my energies trying to persuade London to give me another job in West Africa. And that was an obviously impossible quest. It was four or five years before any government in West Africa came around to the idea of developing pottery; and even then, on the strength of my past record at Achimota and Alajo, no government would have appointed this intransigent and fanatical disciple of the now totally discredited Meyerowitz.

Pottery in West Africa, the cause that had become so dear to me, had been irrigated with tears (without that water nothing can grow) and it seemed to my heated brain that it had even claimed a martyr. Nobody cared now whether it survived or not; it had become a matter of no importance whatever, whether public or private. The only man who had cared as much as I did was dead; and I could not shake off the feeling that his death had been partly my fault. As well as all the other things the pottery at Vumë meant to me, it was to be my way of repaying the debt I owed to Meyerowitz, a vindication of his memory and an act of defiance against the fact of his death.

The timing of my attempt to found a pottery at Vumë was lucky. In 1945 it was still possible for a white man to start a small one-man business in West Africa, with no embarrassing questions asked about how much capital he had behind him. But I was only just in time: a few years later new laws and regulations came in, which would have made it impossible for anyone to embark on such an enterprise.

The great migration to Vumë was fixed at last for Tuesday, 23 October. Kofi and Yawo Kuma were to come with me. Our quarters at Achimota were already closed, and I spent the last night in a room in Accra. At the appointed hour, Yawo Kuma was there, his usual cheerful self, but no Kofi. I did not take Kofi's absence in any tragic spirit, telling myself 'This is West Africa, unpredictable as usual. Kofi will come along later, in his own time.'

Travelling to Vumë in the lorry was a rather unnerving experience. The load was heavy, and the lorry had no brakes. Fortunately the road was dead straight and the slopes were gentle ones, following the slight undulations of the Accra Plain. Whenever we reached the top of one of these slopes the driver switched off the engine to save petrol, and coasted down the long incline. We reached Vumë safely, unloaded all our things – furniture, bricks, timber, potter's wheels – and I began to settle myself into the thatched round-house.

Then I heard that Kofi had been taken to Kole-Bu hospital, with meningitis. He had already been sickening on the day we left for Vumë and had been too ill to join us. I went there in great alarm, and asked for news of him; and we found at last that he had been entered under the name of Clement-Cofie. When Kofi reached the hospital he had been unconscious, but after an hour or two had woken up in a bout of violent delirium, trying to attack the nurses and eventually falling down and hurting himself in his convulsions. But the doctor had at last succeeded in making a lumbar puncture of the spine and giving Kofi what he himself described as 'danger-line' doses of drugs. He assured me that

Kofi was now definitely out of danger and would make a complete recovery, and he was confident that in those cases where a man survived cerebro-spinal meningitis there would be no lasting damage or after-effects. The nursing sister in charge was also wonderfully reassuring, saying that his had been the quickest recovery from meningitis she had ever seen.

She took me to his bedside; and though he recognized me at once he still looked appallingly ill and weak and exhausted and was complaining of pain in his head and neck and in his lower spine, where the lumbar puncture had been made. I stayed on in Accra and visited Kofi every day, bringing him books to look at, and the oranges and bananas and slabs of chocolate he was now allowed to have. On the fifth day (the thirteenth since his admission to the hospital) he was at last beginning to look better; and the next day I said goodbye, promising to send Yawo Kuma to him in a day or two.

The memory of those days of tribulation remains indelible. I was haunted by the feeling of an incurable remorse at having abandoned him on the day of our long-planned departure for Vumë. I ought to have known, when he failed to join us, that something serious was wrong. I knew at last that I could never abandon him in a time of need. Two days later Yawo Kuma went to Accra with a letter for Kofi and two books – Shakespeare's *Sonnets* and Blake's *Songs of Innocence*, both of which I had found in the Methodist Bookshop in Accra.

At last Kofi was well enough to leave hospital. He came to Vumë on the lorry and arrived looking tired after the long, dusty, bumpy journey, but still very much better than he had in the hospital. I took him over to the bungalow and put him to bed there. When he woke later, I brought tea, and jam, and toasted some of our hard bread for him. Yawo Kuma and I made up a temporary bed for him, with my old mosquito net over it, in the little spare room. In a very short time he was up and about again, his old active self, but from time to time he complained of pain in the lower spine, and then I used to make him lie face down on his bed, and give him amateur massage, carefully avoiding the small round wound, now perfectly healed, where the life-saving lumbar puncture had been made.

The first thing we needed at Vumë was bricks for the kiln and sheds. I calculated that we should need about thirteen thousand in addition to the six thousand I had brought from Alajo. Bricks were already being made for the lime-kilns by a beautiful old man from Togo. He was an interesting person who had grown up in Togo when it was still under German rule, and on the occasions when he had taken plenty of palm wine he used to sing 'Deutschland über Alles' to us in German, in a wild but note-perfect version. He agreed to make bricks for us, and I fired them in a disused lime-kiln. The whole place was at last beginning to look more like a pottery.

After my experience with the big 12 foot (3.5 metre) kilns at Alajo, I was cautious when I came to design the kiln for Vumë. It was to be only 6 feet (1.8 metres) in diameter inside, which gives a capacity of about 100 cubic feet (2.8 cubic metres). I did, however, introduce one experimental new feature – a second chamber which I hoped would reach about 900°C or more, from the waste heat coming from the main chamber when it was fired at stoneware temperature.

By the time we reached the level of the top of the fireboxes, all our Alajo bricks had been used, except for a few hundred which I reserved for the chequer and bag-walls of the high-temperature chamber. From now on we used only our local Vumë bricks – even for the hot face and for building the dome. The bricklayers were Kofi and myself and a young boy called Ketani.

After we had completed the fireboxes and fire-arches our progress was quicker; when we came to build the dome we made ourselves a guide stick to make sure the curve was true. About a week later we began building the second chamber. This was comparatively quick work until we reached the top of the chamber and had to start on the chimney. To obtain a regular taper for it – from a diameter of about 6 feet (1.8 metres) to the top, where it was only 3 feet (90 cm) – we had to invent a simple expedient which we called the 'maypole system'. We found a straight pipe of galvanized iron, about 20 feet (6 metres) long, and we planted it in a tub of dirt and rocks in the middle of the chamber floor. We plugged the end of this pipe and nailed a round board to it and tied ten or twelve long pieces of string to the circumference at regular intervals. After this pipe had been set up and carefully made perpendicular we tied the ends of the twelve strings to twelve little wire loops which we had built into the last course of brickwork. As the height of the chimney increased, so did our problems with the scaffolding. At first this consisted essentially of posts firmly fixed in the ground and other sticks, horizontal and diagonal, to stabilize the uprights, with a few 2 inch (5 cm) thick planks bridging the angles. On these we stood and worked, our bricks and mortar boards beside us. But when we reached the top of the first sticks we had to get big oil drums, fill them with more dirt and stones, and put a second lot of posts in these. Occasionally we found we could stabilize this shaky erection by pushing a heavy board against the brickwork of the chimney itself, but for the most part we were content to sway slightly from side to side as we worked – it felt rather as if we were laying bricks while perched in the upper branches of a tree.

The day came when we had nearly reached the planned height, and we had the problem of removing the central pipe without damaging the brickwork; so we cut the strings, extracted the pipe from its bedding in the tub below, and carefully pulled it up by hand until its top must have been nearly 50 feet (15 metres) up, and then carefully lowered it to the ground outside. Nobody lost their balance or fell, and the brickwork was undamaged.

The last course was laid – it consisted of left-over arch bricks laid flat and sloping outward; over them we put a capping of lime mortar, and next we took down the scaffolding and cleaned up inside the chamber. Ketani set to work happily pointing all the outside brickwork with lime mortar. Everyone felt very pleased to see the kiln completed and looking so nice.

Among the supplies I brought from Alajo was a liberal quantity of glaze materials – enough water-ground pegmatite, calcite and quartz to see us through the first few glaze-firings. But I knew that when these were used up we would have to grind our own materials, and I had asked a friend of mine, Philip Varcoe, to send two pot mills out to me from England. When I came to consider the question of what power we would use to run the pot mills, I was struck by the thought that it would be nice for the villagers (and possibly also profitable for me) if we could use the same power to run a corn mill for the village. Most of the larger villages had a mill for grinding their maize and their dried cassava roots. (The ground cassava was made into a sort of pudding called *kokonté* – a poor, unappetising food which was the staple of the local people.) But the people at Vumë depended entirely on the mill at Tefle, about two miles away.

The pot mills were safely landed at Accra beach and I was able to buy a diesel engine and a corn mill in Accra. The price of the engine (£150) included the services of a fitter who would come down from Accra to mount and install the whole mill.

All went according to plan. The fitter was a quick worker; and everyone helped. When he had set up the engine and mill, he almost at once began to give a demonstration, while the concrete foundation was still damp. We offered free milling for the first run, and half the village came along to celebrate. But though it was popular with the village people, our mill never came near to making a profit. It was not surprising that Vumë had had no corn mill before. Anyone with the capital and enterprise to start a mill would have gone to some more prosperous place. In Vumë the people grew hardly any corn; almost all they had to bring for milling was the nauseating dried cassava. Their poverty, as is usually the case, was circular and self-perpetuating. Even the hardest-hearted village capitalist would have found it nearly impossible to wring any profit from that rock-bottom state of want. What Vumë needed, in fact, was a philanthropist, not a poor struggling potter.

However, the mill was useful to the pottery. The engine turned the pot mills; and we soon discovered that when the corn mill was not grinding cassava it could be used to break up various materials for us. For example, we used it in making soft grog.

One of the most interesting features of the pottery tradition in Vumë was their use of low-fired grog. They used to pile clay in a heap and when it was dry, burn it in a bonfire. They brought the fired clay back to the village. Here, on days when the women were out farming or digging fresh clay, one could find some old lady who had stayed at home to mind the younger children, busily pounding the lumps of fired clay in a wooden mortar and shaking it through an improvised sieve to make soft grog. I had read Schurecht's account of experiments made in America on the use of low-fired grog in brickmaking, in which he found that the mix containing the low-fired grog produced the greatest mechanical strength in the resulting bricks; and it struck me that here in Vumë was an example of apparently 'primitive' clay-workers practising something which we in the West had just recently rediscovered for ourselves. At the pottery we imitated the practice of the village potters. We fired lumps of Vumë clay in the second chamber of the kiln, and after breaking them up with a hammer we fed them into the mill to make low-fired grog. The potters in the village soon heard about this and approached us to ask if we could grind their grog too. This was a pleasing example of a two-way exchange of ideas between the new pottery and the old. I had taken the idea from them in the first place, and now they were proposing to get their grog made in the mill. Traditional potters in West Africa, in most ways extremely conservative and strictly ritualistic in all their practices, are sometimes refreshingly open to new ideas.

21

THE SUN IN AFRICA

Our two-chamber kiln worked very well for the first few firings, which were entirely devoted to bricks, this being a good way to give the kiln a thorough drying-out. We still needed bricks ourselves, for various works around the pottery, and the local branch of the United Africa Company had asked us for 4,000 'burnt bricks' to build a storehouse. After that, we filled the first chamber entirely with bauxite, of which we had bought a few tons from Alajo, and in the second chamber we fired our newly made saggars and water-coolers. In their raw state the lumps of bauxite were as hard as limestone. We simply filled the first chamber with these boulders, intending to fire them as high as we could, preferably to stoneware temperature, to provide a good refractory grog for future saggars. But when the kiln reached about 1150°C, we could not get it to go any higher. The draught seemed to be blocked, and since the things in the second chamber were already at a good red heat, we decided to stop.

When we opened the kiln we soon saw why the draught had failed: the weight of those boulders had pushed the bag-wall out towards the wall of the kiln itself, closing the main fireway almost completely; and when the kiln had been emptied we found that all the bag-wall bricks, and most of those in the chequer too, were crushed and broken. These were the last of our stock of Alajo bricks, which up till then were the nearest approach we had to any kind of refractory brick. It was fortunate that the temperature did *not* go too high, because later on I found out by experiment that if you fire bauxite at full stoneware temperature, it becomes almost impossible to break it up into grog; in fact it turns into a sort of corundum, the hardest mineral after diamond.

Not counting myself, there were in our first year nine people working in the pottery: Kofi Athey; Yawo Kuma; Karimu Busanga, who came from Upper Volta; Gabriel Agbodzivi, whose home was at Dabbala, beside a lagoon somewhere between Sogankope and the coast; a Vumë man called Kofi Ntakor; and Atta Gayi, a very bright young man who mostly worked as a part-time carpenter. Atta was also a local man, though he did not come from Vumë itself, and his aunt, an old lady named Adehé, was one of the women potters in Vumë. Then there was Kwami Agbedanu, who had turned up looking for a job at the pottery. He had been one of the men at Alajo, a tall, good-natured man who like Kofi himself and many others at Alajo came from French Togo. There were also two Vumë girls who sometimes turned our wheels or carried water.

But Yawo Kuma fell sick with dysentery and fever. I fed him with what remained of my Bovril and wrote to Kole-Bu hospital asking for medicine for him. Still the weeks went by and he did not get any better. I asked Kofi what he thought about it, and he said that perhaps the persistent sickness was 'because Yawo has not been taking care of his family stool', and that perhaps he ought to go back to his home, which was in Togo. And when Yawo was well enough to travel he left us, taking the small amount of money that was due to him, and his book of Post Office savings which I had been holding for him. That was the last I ever saw or heard of him. We sorely missed him; he was always cheerful and amusing, as well as being a wonderful worker.

Life for me that year was full of ups and downs of sickness and health, failure and success, moments of total despondency followed soon by sudden waves of confidence. No half-tones were admitted, everything was extreme: ineffable exaltations, or else black despair that could be brought on by some apparently trivial event – such as the loss one day of my gold wedding ring. It was a nice ring made by a jeweller friend of Mariel; but it was extremely thin, because we had been too poor for a more solid one. Kofi helped me in the unsuccessful search for it by the light of a hurricane lamp while supper was cooking, or burning. But it was lost. There were also moments of sudden unforgettable happiness, when the beauty of the surroundings wiped away all miseries large or small.

The first pots we made at Vumë were saggars for the future glaze-firing. For these we used ordinary Vumë clay tempered with plenty of the coarse low-fired grog which we had made from the same clay. At first we only made three sizes of the saggars: but plenty of each, more than enough to fill the kiln. After saggars, I went straight on to 2 pint (1 litre) pitchers, and that was a terrible shock at first. I felt as if all the skill which I had acquired over so many years had vanished for ever. I had got into the habit of assuming that pitcher-making was my special thing, my strongest point, something I had mastered so well that it had become part of me, so that I knew more about pitchers than any contemporary potter. Yet now here I was, struggling with the most elementary difficulties of a beginner. I had not made a pot, except for the saggars, since August or September 1945. But my problems were not entirely because I was out of practice; I was not yet used to the Vumë clay, nor to my Vumë wheel-turner.

After two or three days I began to improve, and from then on, I was able to do some throwing for at least part of every day. After the 2 pint (1 litre) pitchers I moved to smaller things, restoring my belief in my own competence by making great numbers of 1 pint (600 ml) pitchers and tiny cream jugs; then back to larger things again.

As the months slipped away, so did what remained of my money, and my old familiar panic came back. Occasionally something turned up to relieve the condition of financial cramp. One day, an official order arrived from the Medical Department of Kole-Bu, for 300 2 pint (1 litre) water-coolers, each with its stopper and saucer. The idea was that every patient could have good cool drinking water beside his or her bed. Kofi and I were jubilant; we started making them at once. Very soon, others came along asking for water-coolers. The potters at Achimota and later at Alajo had built up a popular demand for water-coolers all over the country, and now, ever since the closing of Alajo, people had been unable to get them.

Michael Ensor, the District Commissioner at Ada, who was a frequent visitor whenever he happened to be in our neighbourhood, was always interested in what was going on at the pottery, and we used to talk about what I was doing, and why. Soon the inevitable question came up, 'What made you take to pottery?' To which I never had a coherent answer. And that other question, 'Don't you get bored, making the same kind of pot over and over again?' 'A man who gets bored making this shape – any shape – is not fit to make a shape at all – is not fit to be a potter.' For me, making any shape whatever is a continual and progressive revelation of a form which is taking shape through my own hands. The more you enter into a long campaign of exploring the inner character of even a simple form, the more completely and excitingly it reveals itself with each new realization on the wheel. This is what my life is: for me this is what it means to be a potter.

We knew that there were a few crocodiles in the river, but in those first years we never saw one, and except for taking care not to go too far from the shore, I scarcely gave them a thought while I swam in that illuminated world. It was easy, effortless, voluptuous swimming in that caressing water which never gave the swimmer any of those gasping, galvanic shocks with which one is hit when swimming in northern oceans, lakes or rivers. The clouds overhead were crimson, and orange, and a shaggy sort of purple; towards the western horizon there were zones of clear sky, lucid green and pale blue. The reflections in the water were the same, but dappled and broken up by the ripples. While I swam I dreamed about future glaze-firings. I swore to myself that I would astonish the cold grey world of Northern Europe with a new West African stoneware of a richness and a warmth of colour never seen before

– deep celadons like the river, glowing black-blue masses like the clouds when a tornado approaches – the blue-blackness of the sky before rain, that most characteristic of all West African skies. There would be flashes of red, green, and yellow in the iron-oxide decoration. Such pots, I told myself, would vindicate in the eyes of the world what I was doing here, and would convince my friends at home that what I was doing was, after all, right.

For the first glaze-firing I had carefully worked out the batch recipes for the glazes, among them a clear celadon, an iron glaze, a copper red, and what I hoped would be a really good cobalt blue. I was determined to have clear, bright, honest, glazes. Those were what my African friends liked, and the only ones I liked myself. I had a horror of all 'art' glazes. I wanted none of these dirty colours or contrived surfaces, those sinister patches of scum looking like something on the crust of a badly managed cesspool, nor any of those thick, suffocating matt glazes which seemed to me like expensive fur coats designed to cover up the beauty of the naked pot. As for copper red, I had never been much of an enthusiast for that either, because iron reds look more natural; but I thought it might be much admired locally. So I took precautions to make sure of a completely reducing atmosphere, doing all the things I vaguely remembered being told about copper-red glaze by Matsubayashi at St Ives, such as placing each pot in a saggar whose walls were painted with a coating of the same glaze, and then putting this saggar inside a larger one and filling up the space between them with pulverized blacksmith's charcoal (made, in this place, from the hard shells of palm-kernels).

We finally lit the kiln on the last day of September. The firing seemed to be going well, up to the moment when I opened the spy-hole to see the cones and to take out some of the test-rings. But when I looked inside, it was a view of nothing, just a burning, fiery emptiness. It was a repetition, though on a somewhat smaller scale, of that fatal occasion at Alajo in 1944, when all the saggars in the big kiln had squatted. When, about a week later, the kiln was cool enough to unload, we found that the disaster was not quite so total as it had been in Alajo, but we did not get many undamaged pots. One or two of the bungs, where the temperature had been slightly lower, gave us a few jars and pitchers which came out with a nice grey-white glaze on which the painted decoration took well without any blurring at the edges. Among other relatively undamaged pots were those which, unfortunately, had been given the blue glaze. The result of the experiment was appalling, the colour much too dark and the glaze anyway too thickly applied. The copper reds also escaped disaster, but they were a disappointment in another way: they had produced, not the bright red I had hoped for, but a dark suffused mahogany colour; actually they were rather beautiful *peau-de-nègre*, as I realized next day, when I saw Kofi carrying one of them in his bare arms. Beautiful, perhaps, but not what I had intended.

The melting of the saggars in this first glaze-firing gave urgency to the implacable question which faced me: what on earth were we going to do for refractory materials with which to make new saggars; to say nothing of bricks, which were just as urgently needed to replace those which were now altogether broken up in the chequer and the bag-wall? Sooner or later we should be needing enough bricks to reline the whole hot face of the kiln. Evidently, the situation, which already seemed as bad as it could be, was likely to become even worse as time went on.

I tried desperately to think what we were to do next. Meanwhile Kofi and Atta Gayi were tackling the problem in a more practical way, asking the local people if they knew of any white clay in the neighbourhood. One day the two of them came in with a sample of gravelly material which contained large chunks of white clay. Some well-diggers at Kungbor, about eight miles away, had thrown up a great heap of the stuff, nearly 10 feet (3 metres) high, and were still going deeper and bringing up more. We managed to get hold of about 5 tons altogether, enough for at least the next year. This Kungbor fireclay was almost like a true fireclay, except that it contained too much of the coarse gravel. We had to dry it and put it through a coarse sieve before we could use it for saggars and bricks. We made the new saggar body from a half-and-half mixture of this clay and bauxite grog; and to improve the plasticity we added 10 or 20 per cent of the finest fraction of the washed Vumë clay in the form of slip. These saggars behaved quite well, though, as was to be expected, they were always rather brittle, and had to be handled with care.

Although the first glaze-firing had been so disastrous, it did provide us with a few saleable pots. Those members of the white community in the Gold Coast who knew of the existence of the pottery, and took an interest in it, soon began to ask for them. Vumë was accessible from Accra by road, an interesting day-trip for Sunday mornings, and such visits soon became a feature in my life. Theo Müller, who ran the Union Trading Company's shop in Accra, was one regular visitor who became a friend, and a great support to the pottery. As long as he was at the Union Trading Company he would always buy any glazed pots we had for sale in the shop, and would see that they were properly displayed.

We pressed on to the point where we could have another glaze-firing. But when we lit up the kiln, at the beginning of December 1946, we had more trouble. The bag-wall shifted and blocked the draught yet again, so that we had to stop the fires before the full heat was reached. However, when we came to unload, we found that under-firing was the least of our troubles. The real disaster was that the clay which I had tested at Alajo before deciding to settle in Vumë was now shivering and shattering, almost as badly as the Alajo clay itself. Yet again I had been deceived by tests fired in a tiny kiln. Now the pots were being fired in a larger kiln, on a much longer time–temperature schedule, and there was much more time for cristobalite to be formed.

I can see clearly, with the useless wisdom of hindsight, that after this firing had proved that the Vumë clay – like the Alajo clay – would not stand up to glaze-firing temperature, the prudent course would have been to throw away all the pots which had been biscuit-fired and dipped ready for another glaze-firing; and to use up all the prepared, washed clay – we had a cellar full of it – for water-coolers, since it was perfectly good for that purpose. Then, new batches of experimental body should have been prepared by washing Vumë clay with suitable admixtures of pegmatite. Instead of doing that, I stubbornly went on using the old clay; absurdly persuading myself that if I kneaded a generous amount of the soft-fired grog into the clay it would not shatter.

The inefficient way we fired also contributed to the shivering. At that time, I had only the haziest idea of what was meant by 'secondary air'. Whenever we fired, it all went well until we reached about 1100°C, when there was a tendency for the ashpits to become overfilled with embers. The fuel in the fireboxes was liberating quantities of combustible gas which was unable to burn for want of air. (This helps to account for the intense and beautiful blue-green colours of those few glazed pots which came out in one piece and subsequently remained in one piece.) When the combustible gas reached the second chamber, it began to burn, thanks to small cracks in the walls and door, giving rise to over-firing in that chamber; and when it eventually reached the top of the chimney, it burst into triumphant flame and a huge beard of fire suddenly appeared there. I remember similar gas flames shooting out of the blow-holes of Bernard Leach's three-chamber climbing kiln at St Ives. These gas flames were taken by all of us to be a welcome sign that good reduction of the glazes was taking place. Indeed it was; all reducing-fire is after all a case of imperfect combustion. But at Vumë I was taking it too far altogether, because after 1100°C–1150°C the temperature stubbornly refused to go up and the ashpits became more and more clogged with embers.

I went blindly ahead, and had another glaze-firing in March 1947.[1] This was of course another terrible failure, and it was made more painful by the really beautiful quality of the pots which fell to pieces so disastrously as we took them from the kiln.

---

[1] 'What not to do, by one who has done it', to quote Katharine Bouverie's golden phrase.

Looking back now it appears as if I must have been possessed to have undertaken this third firing, knowing from the previous ones how unlikely it was to be successful. I can only think it was yet another example of the almost hysterical excitability which attacks some white people in West Africa, making them act in ways they never would in sober England.

That third bad firing did convince me that we must somehow obtain kaolin. I had been unable to find any kaolin at all in the Vumë area. But I remembered that among the many samples of clays which the Geological Survey Department had sent to Alajo at Meyerowitz's request there had been a pure white non-plastic kaolin, which came from a trial pit near a place called Benso, between Sekondi and Tarkwa; the sample we had was free from sand or gravel. I decided that the best thing for us to do was to try to get hold of some of this. Kofi and I went to Benso, where we found the pit and managed to hire several carriers to help us. We spent nearly three days digging and carrying the clay. When all our bags were full they were weighed at Benso railway siding and came to not quite two-thirds of a ton. I cannot imagine why we did not go on and get at least two or three tons of the stuff while we had the pit open and the men to carry it. We could have emptied our bags into a truck and refilled them several times. What had become of the energy I used to display when clay-digging four years ago? Tiredly we returned by train and lorry, with our precious load of kaolin. There was plenty of work to be done. We had another order for 300 water-coolers from the Medical Department, and there were new body experiments to be made with the Benso kaolin.

The next problem was the need for a canoe, the old one belonging to the limeworks having fallen to pieces. Whenever we needed to bring firewood from the riverside we had to hire one at a ruinous cost. Kofi and I had long consultations about this, and his proposal was that he and Gabriel should go down to Ada on the launch, and thence to the seashore, to see if any of the groups of sea-fishermen in the villages there had a secondhand dugout canoe to sell us. These canoes were strong sea-going vessels carved out of a single tree trunk. After many rough landings in the surf, they eventually developed cracks and the crew would 'sell it up the river', and buy a new one. Such secondhand canoes, though no longer reliable at sea, were perfectly satisfactory for the river trade. Kofi and Gabriel took the launch on 20 May 1947 – which was unfortunate in a way, since it meant that I was unable to share with them the most wonderful and memorable event of my years in Vumë. This was a total eclipse of the sun. There had been a total eclipse of the sun in 1927, visible from some parts of Britain, and I had travelled from Winchcombe to North Wales hoping to see it. Arriving in the early morning at Conway, we climbed a small mountain to get a better view. But it was raining, and the sky was covered with heavy clouds. We could just see the outline of Snowdon and the other mountains of Caernarvon, and when the few minutes of totality at last came it was impressive even in that murky light. Suddenly the summits and flanks of the mountains in the west were drowned in a dark shadow which raced across the intervening country at what seemed a supernatural speed, quickly enveloping the hill we ourselves were on. We watched and waited for two minutes or three, until, just as suddenly, Snowdon and the mountains were in light again.

At Vumë there was no mountain to climb, but the next best thing was the ridge of the thatched pottery roof, and we waited for it there. Atta and Kwami Agbedanu hesitated slightly but I assured them we would come to no harm. I wrote a long letter to Mariel when the eclipse was over.

I must write now, before I forget *anything*. Atta and Kwami and I climbed up to the roof ridge to wait, half the village and hordes of children standing in the roadway below us obviously rather disapproving that we should so wantonly expose ourselves at a time when all sensible people should keep within reach of a safe bolt-hole. . . . As the sun's crescent grew thinner and thinner the light turned a more and more sickly yellow, and curiously 'dead', like an acetylene gas-light. But the insensitive Vumë sheep went on nibbling, noticing nothing. Only the buzzard which lives on Mrs Christian Dedor's chickens seemed to be upset. Just when the sun seemed to be shrinking down into the last desperate thread of blazing fierceness some small clouds swept across it, and I thought, when the cloud passes, that last thread will be gone. But the cloud passed, and there was still that amazing shred of sun. And then (this was when I was so glad we had climbed on to the roof) quite suddenly the whole sky looked as if it was about to die in an agony, a ghastly, grey, *metallic* shadow spreading over the whole sky at once, like a hundred thunderclouds. Yet they were no clouds; it was the entire sky looking like all the thunderstorms there have ever been, rolled into one. Not the weight, or mass, or *impact* of thunderstorms; but something that was the distilled ominousness of all thunderstorms. (All this was in total silence: the thunder seemed to be in one's head.) Now the people who had been chattering gaily down below started running for home, and I was almost terrified, and Atta Gayi made a slight move as if he would like to hide too. But I told them, 'Don't fear, there's no danger AT ALL.' They sat on, solidly, and in less time than it takes you to read this, the real darkness had come, and there was that amazing black or metallic-grey disc where the blinding shred of fire had been, and round it we saw flames and ghosts of flames, which all the time were moving and shifting; and suddenly there would be red flashes close to that disc; and beyond we saw bright small stars, and a resplendent planet in the west (we were looking west of course), and all overhead a night sky. . . .

And now, if you looked away from that central drama, if you looked north, or to the south, you could see that as it were side by side with our 'night' there was a sort of dawn all the time accompanying it, because the 'path of totality' was only one hundred and twenty miles wide, and we were nearly in the middle of it; and so, about sixty miles to the north or south, there were bright clouds and a strip of gamboge-yellow sky, such a colour as you never see even in the rainiest of English sunsets. . . .

And all the time, high overhead and above all these mere side-effects, there was this *celestial geometry* going on. You had to call it 'geometry' because of the perfect circle of this black disc; but above all, it was a *cosmic violence*, a terrific Promethean struggle between light-and-fire, and the bulk and mass of matter. It was the nearest I've ever been to an irresistible force meeting an impenetrable object. And yet I suppose it is going on every day for twenty-four hours a day – only the shadow just exists in empty space. . . .

It's a curious thing: during the minutes of totality while we were on the roof, I felt I *must* say something – like those moments in dreams when you are sure you have suddenly seen some wonderful, significant glimpse of truth: yet when you remember it next morning, it seems to mean nothing. What I succeeded in saying to Atta Gayi was '*There now, Atta! Now you know what we're made of!*'

Two days later, about a quarter past seven in the evening, when I was sitting by the waterside I heard familiar singing which came from somewhere down by the river. I went to call Kwami Agbedanu, 'Kofi has come.' Now we could hear the bumping of their paddles; we waved the hurricane lamp to show them we had heard, and we began to take up their song. They were tired, having left Ada at eleven that morning and paddled most of the way up, though at one place where they had a favourable breeze they had cut a small tree by the riverside as a temporary mast and had hoisted Kofi's cover-cloth as a sail.

During the next few days we all worked on the canoe: we got a friend who had a sewing machine to cut out and hem the grey baft sail; and Kofi reinforced the holes for the ropes with careful double-stitching. We cut ourselves a fine mast, and Atta and Gabriel trimmed it and fixed it. It was only 12 feet (3.5 metres) long, but it looked just right. We also cut another stick to make a yardarm to carry the sail. Atta Gayi made an excellent steering-oar, which enabled us to sail in a side wind without too much drift; and Gabriel stopped up the cracks with his special paste made from burnt lime, cotton lint and red palm oil. We went and loaded it with two cords of firewood. On the return journey we sailed the whole way. I was so elated that I jumped overboard for a swim, and was nearly left behind.

In May, June, and July we mixed experimental clay-bodies, modifying the Vumë clay with substantial additions of the Benso kaolin, or water-ground pegmatite, or calcined water-ground bauxite. Meanwhile Kofi and I were busy making more pots: plates, bowls, beer mugs and large jars, in addition to water-coolers, for which the demand was still as brisk as ever. We fired water-coolers and biscuit early in June, and by the end of that month we were ready for another glaze-firing – our fourth.

As usual the firing took fifty-five to sixty hours. This time I was determined to wait until the pots inside had cooled almost to the temperature of the outside air, mistakenly believing that if an abrupt temperature-shock could be avoided they would not shatter. So we waited almost three weeks before unloading – we had plenty of other things to do while we were waiting. The new body-mixes worked better than the 'straight' clay. This time there were not nearly so many shattered pots, and some of those which came out sound had a more beautiful colour and quality than I had ever thought possible in stoneware. I remember especially some barrel-shaped beer mugs with a beautiful glaze – a rich glowing matt green with persimmon-brown flecks.

Michael Ensor was going home the following month on leave and offered to take a box of pots for Mariel as part of his own baggage, so they could travel free. Next day, he called in on his way from Kéta, picked up the box of pots and went on to Accra. A few days later he would not have been able to get through, because flood water had reached the motor road. The flood-gauge which had been set up beside our landing stage was knocked over on 12 September – the last reading had said 14 feet (4.2 metres). I didn't see it go; when I looked, it was no longer there. A new flood-gauge was set up and was marked up to 20 feet (6 metres). The level of the cement floor in the house was 19 feet (5.7 metres). The flood level was still rising in the north.

On Wednesday, 17 September, I suffered from earache, so I went to bed early. But I was almost immediately woken up by a succession of excruciating pains, striking somewhere deep inside my ear – so deep that there seemed to be no hope of ever reaching them. There would be an interval of perhaps a few minutes and then the needle – or rather knife – would strike again mercilessly, unbearably and without warning. I lay in a sort of panic, apprehending the moment when the torture would return, which it always did, after a few moments during which I had begun to hope it had gone away. All that night it kept returning; but at one point I forced myself to get up from the bed for some sulpha tablets I knew I had. There were eight of these. Having no idea what the proper dose was, I took two. The next day, I lay inert on the bed, and took two more. The stabbing of that knife had stopped; but I still could not get up, or move, or call for help. Friday was the same. I took two more tablets. On Saturday I had only two left; I took one, and on Sunday I took the last one. The only medicine I had now was castor oil. I forced myself to take some of that, and slept intermittently.

By the Tuesday, 23 September, I felt better. I got up and saw that the flood was still rising – 15 feet 8 inches (4.7 metres) now. I walked over to the pottery and painted some small bowls and one big jar. But almost at once I felt sick again. In the evening I had alarming, unpredictable attacks of giddiness and fainting. On Wednesday, the flood-gauge was well over 16 feet (4.8 metres). In the afternoon I waded across to the pottery, where Kofi and Kwami were rebuilding the bag-wall. The way they were doing it made me so furious with them that I crept back to bed again.

When I woke on Thursday, 25 September, I looked across towards the pottery and saw a curiously exotic spectacle. Our canoe, carved out of a great tree and designed to brave the Atlantic Ocean, was being paddled by Kofi among and between the stems of oil palms, and sitting on one of the thwarts was the new District Commissioner, Michael Ensor's successor, whose name was Tony Frank. I immediately took a great fancy to him, partly because he looked fat and happy but chiefly because he liked pots and bought them for the best of all reasons, because he wanted to use them. He had come over to investigate the state of the road; the ferry was still in action, so he was able to get as far as Tefle; and there he had heard that the white potter was lying sick. He bought four pots, which made me feel better at once, and tried to persuade me to go back with him to Kéta so that the doctor there could take a look at me; but by now I was so confident that there was 'nothing much the matter with me' that I declined.

Meanwhile I had had two long letters from Mariel. She had got herself a very good job, as art teacher in the City of London School for Girls; and this, though it meant she would be able to keep the boys at school, also meant that she would have to leave Wenford and live in London. She implored me, yet again, to come home. I wrote back,

> Of course I want to, and will, come home as soon as I can. The choice I had to make in 1945 was a terrible one, and the consequences are and will continue to be terrible; but I go on clinging to the hope that, given time,

this place will be successfully established in the five years which I planned at the beginning; and that in the meantime you will, *somehow*, be able to carry on, and somehow, keep Wenford – because Wenford is our beloved home and symbol of a united family, and therefore to be held on to, for the sake of the boys and all the work we did there. . . .

That decision in 1945, which I can now modify, even drastically, but can't reverse, meant to me two things: first, a chance for me to make pots. The temporary or even permanent (there is always the risk) abandonment of a man's home, wife, children, friends, anything else, can sometimes be necessary if those things happen to be inconsistent with what he has to do. Secondly (a thing nobody recognizes now but I dare say someone may do so some day), it was necessary for me to pay some kind of debt, inside myself, to what you might call the *idea* of H.V. Meyerowitz. He having by his suicide presumably told the world that he no longer believed in his own idea, someone had to pick it up and prove how mistaken he was – supposing that that was what he meant. Or, to put it in a personal instead of a general way, a debt to myself and to Kofi, the repudiation of which I never for a moment contemplated.

Now that that debt is already (perhaps) partly paid, it is easier for me to tell myself I might have evaded it; or compounded for a part of it only; as for example, if I felt such a debt why didn't I give Kofi a part of the money I received, with which he could have set himself up as a potter: then I could have gone straight home in 1945. But that is something I would not do. It cannot ever have been otherwise than it has been and is. This 'debt', or vow, was not to 'set Kofi up as a businessman on his own' (why should I of all people want to do that of all things?) but to teach him and train him truly and thoroughly, as a potter – as the best of all the West African potters. And that is the only way in which I, being the absurd, limited creature I am, can do *the work for which I was called*, in 1941. And that coincided with the best commonsense way of getting on with my own work, which had been at a standstill ever since 1941. . . .

The flood subsided slowly. My ear was no longer painful, but it was stopped-up and more or less continuously thrumming. Whenever I tried to begin any kind of physical activity the thrumming became louder, accompanied by alarming fits of dizziness. It was the end of October before I was able to do any throwing. Then, on 22 November, at the suggestion of Tony Frank, the doctor from Kéta came to Vumë. (It was now more than nine weeks since I had been struck down with this sickness.) He asked many questions, and told me I had had *otitis media*; that it is not normally a disease which kills you, but is quite as serious as, for instance, pneumonia; and that it takes people quite as long to recover from it. He sent me some ear-drops and some tonic.

Two days later, the dry harmattan wind suddenly began to blow; everything began to look more cheerful. On the following Sunday Dodo Nash, who was on the staff of Achimota College and had become an occasional weekend visitor to Vumë, arrived from Achimota with a large party. Among them was Isobel Browne, the new representative at the British Council in Accra, who immediately proposed that she should put on an exhibition of my work at the British Council, in December. I told her that this was absurd, because most of the pots which *should* have been good were shattered, and most of those which were good were already sold to the Union Trading Company. But she insisted. The exhibition did not have to be enormous; the U.T.C. would lend their pots; there could be photographs, and specimens of materials, and documentation about the traditional pottery industry. Before the party left for Accra it was all settled.

On 8 December 1947 I went up to Accra with all the pots I could muster for the Volta Pottery Exhibition. I concocted a few non-committal, colourless words as an introduction to the catalogue.

> This small exhibition of pottery by Michael Cardew has been selected from the first year's output of the Volta Pottery which he founded in October 1945. The pottery is at Vumë, a village on the Lower Volta long known for the great quality of its native water pots.
>
> Volta Pottery was planned as an experiment to explore the possibility of establishing a small local industry on a permanent basis. It is a purely private enterprise and makes no attempt at establishing a large-scale industry.

I also wrote, to accompany the exhibition, a thing which I called 'Why Don't You Make White Plates?', a curious defensive document which I began by saying that 'This is by far the most frequently asked question I hear at Vumë', and in which I tried to vindicate what to my critics probably seemed a pig-headed prejudice in favour of Oriental ways of making porcelain and stone-ware, against the methods used in England in the industrial manufacture of tableware. I explained how industrial methods of plate-making differ from those of a craft potter – or an ancient Chinese potter. The methods first introduced by Josiah Wedgwood in the eighteenth century were designed to minimize the hazards of plate-making. The jigger and jolley was used in place of the potter's wheel, as jiggering is faster than throwing and turning, and requires less skill. But the really revolutionary innovation was to give the ware a bisque fire at a temperature (usually above 1150°C) considerably higher than that of the subsequent glost fire. The plates kept their shape in the glost fire, because the high-temperature bisque fire had stabilized them. By contrast, in the method used by the Chinese and by continental European plate-makers, the plates were given a low-temperature biscuit firing and then dipped in a porcelain glaze which required a much higher fire; the body became pyro-plastic in the same temperature range at which the glaze melted, and it was therefore much more likely to warp if there was any fault in the throwing (or jiggering).

I stated that my chief objection to the factory plate-making system was that it 'killed the beauty of the ware'. In glazed pottery more than half of the beauty lies in the material and the reaction between the glaze and the clay. In the Chinese method, both of them undergo changes during the final firing, and therefore act upon each other. Part of the clay dissolves into the liquid glaze and slightly modifies its character; and the glaze etches the surface of the clay. Plates which have received the industrial treatment enjoy very little of this commerce or intercourse between glaze and clay; the glaze is like a thin coating of varnish over an inert ground of hard, unyielding fired clay. The only beauty that can come to this kind of plate has to be added on afterwards, in the form of colour and decoration, and at best is only skin-deep, not arising naturally from the way the materials are used.

I doubt whether many, black or white, read this manifesto. But the exhibition itself was a success, though it was open for only two days, 22 and 23 December. Almost all the pots were sold, and we took lots of orders. On the first day, just as people were beginning to leave, dear Dodo Nash came up to me and pushed a fat envelope into my hand, saying, 'Now take care of this, and you mustn't open it till you reach home.' When I opened it, I found inside £30 in £1 notes, and a touching letter from Mr Joseph, one of the senior masters at Achimota College – a Sinhalese, whom I hardly knew.

Achimota, 20 December 1947

Dear Cardew,

When some of your friends heard that there was to be a small exhibition of your pottery at the British Council House, they resolved to give you a surprise in return for the great pleasure and joy you are providing them.

For long we have admired your Art and your Craft. We know how unkind fate has been to you in all your endeavours to produce the best work with local clay under the most trying conditions.

We have decided to present this Christmas gift to you as a mark of our genuine appreciation of your art, in the earnest hope that our little offering will enable you to get home as quickly as possible, for the rest you so richly have earned.

On behalf of all your friends,

A.H.R. Joseph

Whenever I think, as I often do, of the kindness shown to me, not only by friends but sometimes by total strangers, at times when I have been sick, or unfortunate, or homeless, I am speechless with gratitude for people's goodness: especially that of people in Ghana.

On the second and final day of the exhibition I left Accra in the evening, for Vumë. The journey was typical. Our lorry left at 5.30 p.m., but only went about three miles before being stopped by a flat tyre. We finally reached Vumë at 11.30: six hours to cover less than seventy miles. No wonder it seemed a different world. Kofi and the other pottery people – Atta Gayi, Kwami Agbedanu, Karimu Busanga – gave me a lovely reception on my return from Accra; they gave me Christmas presents, and improvised a touching song of welcome. How beautiful and yet how confusing life was. I knew I must go home fairly soon, and yet I wanted to stay; or if I went away, to come back again. Kofi used a formula whenever he was going away, but intending to be back soon, 'I will go and come.'

22

DISTURBANCES

I was now in good health again, and all went well until, on 21 January 1948, the day we lighted up the kiln for another glaze-firing, I began again to have pain and inflammation in my ear. This time the pain was not so intense, nor so frightening, and I managed to keep going until, on the fifth day, it drove me to bed again. I was lucky: that very day, the doctor happened to call at Vumë, took one look at the ear and told me to go to Accra for treatment.

In the bed next to mine at the hospital was a young white man, who had been working for one of the mines in the Western Province. His conversation, which was unending, was amusing up to a point; it seemed to be that of an extremely naïve and open-minded adolescent; but little by little I began to recognize that most of what he was saying did not make any sense at all. Not having had any previous experience of mental disorders I had listened to him as if he was a normal person who seemed to have somehow kept open some of the windows which established, 'normal' citizens take care to keep shut. This made his conversation amusing and even fascinating, until he began to tell you about all the diamonds he had picked out of the gravel and was going to take home with him.

Next day, they put him on an aeroplane for London. The patient in the bed on my other side was explaining to the male nursing attendant what was the matter with the unfortunate youth: he was suffering from something he pronounced with special care: 'scripturephrenia'. Giving thanks that my own trouble was merely a small disturbance among the members of the crew and not a sudden failure of the man at the helm, I emerged from the hospital and went down to the lorry station in Accra to look for a truck back to Vumë, and was met there by a miracle. As I waited, my ears were greeted by the sound of the third movement of Mozart's Quintet for piano and wind instruments. It was my favourite work and I had never heard it performed. I found it more than twenty-five years before, in the Holywell Music Room Library in Oxford when I was looking for clarinet music by Mozart; but I had long ago given up hope of ever hearing it played. It seemed specially wonderful that the dream should have come true in, of all places on earth, the lorry station at

Accra; a result made possible by the proliferation of records during the years just after the war, plus the necessity for radio stations to fill up time with music. During that last period of colonialism the radio stations were partly manned by highly cultivated Europeans who, whenever they saw the chance, put good music on the air, on the excellent principle that it did them good to hear it and could not possibly do active harm to the local listeners.

On that visit to Accra I heard a good deal about the boycott of European goods which had been going on more or less since the new year began. This was partly commercial, partly political. The war had now been over for nearly three years and still supplies of imported goods were unequal to the demand. A buyers' boycott was organized. This proved an effective protest against the shortages; it also built up a tremendous hunger for imported goods which could be, and was used for the political purpose – which was, of course, to achieve self-government and independence for Ghana. The people who pursued this aim most actively were the newly returned demobilized soldiers who had been recruited during the war for service in India, and Burma; in these countries they met like-minded Indians and Burmese and began to have 'dangerous thoughts'. Both India and Burma had now achieved their independence. Why not West Africa?

Back in Vumë, my ear cured, I started to make a run of two hundred soup pots with lids, a popular line with the Europeans in Accra. We opened the glaze-firing we had had before I went to Accra. It was an improvement on our previous record: some of my new bodies came out well, including some pots which are still extant.

On Sunday, 29 February, Kofi came in with news, brought by lorry drivers, that rioting on a large scale had started in Accra; the whole town was said to be a scene of shooting, looting and murder. At 7 p.m., when I as usual was practising the recorder in the bungalow, Kofi came in with more tales of rioting and violence in Accra. At 9 p.m. I went over to my bed in the pottery. Two hours later I awoke out of a miserable nightmare about what was going on in Accra, and twice again before dawn I was woken up by evil dreams full of a sort of generalized vision of the ugliness of what was happening. When the first glimmer of dawn appeared I got up and went back to the bungalow. The door had been forced open and most of my belongings had been taken, including my beloved Dolmetsch recorder (made in 1926 and acquired by me in the same year), which I had left lying on the bed after cleaning it the night before.

At Kofi's suggestion I made a list of the things I had lost, and he took it along to the police at Sogankope. About an hour later the clerk of the local government court and a Native Administration policeman arrived. As soon as they entered the bedroom they began to look serious, because the strong green American-army mosquito net that hung over the bed had been slashed with a cutlass right down the middle. This suggested to the clerk and the policeman that the intruders' first act had been, not to help themselves to any property they found, but to assail the body of whoever was sleeping on the bed. They roundly declared that the raiders might have taken loot, but were chiefly out for blood. 'I wonder', says my diary.

Personally, I prefer to imagine that the intruders, failing to find money or anything much worth taking, had slashed the mosquito net as a parting gesture of frustrated vindictiveness. In any case, I did feel quite glad that I had not been in the house to confront them.

Happily, the recorder was discovered by two little boys, under a culvert on the roadway between the bungalow and the motor road, quite unharmed and still wrapped in its piece of Assam silk and the small Hausa cotton loincloth which was what I wore when I was throwing. I think the raiders must have decided that this primitive musical instrument belonged to the Hausa night-watchman employed by the Europeans. There were also a few other belongings of mine which had been left behind on the same principle, that no white man could possibly be the owner of such things: for instance, two extremely thick and heavy shirts, which Mariel had made out of some Irish flannel.

The young Chief at Vumë came to see me, in a state of great concern, and agreed with the others that I must give up sleeping in my bed in the pottery. There was a nice bedroom in his house which I could occupy and he, meanwhile, would spread a rumour that I had gone away.

I learned later that the sequence of events in Accra had been more or less as follows. On Saturday, 28 February, a group of ex-servicemen marched through the streets of Accra. They turned then towards Christiansborg Castle, the Governor's Residence, intending to present their demands to the Governor. (These demands, for example for dominion status for Ghana, seem today to be perfectly level-headed, reasonable proposals.) At a road junction on the way they were stopped by police. When it became obvious that they were not going to be turned back by peaceful persuasion, a police officer, a white man, in a fatal moment of panic fired his gun. Two of the marchers were killed and several others wounded. (The spot where this took place is marked now by a monument erected by Kwame Nkrumah, Ghana's first Prime Minister, to commemorate the moment and the event which signalled the coming of Ghanaian independence.)

After the shot had been fired, the column of protesters turned back towards the town; and *simultaneously* (it was maintained by the police) the looting began there. Was the complete breakdown of civil order in Accra the consequence and result of that fatal shot on the Christiansborg Road (as the African Nationalists maintained); or had the looting been planned in advance (as the case for the Government and the police maintained)? The looting, the police said, began either before the shot was fired, or so soon after that it could not have been anything but a previously agreed response to an expected signal. The defence replied that an outbreak of lawlessness on such a scale could only be the result of the dreadful crime which had been committed on the Christiansborg Road.

When the last shop had been looted and the rage of the people had temporarily burnt itself out, something which is called Law and Order was eventually restored. The Government named four politicians as being responsible for the outbreak, and invented for their peculiar benefit Preventive Detention, which provided for their being tried in the Courts without the necessity for arresting them on any specific charges. One of these men was Dr Danquah (Meyerowitz's old friend) – the most improbable of all villains; another was Kwame Nkrumah, at that time a name new to British ears. The other two I have forgotten.

They hired an English barrister, who defended them so successfully that at the end of the trial when the verdict was declared, the people of Accra carried him shoulder-high in triumph through the streets. About a year later, I had the good luck to meet this barrister, Mr Dingle Foot, who was standing as Liberal Candidate for the Bodmin division: I exclaimed in my confusion, 'You must be the man who was carried shoulder-high through the streets of Accra!' 'Yes,' he said, 'but don't tell that to the Law Society.'

Dingle Foot went on to tell me how the affair had struck him. Three of the defendants, he said, were simply well-meaning academics, no possible threat to anyone or anything. 'But the fourth, Kwame Nkrumah, is obviously a very able man, and a real threat to anyone who thinks colonies should not be liberated.'

The 'Accra Disturbances' of 1948, as they came to be called, were a true watershed. From 1948 on, the thinking of white men in West Africa, and of the infinitely more powerful white men in governments and big businesses in Europe, underwent a salutary change. West African independence, from having been thought of merely as a distant consummation, devoutly to be wished of course, but always to be indefinitely postponed, now dominated their thinking: from then on, all policies had to be judged by the criterion of whether they contributed to that end. The hard heart of big business, especially, saw not only how necessary but how desirable that end was. Did not the United States of America enjoy, in Liberia, all the advantages of 'owning' a colony with none of the expense and responsibilities and above all, none of the odium in which colonies involved you? (All through the Second World War England had been abused as a colony-exploiting Kettle by the lily-white Pots across the Atlantic.)

The main effect of those events on me personally, was that they cured me of any romantic attachment I may have had to philosophical anarchism. It is a doctrine with a natural appeal to all who call themselves artists. Artists suffer more than most people from all the machinery of government, such as filling out forms, or paying taxes; but their sufferings are more temperamental than substantial.

Politics is a coarse kind of work, but necessary; and therefore we pay politicians well, in both money and fame, for doing our dirty work for us. An artist is a person whose most important desire is to be allowed to get on with his work without interruption; and the great merit of government is that it provides a reliable framework, the function of which, from your point of view, is to enable you to conduct your life without having it interrupted at unexpected or inconvenient times by (for instance) irrelevant interviews with angry armed men. From an artist's point of view government is a necessary evil. It is not part of his responsibilities to take part in it: he has other responsibilities, of quite a different kind. If we are artists our time is best spent getting on with our own work, leaving the world to sort itself out as it has always sorted itself out – even when it transparently aims to allow the rich to flourish at the expense of the poor.

John Milton would have called this an ignoble philosophy, a case of preferring 'bondage with ease' to 'strenuous liberty'. But ease hardly enters the question. It is more a case of accepting a certain amount of bondage as a condition of being allowed to go on doing your work – the alternative being, to be prevented or hindered from doing it at all.

In Vumë we quietly went on potting. On 29 April we fired the kiln again. It was a fifty-one hour firing, and seemed quite normal. On the last day of the firing, the rainy season began: from 9 a.m. heavy rain soaked all our dry firewood and we had to bring it to the kiln through mud and water. I was afraid this would spoil the fire, but it made no difference. The wetter the wood we put into the fireboxes, the more the temperature rose. It was my first experience of something the scientific explanation of which I did not then understand, and did not grasp consciously until several years later. If the temperature in the fireboxes is above 1150°C, the surface water from the wet wood is decomposed or dissociated to become water gas, a combustible gas which produces as much heat energy as is absorbed or lost by the introduction of wet wood.

Even in that wet weather, which always in the tropics makes kilns cool more quickly, it took nearly three weeks before the first chamber could be unpacked. But we were able to open the second chamber in only two. I had been noticing for some time that the temperature near the bottom of this chamber sometimes went up as high as 1150°C or more, so this time I had tried the experiment of putting two or three bungs of saggars with glazed ware in this part of the chamber, where they were underdone but pleasing. When we unpacked the first chamber we found (as usual) plenty of trouble. I had made coffee pots, cups and saucers from an experimental body; but it was no good: they all came out shattered (and such lovely colours!). This was the last firing I had at Vumë, and in spite of the shattering it was the most promising we had had, and it tantalized me to think I was leaving very soon, just when the prospects seemed at last to be propitious, suggesting we were on the brink of success.

Towards the end of May I went to Accra and bought myself a cheap ticket to England on a boat called the *Empire Bure*, which was to sail about 5 July. On 30 June we had a farewell feast for all the pottery people and our friends at Vumë. The next day Kofi and I went by lorry to Accra, where we did some business at the bank and last-minute shopping, and joined 'Adra's Government Transport Bus'. It was my first ride in this vehicle since the fateful and ever-memorable day of my first setting foot in Ghana when I had travelled from Takoradi to Achimota almost exactly six years before.

The Empire Bure, a very old troop ship, was packed tight. The troops, mostly white with a few African N.C.O.'s, were in the forecastle. In our cabin, which had been designed originally for two passengers, ten men had been packed, two of them so fat that it felt like twelve. There was a group of Palestine Police, who had no doubt been hastily summoned a few months before, at the time of the Accra Disturbances: tough people mostly from Northern Ireland. Their leader, Hamish Dougan, somehow reminded me of an early photograph of Baudelaire I had once seen: the bright intelligence, the frustrated sensuality, the same rueful smile. He described himself as a 'natural mercenary'. There was a rabble of railwaymen from Nigeria, our self-appointed entertainers. There was one solitary District Officer from Northern Nigeria, very young, who had an indefinable but vaguely aristocratic resemblance to a horse.

The nights in our overcrowded cabin were claustrophobic. One morning I woke about 5 a.m. to find that we had dropped anchor. Though it was still dark I went on deck, up to the bows of the ship, and stayed watching the dawn and the morning star, until at about 6.30 the anchor was hauled up and the ship began its cautious zigzagging way into Bathurst harbour in a trading, dry, north-west wind. We did not stay long enough for us to land; and that same night we saw on our starboard horizon the lights of Dakar, our last view of West Africa.

One night I dreamed about Kofi. He had grown quite middle-aged, and had a large family, all very plump and prosperous. When I looked again in my dream, he had turned into a white man, asking me where he could buy some petrol. I explained to myself, while still asleep, that he was just trying out what it felt like to be a white man. I woke with that familiar ancient grief clutching yet again at my throat; and wept helplessly, in silence, as if at that moment he had sent out some kind of SOS. I got up and went on deck; there was the faintest glimmer of dawn beginning in the east.

We had left the tropics. It seemed to have happened quite suddenly. The sea, with a stiff north-easterly breeze, became rough, the colour of dark blue enamel, with crests of spray on the waves. Some people were seasick. Rather to my surprise, I found I was feeling extremely well. (I was not used to this feeling.) We saw the Gran Canaria in the distance, high and huge, more like a cloud than any solid land. One evening, the entertainment consisted of a piano recital (Mendelssohn, Chopin, Liszt). Sandwiched between these, the pianist insisted I should play the Handel Sonata in C major for recorder, a sonata by Marcello, and the voice part of Bach's 'Jesu, Joy of Man's Desiring'. The audience was large, and attentive.

On Monday, 19 July, Scilly was sighted: and at 6.30 that evening the coast of Cornwall could be seen on our starboard quarter.

Next day we tied up in Liverpool at about 7 p.m. It was a most beautiful evening: greys on greys everywhere, the sky, the water, the town, the buildings, the smoke, the tugs in the harbour. Lights came on one by one.

We got off the ship about 9 a.m. on Wednesday, 21 July. When I went into the Customs Shed there was Mariel. She ran up to me and gave me a hug and a kiss such that all the rules and regulations of H.M. Customs and Excise were happy to yield before her.

23

BACK
IN ENGLAND

We were able to catch an early train to London. At Euston we hired a taxi (an unheard-of luxury) to take us and all my loads to my brother Philip's house in Regent's Park Terrace. We left the baggage with him, and went on to Fleet Street and down Carmelite Street, past the *Daily Mail* and the *Evening Standard* and the stand-up and sit-down cafés used by the humbler employees of newspapers, to where, incongruously in that environment, the City of London School for Girls lived at that time. Here Mariel taught art. We took the underground to Stepney Green Station, and walked to her cosy, wonderfully cheap and beautiful lodgings in a house in Rectory Square, in which two old ladies and several cats lived. Both of these ladies were deaf; they communicated by shouting at each other, so that the whole house reverberated, whenever they addressed casual – and usually cryptic – remarks to one another.

On Sunday, 25 July, Seth, our eldest boy, came up for the day from his school in Sussex, and we went together to Canterbury to see Cornelius (then, at the age of twelve, at the peak of his early career as a choirboy) and Ennis, who had come to Canterbury from his boarding school not far away. All through the Vumë years I had written letters to them with fair regularity; but three years is an eternity at that age; especially to Ennis, who even now was not quite ten. Yet it was he who had expressed most interest in 'Africa', and asked me for the numerals in the Ewe language, and 'What is Africa really like?' And I used to tell him about the crocodiles, and some of my adventures with snakes. All this had made me feel I was quite close to him, but I realized now that from his point of view I had become a stranger. When I saw him I said cheerfully, 'You see, I did come back at last!' But his reply, in a glum and accusing tone, was 'Can't think why you ever went away in the first place.'

The present incomprehension was a consequence of that distancing of myself from my family which had become necessary when I left them in 1942. I was sorry at the incomprehension, but I did not for a single moment regret that hard decision.

I spent two days in London, looking for some gallery in which to exhibit the few pots I had brought from Vumë. The Berkeley Gallery in Davis Street sounded promising, but the proprietor, Mr Ohly, was out when I called. I had an introduction to Liberty's in Regent Street, but one interview there convinced me that that was out of the question. I went to see (or be interviewed by) Sir Robin Darwin at the Royal College of Art. I was kept waiting for a suitable length of time before being admitted into his presence. When I got there, he told me bluntly that he had no place for me in the new régime he was setting up. I went out and wept quietly in the gallery for a few minutes. Then I pulled myself together, and went over to the Geological Museum across the street and began to instruct myself about zircon and how to recognize it, next time I met it.

The first few days back in Cornwall were occupied with slowly unpacking the various treasures I had brought home – West African textiles, red morocco goatskins, leather purses and similar things.

A fine August is one of the most beautiful months in Cornwall, even though one has to share it with far too many of one's fellow creatures. Every morning I got up mentally singing to myself a new tune for the words which continually welled up inside me, 'My cup runneth over'. The three boys and I went out in a hired boat from Port Gaverne to celebrate Ennis's tenth birthday. We rowed until we were out of sight of land and then we all jumped into the deep water.

I was taking a new delight in the contemplation of our house, which had been ours now for nearly ten years. Especially the details. Every time I entered our little box-like bedroom I stood spellbound, gazing at the window. I had somehow learnt to appreciate the medium, the window itself and the way the small panes were separated by their delicate, nicely fitted wooden frame, and to realize the craftsmanship which had been put into it. There was nothing very special about it, or about the house itself, a typical early-nineteenth-century Cornish cottage. The windows themselves were typical of such houses, slightly taller than their width, and each divided into sixteen small panes. The glass in those panes was slightly irregular in its surface so that it was immediately recognizable as glass, and yet sufficiently regular that it did not seriously distort the shapes of what you saw through it; seen from the outside, the windows reflected the light in a lively way, instead of the black, empty stare of death-like eyes which modern buildings usually present to the world. The beauty of the man-made landscape depends on these small things, the hands of unknown craftsmen working on small particular details everywhere, just as the beauty of the natural scene comes from unseen, minute particulars: from the subdued purple of innumerable unopened alder catkins or the drab

velvet of the hazel tree just before the annual arrival of the moment when, like
Jupiter courting Danae, they turn into a shower of gold.

If that bedroom window at Wenford seems to have led me astray, it is
because at that particular time in my life it recalled me to the true roots and true
nature of our European civilization as opposed to the impoverished version of
it which we exported to West Africa. A white man going there suffered the
(largely unconscious) deprivation of those everyday contacts with his own
past, the small, seemingly unimportant details of craftsmanship which are a
part of daily living and which are neither missed, nor truly valued, until you
come home from a world where, though they exist in great abundance, they
are in forms which are not yours, and therefore cannot speak to you in your
own language.

None of our efforts to find a gallery willing to exhibit my small collection of
pots made in Vumë had met with any success. But I managed to persuade
Philip to let me use what he grandly called the saloon of his house. It consisted
of two fine rooms rolled into one, on the first floor or, as he preferred to call it,
the *piano nobile*. To accompany the exhibition we produced a printed folder
with photographs of the best pots, and, on the cover a snapshot of the pottery
and kiln. I wrote a short introduction about the Volta Pottery, Vumë, which is
dated November 1948. I saw this exhibition and its accompanying folder as a
kind of manifesto addressed to the Establishment – hoping that if they would
deign to take notice of what I had been trying to do in the past three years,
under conditions of such difficulty and against such odds, they might have
second thoughts, and once again begin to smile upon the cause of pottery in
West Africa.

Now, all these years later, I am able to admit it: to say that the Volta Pottery,
Vumë, was a failure. The years at Vumë were the long, necessary, testing
apprenticeship I had to serve to pottery in West Africa, in order to fit myself,
later on, to succeed there. The pottery at Vumë is now a totally abandoned
ruin. Yet it represents a moral foundation without which I would not have
been able, a few years later, to steer a more or less successful course in Nigeria.

But in 1948 I would never have agreed that the pottery at Vumë was a
failure. I was not going to take refuge in saying that the point of it was in the
trying, not in the success. It had got to succeed, in order to prove what it
was founded to prove: namely, that a small country pottery in a place like
Vumë was (unlike the too-large pottery at Alajo) sure to succeed provided it
was nursed carefully during its infancy and was allowed to grow at its natural
pace.

I can see now that there were two major factors in the failure of the pottery at
Vumë. The first of these was the old complaint of potters in Ghana, poor raw

materials. In the course of time I might have evolved a sufficiently plastic body-mix which did not shatter; but it was evidently a fatal mistake to have settled on Vumë in such haste. Carried away by the beauty of the place and of the pots which were being made there, I had left to chance the important question: was there a satisfactory source of refractory clay in the neighbour-hood? This is the kind of sloppy mistake which can wreck a scheme in West Africa.

But in the eyes of people who knew little or nothing about technical matters such as these, the main reason for my failure was (as they would have expressed it) that I 'did not have what it takes' to carry such an enterprise through. I was always falling sick; and if you want to succeed in an enterprise like this, *that won't do.* You need to have what used to be called an 'iron constitution', a higher than normal immunity to most of the ailments to which most people are subject. The failure of great enterprises usually comes, not from an inadequacy of talents or brains in those who undertake them (the end, and the means to it, may have been well seen and properly thought out), but in the brute animal texture or strength of the organism of individual human flesh and blood which undertakes it.

The main thing I brought home with me from the pottery at Vumë was an unquestioning determination that I must return there. I could not leave it unfinished. What it needed, even more than money, was perseverance, and of that I felt I had an inexhaustible supply in myself. I was old enough to know I only had one life, of strictly limited duration, and only enough energy to shape the years ahead, if I stuck to one ruling purpose. In the case of some of my early friends I had seen that the prodigal dispersion of energies which people enjoy in their early twenties may (if one does not have clear, or clearly formulated, aims) be prolonged almost indefinitely – into their forties, fifties, sixties; until, sitting in the late afternoon sun of their life, they realize (too late now to change) that they have been the victims of a romantic view of their own youth, having allowed themselves to follow a variety of interests for short spells, rather than to pursue one aim in depth. No doubt it is a choice which everyone makes for himself according to his temperament; but I always felt an appre-hension lest my life slip away year after year, or decade after decade, and leave me with my one narrowly focused aim still unrealized.

When I was a student at Oxford about 1920, the highest term of praise that my friends and I ever gave anyone, whether he was an artist or a fellow-student or a writer, was 'brilliant' ('So-and-so: *brilliant* man!'); and even at that time I had discovered a fact about myself: I was not at all brilliant. Yet I felt that there was inside me something which, if I could cultivate it, might eventually prove to be as good, or better. Now, after about fifteen or twenty years of that cultivation, I found that critics were still writing the same language ('Mr X, one of our most *brilliant* potters . . .'). How could they bear to allow themselves to go on writing at all, handicapped as they were by this unerring instinct for using the inappropriate word? – mistaking, in this case, where artists are concerned, the part for the whole – and a less-than-essential part. Leonardo da Vinci, Mozart, Picasso . . . certainly they were brilliant; but the important thing about them is not their brilliance but their greatness. Of some other artists – Blake, for example, or Van Gogh – nobody would have used the word brilliant: nothing came easily to them; they had to fight for every inch of their progress, all their lives. Similarly, I knew I was not a brilliant potter, but I thought I might become a good one if I worked hard enough. For three years now all those efforts had been directed to starting the pottery at Vumë, and I was not going to be easily or quickly persuaded to change course.

Above all, Vumë was, in defiance of all logic, part of what I called my 'destiny'. I could not then, and cannot now, define what I meant by destiny; but contrary to all the arguments which proved there was no such thing, in spite of everything that common sense or my friends could say, I still believed in its reality and was bound, hand and foot, to follow it.

POSTSCRIPT

There, apart from some notes for later chapters, my father left his memoirs, when he died. These unwritten chapters were to tell of his return to West Africa, and of the years after he came back to England. Except for visits, he did not return to the pottery at Vumë. But in 1951 he went to Nigeria, as Pottery Officer of the Nigerian Department of Commerce and Industry. At Abuja in Nigeria he built and ran a successful pottery with West African potters, achieving what had been his aim since his first arrival in West Africa in 1942. Then, in 1965, at the age of sixty-four, he returned to England.

His later years were divided between making pots at Wenford Bridge Pottery, writing, and teaching and demonstrating both at home and abroad. (He made extensive lecture tours in the United States, Canada, Australia and New Zealand.) His demonstrations became his chief interest. He would officiate at the wheel, a priest at an altar to clay, making pronouncements on the universality of form and proclaiming lines from Greek and Latin poetry (with English translations for the benefit of unlearned potters). His brown apron, the brown clay and slurry and the great pot revolving and growing under the spotlight made an indelible impression on his audiences.

He left some sketched notes on subjects which the book as it stands does not cover in detail. I think he would have wished that two in particular should be mentioned.

The first concerns his relationship with Mariel. In his account of their Irish 'honeymoon' he refers to the two of them as 'Babes in the Wood'. So, in their relationship to each other, they remained: in a world of dark and hostile adult forces they preserved a child-like innocence. Living in the same house became increasingly difficult and then impossible for them; but this does not nullify their relationship. He was a man's man and she a woman's woman. In an extended family situation, these tensions can be resolved: he works with his men and she with her women. In the years at Winchcombe this was how things were. Soul-searchings about 'retaining one's personal integrity' and 'developing the capacity for a profound relationship' came later, when there were fewer people around; and the two propositions came to seem irreconcilable. My mother, with passionate loyalty, preserved his image as a great man in our minds as children, while he was away, referring to him as the Master, and weeping openly if she broke one of his pots by mistake.

Another thread that was not thoroughly woven into the fabric of the memoirs as they stand, was my father's profound love and understanding of music. He venerated especially the music of Mozart and Handel. He recalled the impression the Mozart Tenor Trio no. 7 made on him as a child – 'going through me like a knife'. When as an adult he came back from Africa to Cornwall in a state of mental turmoil, there were his growing children performing the same work under the devoted supervision of his beloved brother Philip. When he had recovered his composure he took his Dolmetsch treble recorder and joined in with us, playing the Handel Trios. This love of music was one of the noumena behind the forms that emerged when he was working at the potter's wheel.

Seth Cardew

APPENDIX I

ON ART IN WEST AFRICA

Early in 1946 the British Council asked me for my written comments on Leon Underwood's report 'Art in West Africa'. The comments I produced, set out below, interest me now because they show that the ideas about West African arts which I developed later had already begun to take shape in 1946.

As I see it, the only things that can be done about the Native Traditional Pottery are:

1 Leave it alone! Don't *tamper* with it, technically or artistically.

2 In cases where this is possible, discreetly try to *divert* it from what you consider to be false trails. (If this is 'tampering', it is at least a negative kind of tampering.)

3 Use the pots, wherever they are useful, and encourage their use by others.

4 Hold them up as inspiration for the forms and decorations used in more 'advanced' techniques, just as contemporary potters and designers draw inspiration from the Neolithic, Prehistoric and Protohistoric pottery of Europe, Central Asia, the Near and Far East or Ancient Mexico.

Resistance to Thermal Shock   A special property of the traditional pottery is that you can make a wood fire under the belly of a large pot and boil water in it without cracking it. Ordinary glazed earthenware and hard-fired stoneware and porcelain sacrifice this for other desirable properties (e.g., mechanical strength, non-porosity, glazed surface).

Art   Underwood speaks of 'Art in Africa' rather than 'African Art'. Talk of 'African' as opposed to 'European' art is misleading. Art is simply art. Artists and critics in Europe are now trying to recapture and reintegrate into our own arts the spontaneity, vigour, rhythm and harmony which is found in 'primitive' and prehistoric form and expression. The significance of this movement is proved by the sincerity and conviction of its spokesmen. What a few pioneers think and feel now will be felt and thought by most people tomorrow. It is possible that in some spheres West Africans will have to go through some at least of the painful evolutionary stages that we others underwent in the past; but in the arts, the people with the lightest burden of 'historical background' (as at present understood in the West) may be able to pass in a single step into the climate of the present day and of the future.

Fine Art, and Applied Arts   The key to Underwood's findings is that Fine Art (or Absolute Art) is the nurse and protector of all the so-called Applied Arts – i.e., those which cover the whole range of things of practical use whose essential character depends on form, proportion, rhythm, colour, pattern, texture – in a word on humane design and quality. If among a people so richly endowed as West Africans this quality begins to decline, that is due to the religious inspiration having fallen out of their 'Fine' Arts.

Art and Religion   More space might have been given to a point raised by many (both Africans and Europeans) on several occasions. In its most extreme form it was expressed by a well-known English collector of art objects from the Gold Coast, as follows:

He said that the influence of West African arts on the style of many eminent modern artists in Europe was an irrelevancy, the result of a purely intellectual approach completely divorced from the spirit of genuine primitive art; which was always religious – the making of ritual objects the significance of which, for us, is 'purely anthropological'; and that the necessity for this art must disappear as and when African artists discard their ancestral religious systems.

The same point was raised at one of Leon Underwood's lectures in Achimota by a practising African artist. He said, in effect, 'But what are we to do? The old examples you show us were ritual objects with a definite religious meaning for a definite place in a shrine. If we are discarding our former religious beliefs, how can such objects have any meaning, and how can we produce them with any real conviction?'

The proper answer, which Underwood produced briefly at the time but did not develop sufficiently, is that *all* true art is religious. The particular ritual setting is only incidental. The significance of art is universal and transcends the frameworks in which it was produced. When during the same lecture he let fall the remark that 'a second-rate artist is no better than a tenth-rate artist', he was making the same point, namely that art properly understood has room only for what is first-rate – that is, for what is authentic, original, genuine, creative. In a word, art always requires genius of some kind. (When Eric Gill said 'Every man is a special sort of artist', he was saying, not that genius is equal in everybody, but that some sort of genius is universally shared – everybody has it in some form or other.)

In West Africa, art has not yet been separated from ordinary life; it is still the air that everyone unconsciously breathes. Every man and woman is by nature a poet, a stylist, an aesthete, though outsiders like ourselves may sometimes disagree with or disapprove of the ways in which it is expressed. West Africans do not need to make a cult of art – still less, of what we call 'good taste' – because they live with it all the time and, unlike ourselves, have not made the mistake of treating it as a separate 'department'.

ACHIMOTA COLLEGE AND THE WEST AFRICAN INSTITUTE

Achimota College, formally opened in 1927, was the brain-child of the then Governor and Commander-in-Chief of the Gold Coast (now Ghana), Sir Frederick Gordon Guggisberg. The College was a co-educational, non-denominational, highly selective boarding school which included a kinder-garten and junior school as well as the main secondary school and a teacher training college. It was from the start a privileged school training an African élite, and it was granted a large proportion of the Gold Coast educational budget. From 1930 it was run virtually independently by its own Achimota Council, which prided itself on having at least six African representatives on a Council of fifteen members. The College combined Western educational methods with the study of local customs, laws, languages, geography and flora and fauna, but its success was perhaps due less to this acclaimed African element in the curriculum than to the high quality of its staff and its superior resources. In many ways – for instance, the emphasis on organized games – Achimota reproduced the spirit of an English public school.

In 1936 the then Principal of Achimota, the Reverend H. M. Grace, appointed Herbert Vladimir Meyerowitz as the College's art supervisor. Meyerowitz was a product of the German Kunstgewerbeschule system and an admirer of the theories of the educationalist Franz Cisek. When he came to the Gold Coast he had already written an enlightened report on the arts and crafts of Basutoland (Lesotho) based on a survey carried out in 1935 (*A Report on the Possibilities of the Development of Village Crafts in Basutoland*, Morija Printing Works, 1936). On his arrival at Achimota in 1936 he and his wife Eva (who was also to join the College staff) went on a tour of the Gold Coast to survey the indigenous crafts. They found that many skills described by R. S. Rattray in his 1927 classic *Religion and Art in Ashanti* were in decline. At Achimota Meyerowitz swiftly replaced academic painting and drawing classes based on a Western view of art historical development by an arts and crafts approach, drawing on local skills and materials.

As his autobiography records, Michael Cardew had met Meyerowitz when the latter was in England in 1936, just before taking up his post at Achimota.

Later that year Cardew recommended Harry Davis as a suitable potter to run ceramics classes at the College. This appointment was part of Meyerowitz's expansion of the College's art department.

When, in the wake of political unrest in 1938, Grace decided that a research body was needed to study every aspect of Gold Coast life, he had the enthusiastic support of Meyerowitz. From Meyerowitz's point of view the Institute envisaged by Grace would serve to record and conserve native crafts while simultaneously introducing apprentices to modern technology.

By 1939 the school pottery had expanded and Davis was producing bricks and tiles at Achimota and was able to provide for the rebuilding programme following the 1939 Accra earthquake. In 1941 Davis decided to leave the Gold Coast and Cardew agreed to replace him. He arrived in Achimota in September 1942. By then Meyerowitz had formulated plans for a much larger pottery and tileworks at Alajo, some distance from the college. Cardew explains that the Second World War altered the emphasis of the projected Institute. Meyerowitz's belief that the Alajo pottery and tileworks could supply the needs of all West Africa, including those of the army, fitted in with the need for West Africa to become self-supporting as part of the war effort. Meyerowitz broadcast on this theme on Gold Coast Government radio in 1942; this was later published as *The Making of Things*, Sheldon Press, 1942.

In November 1942 Harry Davis left Africa, convinced that the huge expansion of the pottery at Alajo would pose enormous technical problems. In 1943 the College Bursar at Achimota announced losses of £2,000 at the tileworks, but that year the Colonial Development Fund voted £127,000 for the Institute, now officially known as the West African Institute of Arts, Industries and Social Sciences, partly on the understanding that the tileworks would make a profit and help further fund the Institute. It continued to make a loss, and as Cardew records, relations between the College and the Institute soured. The highly literate, educated products of Achimota who came as apprentices to the pottery and tileworks found little to admire in Cardew's studio pottery approach with its artisanal emphasis and their hostility certainly contributed to the demise of the Institute. Grace's retirement in 1940 had meant the loss of a vital ally. The new College Principal, the Rev. R. W. Stopford, retired because of ill health in 1945 and this, combined with the suicide of Meyerowitz in the same year, spelt the end of the Institute, the pottery and the tileworks.

Tanya Harrod, London, *August 1987*

CHRONOLOGY

1901	Born on 26 May in Wimbledon, the fourth child of Arthur and Alexandra Cardew.
1918–23	At Exeter College, Oxford.
1923–26	Working at the Leach Pottery, St Ives, with Bernard Leach.
1926	Moved to Winchcombe, Gloucestershire, where he established a country pottery.
1926–39	At Winchcombe, producing mainly slipware.
1933	On 24 December married Mariel Russell. They had three sons: Seth, born 1934, Cornelius, born 1936 and Ennis, born 1938.
1939	Moved with his family to Wenford Bridge, Cornwall, to start a pottery there.
1939–42	Built a kiln at Wenford Bridge and produced a small amount of slipware.
1942	Appointed by the Colonial Office to go to Achimota College, the Gold Coast (Ghana), to build and run Alajo Pottery and train West African potters.
1945	When Alajo was closed, moved to Vumë, on the River Volta, to start a pottery to produce stoneware.
1948	Returned to England.
1948–51	Working at Wenford Bridge Pottery, producing stoneware.
1951	Appointed by the Nigerian Government to the post of Pottery Officer.
1951–65	Set up a pottery and training centre for Nigerian potters at Abuja in Northern Nigeria and worked there, producing stoneware and teaching, for 14 years. Appointed MBE (1964).
1965	Returned to Wenford Bridge.
1965–83	Worked at Wenford Bridge, producing stoneware, teaching and demonstrating, and writing *Pioneer Pottery* (published 1969). Also made lecture tours in the United States, Canada, Australia and New Zealand. Appointed OBE (1981).
1983	Died in Truro, Cornwall, on 11 February.

INDEX